D1293205

TROUBLED PHILOSOPHER

Kennikat Press

National University Publications

Series in American Studies

General Editor

James P. Shenton

Professor of History, Columbia University

CHARLES F. HOWLETT

TROUBLED PHILOSOPHER

John Dewey and the Struggle For World Peace

National University Publications
KENNIKAT PRESS // 1977
Port Washington, N. Y. // London

Manufactured in the United States of America

Published by
Kennikat Press Corp.
Port Washington, N. Y./London

Library of Congress Cataloging in Publication Data

Howlett, Charles F.
Troubled philosopher.

(National university publications) (Series in American studies)
Bibliography: p.
Includes index.
1. Dewey, John, 1859–1952. 2. Peace. I. Title.
JX1962.D48H68 327'.172'0924 76-22784
ISBN 0-8046-9153-3

FOR MY MOTHER AND FATHER
AND JOAN

CONTENTS

	PREFACE	ix
	INTRODUCTION	3
1.	THE MAKING OF A SOCIAL CRITIC	10
2.	DISAPPOINTMENT	20
3.	DEMOCRACY'S AMBASSADOR TO THE FAR EAST	43
4.	EDUCATION FOR PEACE AND DEMOCRACY	58
5.	EDUCATION FOR UNDERSTANDING, NOT FOR WAR	71
6.	OUTLAWRY OF WAR: A NEW APPROACH TO WORLD PEACE	80
7.	DIVERGENT PATHS TO PEACE	96
8.	SOCIAL JUSTICE AND THE EMPTY POCKET	114
9.	A SHATTERED HOPE	129
10.	TROUBLED PHILOSOPHER	144
	NOTES	154
	A NOTE ON SOURCES	165
	INDEX	176

PREFACE

In America today we worry, perhaps more than ever before, about maintaining peace throughout the world. Almost daily we read in our newspapers, hear over the radio, or watch on television stories about increasing violence in the world. Whether it is in the Middle East or Southeast Asia, the evidence of bloodshed remains as a constant reminder that people learn very little, consciously, from the past. Old mistakes are continuously repeated; the lessons of experience, if they are learned at all, are all too quickly forgotten. Perhaps the sad conclusion is that the one way to peace on earth may be as a result of an invasion from Mars—if such is possible. Only then will the peoples of the world unite in a common cause.

The struggle for peace has been a long, tedious, and tragic one. Time and time again the efforts of sincere peace advocates have gone by the wayside when the trumpet of national honor and patriotism was sounded. Yet the struggle continues, and will continue so long as concerned individuals place peace above war. The hope, no doubt, lies in our ability to convert past mistakes into future gains. Indeed, no one was more aware of this than Merle Curti when he wrote:

> Many wise students of history have come to expect very little of mankind, so far as any learning from the past goes. Perhaps this is the sad, deplorable truth. But no merchant would ever try to keep shop without a ledger, to be consulted and studied on occasion; and no mariner would dare sail a vessel without carefully scrutinizing his day-by-day log. So it may well be that those who today hope and pray and work for a warless world may orient themselves somewhat better by relating their ideas and programs to the historical struggle against war of which they themselves are a part. (*Peace or War: The American Struggle, 1636–1936*, p. 14)

One such person who finally did straighten out his ledger and who began steering a course for world peace was John Dewey.

The life of John Dewey offers one of the most remarkable careers in twentieth-century American intellectual history. Author of nearly twenty major books, he is perhaps best known and remembered for his interest in the study of pragmatic philosophy and his application of progressive ideas to the field of education. In many respects, Dewey remains an important intellectual figure. His long life and voluminous writings have helped to perpetuate this tradition. Yet, even though a great deal has been written and is continuing to be written about the man and his life, there remains one side to this magnificent career which has received very little attention. This is Dewey's relationship to the peace movement after World War I.

Many students are familiar with Dewey's role in World War I. His outspokenness in support of American war aims and his willingness to allow his pragmatism to be tainted by the martial spirit have been vividly recounted and roundly criticized by academicians such as Morton White, Arthur A. Ekirch, Jr., Christopher Lasch, and Charles Chatfield, to name just a few. Their criticisms have demonstrated the shortcomings of Dewey's philosophy in a time of crisis. Yet such criticisms have tended to obscure Dewey's later change in attitude with regard to the issue of war and peace. A great deal of attention can and must be directed toward analyzing Dewey's conversion to pacifism after his wartime experience of 1917–18. Indeed, Dewey's switch from "intellectualizing" the use of force in support of war to his interest in educational peace research in the twenties and thirties remains a subject of considerable historical importance.

It is important to remember, when discussing Dewey's peace psychology between the wars, that the doctrine of pacifism became a basic part of his pragmatic approach to social affairs. It was not until after the war, however, when he reexamined his own philosophical beliefs, that he discovered the usefulness and practicality of pacifism. Thus, the purpose of this work is twofold. First, it is to point out that from a philosophical view pacifism became an inherent aspect of Dewey's method of socialized intelligence. In more specific terms, the interrelationship between intelligence as the means and peace as the end came to be based on a pacifist approach to human relationships. Second, it is to point out that Randolph Bourne's criticisms of Dewey's own revaluation of his philosophical beliefs forced him to reconsider the interrelationship between pragmatism and pacifism. Both points are demonstrated in Dewey's relationship to the peace movement after the first World War. Here Dewey acted out his belief in the role of an intelligently formulated public opinion, based on pacifist ideals, as a useful and viable instrument for achieving world peace.

Because many of Dewey's writings are at best, in the words of William James, "damnable; you might even say God-damnable," it is important to help the reader understand Dewey's complete approach to the critical social issue of war and peace. Richard Hofstadter once wrote that Dewey's "style is suggestive of the cannonading of distant armies: one concludes that something portentous is going on at a remote and inaccessible distance, but one cannot determine just what it is" (*Anti-Intellectualism in American Life*, p. 31). Despite such problems, I hope to bring the echoes of the clash a little bit closer so that we may all learn something from Dewey's experience with the problems of war and peace.

This book had its genesis in the spring of 1966, when, as a sophomore in college, I had the unique opportunity of listening to A. J. Muste, Staughton Lynd, and others speak out against the Vietnam War during one of the many teach-ins then taking place on college campuses throughout the nation. Later my convictions on world peace and human cooperation were strengthened while serving in the United States Marine Corps. It was at that point in time that I came to realize how seriously we need to educate the mind to think in terms of peace rather than war.

In the course of this study I am indebted to a number of persons for their help and advice. I am immensely grateful to Professor Arthur A. Ekirch, Jr., of the State University of New York at Albany. He taught me most of what I know about historical research, encouraged me to pursue my interests in peace research, and critically read the original manuscript. I also wish to thank: Kendall Birr, Robert Wesser, and Richard Kendall of the State University of New York at Albany; Mr. Thomas Casey of Marist College; Dr. Edward J. Bordeau of Sacred Heart University; Professor Charles C. Griffin (emeritus), Vassar College; Professor James P. Shenton of Columbia University; Professor Lawrence Cremin, now president of Teachers College, Columbia University; Professor Alan Lawson of Boston College; Professor Stephen Gottschalk of the Naval Postgraduate School at Monterey, California; Professor Paul Bourke of The Flinders University of South Australia; Dr. Edward Cashin of Augusta College; Dr. Jo Ann Boydston of the Cooperative Research Center on Dewey Publications at Southern Illinois University; Mrs. Charity Roth of the Inter-Library Loan Office at the State University of New York at Albany; Mr. Stephen Tannler of the Joseph R. Regenstein Library at the University of Chicago; Dr. Roy P. Basler of the Library of Congress; Mr. Kenneth Lohf of Butler Library at Columbia University; Miss Elizabeth Bonnell of the Seth Low Library, Columbia University; and last, Mrs. Barbara Loatman of Mechanicville, New York, and Mr. Charles H. Brown of West Islip, New York. Mrs. Barbara Stephen cheerfully assumed the chore of typing the final draft of the manuscript. A research grant from the State University of New York Research Foundation also helped to make this study possible.

Finally, I would like to thank my parents for their patience and understanding. No words can properly express my feelings toward them.

TROUBLED PHILOSOPHER

Before, a joy proposed; behind, a dream.

Shakespeare, *Sonnet 129*

INTRODUCTION

At 7:45 P.M. the doors opened. The crowd, unusually quiet and somber, began filing past the doors and into the auditorium of the Great Hall at Eighth Street and Astor Place in New York City. Stunned by the events which had already taken place earlier in the day, they sensed that this speech tonight would have significant meaning for their future lives. The atmosphere was tense with uncertainty. No one cared to smile or offer any words of joviality. Signs of weariness and despair were easily noticeable on the faces of the crowd as it nervously waited for the guest speaker.

Backstage, meanwhile, an aged philosopher began looking over his prepared speech, "Lessons from the War: In Philosophy." How ironic, he thought to himself, that on this cold, brisk evening of December 7, 1941, he would be talking to an audience struck by "pain and pathos at the news that war had been declared."[1] How is it possible, he kept saying to himself, that mankind, with all the knowledge it now possessed, could resort to war? What must we learn from philosophy? What needs to be done to make the world a better place to live in? These questions and many more rushed through John Dewey's mind before the clock read 8:15 P.M.

The time arrived for the eighty-two-year-old former Columbia University philosopher to go before his anxious audience. Slowly and quietly he approached the podium inside the huge auditorium at Cooper Union. His face appeared strained and pale. Nervously—his hands shaking and his voice cracking at times—he began to read his speech. Signs of perspiration suddenly appeared on his forehead and below the frame of his glasses. As he gazed out upon his attentive listeners, his mind began to drift backwards to that period of time when he had supported American military involvement in the first World War. Such memories made the present situation more difficult to bear. It was even harder for him now to comprehend that it was happening all over again. As he neared the end of his brief but important speech, his voice became louder.

> And now my friends [he concluded], I should say that what philosophy has to learn from the war is at least the importance of facing the problem of getting some kind of unified view of human beings in which ideas and emotions, knowledge and desire, would cooperate with each other instead of either going entirely separate ways or [of] being brought into harmony with each other only through some outside power.[2]

The impact of the words was clean and hard. Leaving the podium in the same manner in which he had approached it–slowly and quietly–he sadly departed the auditorium and its shocked audience, whispering to himself: "Did we really learn anything from the last war?"[3]

During the first World War Dewey had used his pragmatic philosophy to support American military involvement overseas. As a practicing pragmatist and instrumentalist, he reasoned that war might serve as a useful and efficient means for bringing about the desired end of a democratically organized world order. It was not that Dewey enjoyed war. Quite clearly, he viewed war as socially undesirable. But, given the circumstances in 1917, he had argued that war could not be separated from the system of power politics in international relations nor dissociated from the ends it sought to achieve. Although war on the whole was undesirable it might nonetheless be made useful and educative. Rather than remaining cynical or detached over the state of affairs that existed in the spring of 1917, Dewey had put his pragmatic philosophy to work in support of American war aims.

If Dewey had been more conscious of the wider implications of his support for war, he might have recognized that his justification for the use of military force had nicely served the pernicious motivations of political propagandists. Indeed, had he been more aware of the manipulative effects of patriotic propaganda, he might have understood better that victory at all costs becomes the only end that matters in time of war. Ironically, in contrast to his wartime position, Dewey's entire philosophy had always emphasized the virtues of a peaceful and intelligent solution of problems. At the heart of his philosophy of pragmatism had been an experimental approach to social affairs. The utilization of intelligence and scientific methodology rather than coercive force, Dewey had previously contended, were the means for achieving the goal of a peaceful democratic society. In an essay he wrote early in 1917 before America's entry in the war, entitled "The Need for a Recovery of Philosophy," Dewey had pointed out that "the pragmatic theory of intelligence means that the function of mind is to . . . [peacefully] free experience from routine and from caprice."[4] But was not the function of creative intelligence to free the mind from the routine and caprice of war? Was it therefore not uncharacteristic of Dewey to preach to his *New Republic* readers as he did in "Force and Coercion" and "Force, Violence and Law" that armed force was morally correct and war legally justified?[5] How and in what possible way might war have served as an intelligent and peaceful solution of problems?

According to Randolph Bourne, a former student and the chief wartime critic of the Columbia professor, Dewey's pragmatic-instrumentalism trapped him into miscalculating the relationship of the war to true national interests and democratic values. To Bourne, Dewey's excessive optimism led him to overestimate the power of intelligence and underestimate the force of violence and irrationality. Dewey's emphasis on utility, Bourne contended, afforded him no "elevated value with which to sustain a position in opposition to the predominant trend of vagueness and impracticality."[6] Dewey's support for war, he also argued, had placed technique above values. As Bourne wrote in his famous and oft-quoted article, "Twilight of Idols":

> To those of us who have taken Dewey's philosophy almost as our American religion, it never occurred that values could be subordinated to technique. We were instrumentalists, but we had our private utopias so clearly before our minds that the means fell always into its place as contributory. And Dewey, of course, always meant his philosophy, when taken as a philosophy of life, to start with values. But there was always that unhappy ambiguity in his doctrine as to just how values were created, and it became easier and easier to assume that just any growth was justified and almost any activity valuable so long as it achieved ends.[7]

Bourne's argument that Dewey's support for war was technique-conscious and morally blind did much to sharpen Dewey's views on pacifist ideals after the war. Indeed, one may suppose that Randolph Bourne's article proved to be the most decisive factor in Dewey's conversion to pacifism.

The World War I period marked a transition between Dewey's former support for war and his later acceptance of pacifist values and ideals. Although his pragmatism had always advocated the adoption of "peaceable" means for social reform, Dewey had never before proclaimed himself a pacifist. Perhaps Dewey's own pragmatic emphasis on methodology had blinded him to a true understanding of the importance of social and moral values. It took a war with all its violence, emotionalism, and excessive intolerance to convince Dewey that his own philosophical preconceptions concerning the progressive possibilities of military force were ill founded.

Yet, if the war proved disheartening to Dewey, it also made him a pacifist. Disillusioned by the war's results, he now upheld the position that values were more important than technique. The search for world order based on peace and democracy became Dewey's main passion after the war. His Felix Adler lecture, which he delivered before the Society for Ethical Culture in 1938, clearly demonstrates the transformation from militant patriotism to democratic pacifism:

With our fortunate position in the world I think that if we used our resources, including our financial resources, to build up among ourselves a genuine, true and effective democratic society, we would find that we have a surer, a more enduring and a more powerful defense of democratic institutions both within ourselves and with relation to the rest of the world than the surrender to the belief in force, violence and war can ever give.[8]

His statement was sincere and compelling. The substitution of the "intelligent use of pacifism" for the "intelligent use of armed or coercive force" became his new rallying cry—a cry that he would echo throughout the rest of his life. Thus, his pacifism was marked by a curious blend of moralistic beliefs, democratic ideals, socialistic values, and nonreligious ethics. It contained none of that individualistic Christian fervor which characterized many of the nineteenth- and early twentieth-century disciples of peace. His was a corporate pacifism that he sought to apply to his own social philosophy—a philosophy that encouraged the individual to employ his intelligence in the best interests of the community. The basic thrust of his pragmatic philosophy after 1918 was to formulate the method of intelligence in such a discriminating fashion as to minimize the increasing influence of patriotic and nationalistic propaganda. "The power of voluntary action based upon public collective intelligence" was Dewey's answer to a burgeoning martial spirit.[9] It was also a pacifism that stressed the importance of education and the role of public opinion in the peacemaking process.

Dewey proposed to champion his pacifist beliefs and values through the use of his pen. To Dewey, war came to represent an unpragmatic method of the use of intelligence. Admitting his own susceptibility to the emotional appeals of nationalism and patriotism, Dewey now reached the conclusion, as a result of his own painful conversion, that the pacifist method was not only rational but also very realistic. He came to look upon pacifism as an effective means for counteracting the emotional aspects of chauvinism. Thus, in the 1920s he argued that the League of Nations was pragmatically unsound because it advocated the use of sanctions or military force. Indeed, this was a far cry from his World War I thesis that armed force might be employed more economically and easily and with little waste if all Americans vigorously and conscientiously backed the war effort. During that same decade he also linked his pragmatic philosophy to the outlawry of war crusade in which he urged that the people and not the diplomats assume the leadership in the movement for world peace. In terms of his pragmatic methodology, Dewey envisioned "outlawry" as an educational mechanism that would actively unite the moral sentiments of mankind in their search for the right road to abolish war, end poverty, and create a democratic world order based on freedom and equality. He was convinced that until people stopped thinking in terms of war, the path to peace would remain at best an ideal. Outlawry, as a noble experiment for world peace, afforded some measure of hope. By the 1930s Dewey, despite his own sympathy for their program, counseled his fellow Americans to ignore the socialist appeal for the destruction of the capitalist system through violence. At the same time he supported the essentially socialist platform of the Keep America out of War Congress. The transition from a patriotic progressive in 1917-18 to a peaceful socialist during his remaining years is, to say the least, striking.

John Dewey's close friend and colleague at Teachers College, William Heard Kilpatrick, has described him as a person with "a common sense attitude towards life's problems, a strong dislike for class distinctions, and a strong moral background. Out of his family setting came, we must believe, his initial inclination towards democracy, his common sense thinking, and his interest in morals."[10] Yet he was more than just an average individual—he was also a great spokesman pleading for a society based on intelligence and democracy and unwilling to settle for less. Dewey was neither an appealing orator nor an exciting or stimulating classroom teacher. But he was an influential writer arguing for a better world, free of hunger and despair, war and injustice, a world where all men would reason together and work with one another in building a democratic society. It is not his style, but his determination to make known his views, that deserves consideration.

Yet who was John Dewey? What type of person was he? Dewey, it appears, was a rather complex person. He preferred the quiet solitude of academia to the hectic, sometimes disturbing, role of social critic. His own dislike for the limelight, however, conflicted with a compulsive urge to speak out against social injustice and economic oppression. His complexity was further compounded by the fact that he was both a twentieth-century Jeffersonian democrat and an eighteenth-century moralistic optimist. Individualism, liberalism, enlightenment, and social cooperation are the key words characterizing Dewey's philosophy—a philosophy that ran counter to the impersonalized society of his day. As a philosopher, he was not contemplative in the same sense that Bertrand Russell, William James, and George Santayana were. He was a man who looked ahead rather than back. He was more of a doer than a thinker, which may account for the reason why he did not write much "philosophy" but wrote a great deal about philosophy. His social philosophy was a reflection of that desire to equate moral values with democratic libertarianism. His goal was a continuous, progressive "qualitative adaptation" of man and environment on a reciprocal basis:

> There is an old saying to the effect that it is not enough for a man to be good; he must be good for something. The something for which a man must be good is capacity to live as a social member so that what he gets from living with others balances with what he contributes.[11]

He was an intense and serious-minded person who always argued that the unattainable was attainable, and the impossible possible. But it was this optimism on the part of Dewey that proved so disconcerting both to himself and to those around him. Despite what he wrote and believed, he remained a troubled person. His trouble stemmed mainly from his own fear and realization that the struggle against war would not be easily won. Past experience, he sadly noted, dictated future actions. He also knew that the acceptance of pacifism as a working disposition of the mind was at best a forlorn hope. Thus, his writings portray an individual wavering between buoyant optimism and conscious pessimism. His being trapped, therefore, between the realities of present-day social disorders and his own conscious efforts to eliminate them in the face of overwhelming odds, best accounts for the descriptive title "troubled philosopher."

Although he remained troubled, Dewey nonetheless recognized that participation rather than apathy was the only course for people to pursue. He was correct when he pointed out that the failures of our democratic system were directly related to the willingness of the American people to leave every decision-making process to its leaders. Such "blind faith," Dewey was quick to point out, would surely lead to despair. Only by assuming an active role in the governing of society could people overcome the plaguing problems of war and social injustice. The race between the socialization of intelligence and catastrophe dictated how fast Dewey was willing to run when it came to calling for a basic restructuring of the existing social order. To Dewey, time was of the essence and participation advantageous.

Small in stature and inclined toward shyness, Dewey looked every bit the university professor who wished to be read and understood but not seen. But seen he was. Beginning with a critical analysis of the society in which he lived, he would rise to the occasion whenever it seemed necessary to assail the inhumanity of a social order that abused the principles of democracy by permitting its young to die in battle in far-off places, by ignoring its poor, and by encouraging its scientists to develop weapons that could conceivably destroy all forms of life on earth. He was, to quote a fellow philosopher, "ready to join with others in forming activist organizations, against war, on behalf of intellectual freedom and social justice, for education and social change, and for the cause of liberalism in social institutions."[12]

The object of this book is to explore that alliance in order to understand more clearly why, on that cold, brisk evening of December 7, 1941, Dewey no longer shared the enthusiasms and optimism he had demonstrated only twenty-four years earlier.

CHAPTER ONE

THE MAKING OF A SOCIAL CRITIC

> In sum, I believe that the individual who is to be educated is a social individual, and that society is an organic union of individuals.
>
> Dewey, *My Pedagogic Creed*

There was little in the small town where John Dewey was born and raised or in the orthodox Protestant household of his parents to foretell his later role as a social critic. Burlington, Vermont, where Dewey was born on October 20, 1859, was a typical small town with a population of about six thousand, which served as the commercial center for the rich farming and lumber area of the greater part of western New England. Although it had been at one time composed mainly of small dairy and cattle farmers, a recent boom in the lumber trade had gradually transformed the physical features of Burlington within a very short period of time. With the expansion of industry came people. Within three years after the start of the Civil War, Burlington's population jumped from close to six thousand to over fourteen thousand. Mills and railroad engines belched smoke and ashes, horse carriages and wagons moved swiftly through the dusty streets, and the town was a center for a number of small but very successful businesses. As in many other small industrial cities of that era, there was ample opportunity for young men on the make to reap extensive profits.

Archibald Dewey, John Dewey's father, was quick to follow the example of other Horatio Algers of his day. The burgeoning lumber business, which made Burlington the second largest lumber depot in the country by 1835, provided him with a golden opportunity to move from his family's farm in Fairfax to Burlington, where, along with a friend, he established his own grocery business.[1] The city's rapid commercial expansion, accompanied by a growing population, netted Archibald and his partner a handsome profit. By the time he was forty-four years old, he was a prosperous merchant—a perfect illustration of the self-made-man principle. At the same time he was also ready for marriage.

In the middle of the 1850s Archibald Dewey married Lucina Artemisia Rich, twenty years his junior. The marriage was made considerably easier by the fact that Dewey's drive and economic ambition proved socially acceptable to his wife's parents, who were both economically successful and politically prominent. Lucina's grandfather, Charles Rich, served for ten years as a congressman from Vermont, while her father, Davis Rich, was a respected and well-liked member of the Vermont General Assembly for five years.

John Dewey's parents were typical of that new breed of New England Yankees who cherished the Protestant virtues of industriousness, thrift, patriotism and Republicanism. To them the ability to get ahead and achieve some form of social distinction was a sign of God's blessing. Hard work, love for God, and a strong respect for one's neighbor and country were just a few of the commandments recited in the Dewey household. It was a deeply religious, politically conservative family, that bore all the earmarks of pecuniary success.[2]

The house on South Willard Street where Dewey was born exemplified that success. Located in the more prosperous section of Burlington, overlooking Lake Champlain, and watched over by the Green Mountains to the east, the Deweys' home stood as a model of aristocratic magnificence. There existed none of the depressing demeanor of social poverty that Dewey himself would later encounter while working with Jane Addams at Hull House. Here were beauty and wealth at their best. The aristocratic trappings of prosperity were there for all to see. Only the Civil War interrupted what might have been a relatively quiet and happy time for the Dewey household.

With the onset of the Civil War, John's father immediately gave up his grocery business and enlisted with the First Vermont Cavalry as quartermaster. His urge to defend the Union from the rebellious states south of the Mason-Dixon line derived largely from an attitude of New England Yankeeism which prided itself on its patriotism and moralism. The belief that the union was divinely blessed and must be protected at all costs was so strong on the part of Archibald Dewey that he left for combat shortly after President Lincoln's call for volunteers, For nearly six years family life and business were interrupted by the "call to duty."

After the war Archibald Dewey relocated the family, moving them from South Willard Street to Pearl Street. At the same time he invested in a new business enterprise. This time he bought a share in a cigar and tobacco shop.

A few years later, as a result of his own ambition and determination, he became the sole owner. Once again the Dewey household enjoyed prosperity.

The second of three Dewey children, John was shy and introspective with a lively curiosity and penetrating mind which only came to light years later while he was attending college. He was an intense boy, rather small in stature but healthy during most of his childhood. He was not easily disposed to reading books, and the archaic conditions of the public school system in Burlington did not help the matter. Like most youths growing up in Vermont, he found the lure of the outdoors more compelling than the urge to learn from books. During most of his grade and high school days, he spent much of his free time wandering along the shores of Lake Champlain, only three blocks from his home. Although he was an able student and one who was respected by teachers and fellow students alike, John's school years proved to be relatively uneventful in terms of academic achievement.

Immediately after John graduated from high school in 1875 at the tender age of sixteen, he entered the University of Vermont, where he suddenly underwent a profound transformation in his attitude toward social affairs. It was during his undergraduate years that Dewey came under the influence of radical writers like Charles Darwin, Thomas H. Huxley, George Tyndall, and Leslie Stephen. The metamorphosis from a rather shy and reserved person, raised in a conservative religious household, to a conscious critic of the existing social system was stimulated by his voracious reading of the radical British periodicals, *Fortnightly Review, Nineteenth Century,* and *Contemporary Review,* which regularly carried articles on the economic, political, and social problems of the day.[3]

Although Dewey excelled in philosophy and the sciences under the tutelage of H. A. P. Torrey, professor of mental and moral philosophy, he was far more impressed with Matthew Buckham, president of the college and professor of political and social philosophy. Despite Buckham's rather obvious conservative bias in politics, Dewey was influenced by his mature and pious wisdom when it came to general discussions of social and political problems. Buckham regularly encouraged his students to ask questions and frequently digressed from his lesson plan to discuss some of the more pertinent issues of the day. Even though Dewey did not agree with all of Buckham's views, he was fascinated by the way Buckham would challenge his students when it came to present-day issues. The lively exchange of ideas which resulted from these encounters provided Dewey with an entirely different view of the role of philosophy. It was in Buckham's classes that Dewey began to develop his own conception of a socialized philosophy. His senior commencement speech, "The Limits of Political Economy," clearly reflects his growing concern for social awareness.

In 1879 Dewey graduated from the University of Vermont with a bachelor of arts degree, a four-year average of 86 percent, and membership in the national honor fraternity Phi Beta Kappa. He was class salutatorian.

Although Dewey would have liked to continue his studies in philosophy, he accepted instead an invitation to teach in western Pennsylvania. The teaching position was offered to him by a relative who was principal of Oil City High School. The three years he spent teaching Latin, algebra, and the natural sciences, however, were for all practical purposes largely unproductive ones in the life of Dewey. Except for a few helpful hints on how to gain profits on investments in the oil business, Dewey came away from Oil City with a feeling of having accomplished very little. He still looked forward, with a greater sense of urgency than ever before, to attending graduate school.

Shortly after his departure from Oil City, Dewey received word that he had been accepted for graduate studies at The Johns Hopkins University. This was a great moment in Dewey's young life. The expectation that after three unproductive and uneventful years he would finally be able to pursue his interest in philosophy filled him with immense joy. In September, 1882, at the age of twenty-three, Dewey began his studies for the Ph.D.

At Hopkins Dewey came under the influence of two very famous philosophers, G. Stanley Hall and George Sylvester Morris. Both Hall and Morris were philosophers with penetrating minds and a deep concern for social awareness. Hall's major contribution was that he impressed upon Dewey the importance of experimental methods for a scientific understanding of philosophy. Yet it was George Sylvester Morris, more than anyone else, who gave Dewey his greatest sense of satisfaction when it came to the study of philosophy.

Morris's courses, particularly those with the descriptive titles "science of knowledge," "history of philosophy in Great Britain," "Hegel's philosophy of history," and "history of German philosophy," were replete with new interpretations of Hegel's idea of interacting organisms. It was under the influence and guidance of Morris that Dewey finally liberated himself from the conservative confines of his New England puritanism. This great awakening for Dewey came in the form of Morris's neo-Hegelianism. Utilizing Hegel's philosophy of history, which presented a world view marked by interaction and change, Morris taught that philosophy was more than an intellectual exercise; it was thought applied to social action. Morris's beliefs, moreover, enabled Dewey to link neo-Hegelianism with the then prevailing concept of scientific Darwinism. The idea that philosophy should be approached on an interdisciplinary basis which combined all forms of knowledge into an organic whole was Morris's major contribution to Dewey's thought. It provided Dewey with an opportunity to incorporate his minor fields of study, science, history, and political science, into his own conception of philosophy as a form of social criticism. The emerging view of philosphy as a method for social analysis, as well as a bridge for overcoming the duality between mind and matter proved to be the most important influence affecting the early development of John Dewey the social critic. His appreciation for a philosophy of social criticism which first captured his imagination at the University of Vermont was further strengthened during his graduate days at The Johns Hopkins University. He was now firmly convinced that philosophy could play an important role in everyday affairs.

Upon receiving his doctoral degree in 1884, Dewey immediately left for teaching duties at the University of Michigan. It was largely through the family's association with Michigan's academic president James B. Angell, who previously had taught and served as president at the University of Vermont, that Dewey was offered a position as instructor in philosophy. His starting salary was nine hundred dollars.[4]

By the time Dewey moved to Michigan, he had begun to witness the pangs and violence of social discontent. Within two years after he had assumed his position in the philosophy department, labor unrest and violence erupted throughout many of America's leading industrial cities. It was in 1886 that a bomb exploded at Haymarket Square in Chicago, sending shock waves throughout the country. The impending struggle between labor and management became a basic part of America's rise to industrial power. Dewey, who by this time had developed his own social philosophy, looked upon this growing problem with great trepidation. He was bothered less by industrial and economic expansion than by its accompanying social problems. The drive for profits which created these problems, he felt, was also directly responsible for the abuse of the principle of democracy. More than anyone else, Dewey was the leading defender of the democratic way of life. To Dewey, democracy, as a social ideal and ethic, was more than a form of government or political process. It was, as he defined it, a method of associated living in which affairs were so arranged that the intellectual and social self-realization of the individual in the community inevitably involved the equal self-realization of every other person. According to Dewey, a democratic community was the "sole way of living" which provided for the "creation of a freer and more humane experience in which all share and to which all contribute."[5] The communal bond of the New England township, with democracy as its covenant, had been deeply embedded in Dewey's consciousness since his early childhood.

In a curious yet interesting way, Dewey looked upon democracy in terms of his own Hegelian sympathies. He believed that democracy was an internally active social organism in which the individual citizen defined his objectives in terms of the social welfare of all its members. In many respects, democracy was a moral ideal for Dewey. It stood as a symbol for shared experience and human understanding and cooperation. Thus, the violence that occurred on the streets of Chicago, Dewey believed, had been a direct result of the desire on the part of the captains of industry to enhance their own welfare at the expense of the rest of the community. The profit motive of the capitalistic ethic had become so powerful, Dewey argued, that it was now supplanting the democratic rights and freedoms of all Americans. This abuse of the individual for the sheer sake of profit Dewey could no longer tolerate. The Protestant ethic upon which he was raised, he sadly concluded, had been deliberately transformed into a vehicle for social oppression.

Dewey's conscience would not allow him to sit still and watch the working man be exploited. His class lectures and his off-campus addresses were ringing defenses of the concept of democratic equality. He pointed out that in order for democracy to remain an effective instrument for communal improvement, all the American people would have to work vigorously for the abolishment of industrial and social ills. Civil and political democracy were meaningless, he noted, without economic and industrial democracy. "There is no need to beat about the bush in saying that democracy is not in reality what it is in name until it is industrial, as well as civil and political."[6] The goal for Dewey was the creation of a state of socialized democracy in which he drew a fine distinction between unrestricted laissez faire and complete government control. It certainly may have been an elusive ideal, but it remained, in Dewey's opinion, the only way to curb the violence which accompanied America's industrial growth. At least this was the message he attempted to put across in a short monograph he wrote in 1888 entitled *The Ethics of Democracy.*[7]

The most important event in Dewey's personal life while at Michigan was his marriage to Harriet Alice Chipman. Alice, as she preferred to be called, was a month older than Dewey. Her parents had died when she was very young, and both she and her sister had been cared for by their maternal grandparents, Frederick and Evalina Riggs. In 1882 she entered the University of Michigan to study philosophy. Two years later, when Dewey arrived, she immediately signed up for his courses. A romance developed between the two, aided by the fact that they both lived in the same boarding house. On July 28, 1886, they were married in Alice's home town of Fenton, Michigan.

Prior to moving to the University of Chicago in 1894, Dewey had already established himself as a first-rate scholar in the field of philosophy. By 1891 he had published two works, *Psychology,* which was published in 1886, and *Outlines of a Critical Theory of Ethics,* published in 1891. It is his *Outlines* that merits consideration. It is in this particular work that one can trace Dewey's movement away from Hegelianism to instrumentalism. In *Outlines* Dewey emphasized the important role intelligence could play in social organization. The role of intelligence, Dewey noted, must become practical. It must not remain merely an academic discipline. Its function is to guide the individual's attempt to adjust to his physical, social, and cultural environment. "The duty of the present is the socializing of intelligence—the realizing of its bearing upon social practice." The role of intelligence, moreover, is to establish the end of a moral community which recognizes the rights and satisfactions of others:

> There is to be found not only the satisfaction of self, but also the satisfaction of the entire moral order, the furthering of the community in which one lives. All moral conduct is based upon such a faith; and *moral theory must recognize this as the postulate upon which it rests.*

In terms of Dewey's own intellectual growth, it is readily apparent that the practical aspects of logic and thought took precedence over the Hegelian conception of divine order. The shift from providential rule to human control was the new development in Dewey's philosophical thought. It is in *Outlines* that the interrelationship and utilization of intelligence, morality, and science as instruments for human employment finally take shape. It is also in *Outlines* that Dewey at last adopted the philosophy of pragmatism, a philosophy based upon a combination of inquiry and values which he preferred to call instrumentalism.[8]

In 1894 Dewey left his teaching position at Michigan for the newly established University of Chicago. Chicago's president, William Rainey Harper, gathered about him a number of brilliant men with the purpose of establishing a veritable think tank in the field of higher education. At the suggestion of James Hayden Tufts, Harper offered Dewey the position of philosophy department chairman along with an annual salary of five thousand dollars.

Dewey's tenure at the University of Chicago marked his complete development as a social critic. The 1890s were a decade of social ferment. In 1892 a strike took place at Carnegie's steel mill at Homestead, Pennsylvania, resulting in workers being beaten and hauled off to jail. Two years later the American Railway Union, headed by Eugene V. Debs, attracted national attention when the union went out on strike against the Pullman Car Company of Chicago. The resulting clash between the strikers and federal troops, and the subsequent incarceration of the strike leader Debs, resulted in more bloodshed. That same decade also witnessed the birth of populism, whereby midwestern farmers heeded the call of Mary Lease to "raise less corn and more hell." A growing demand for social and economic justice was characteristic of this period. No doubt, the anomaly of the existence of want in the midst of plenty which Henry George first publicized in 1879 in *Progress and Poverty,* proved extremely troublesome to most social critics, including John Dewey.

Dewey's first real contact with the abuses of industrialization came while he was working with Jane Addams at Hull House. It was there that Dewey saw for himself the evil effects of industrialization. He served on the first board of trustees, conducted courses in social philosophy, gave lectures, and led discussion groups. Just as significant, Hull House served as a popular meeting place for people with diverse backgrounds and social views. Here were found followers of Henry George and Henry Demarest Lloyd, as well as members with more radical dispositions. Here also Dewey found ample opportunity to engage in lively exchanges with various socialists—he opposed their methodology of violence over intelligence—while at the same time he incorporated many of their ideas into his own social philosophy. Perhaps the greatest contribution Dewey received from Hull House was not the memory of Jane Addams, which he deeply cherished, but rather the more radical views of those opposed to the monopolistic practices of the capitalistic enterprise.

Dewey's association with Hull House helped to sharpen his own ideas on social reform. The relationship between the philosopher and the public man was clearly demonstrated in such lecture courses at the University of Chicago as "contemporary theories regarding ethical relations of the individual and society" and "the sociology of ethics." It was in these courses that Dewey discussed the pressing social problems of the day. It was also in these lectures that Dewey lashed out against the capitalistic abuses affecting the American way of life.

> The natural and individualistic regime instead of producing progressive harmony is producing increasing disequilibration: separation and conflict of interests of capitalists (owners of the means of production, distribution and exchange and hence of means of access of the laborer to work), and laborers. Low wages, labor of women and children . . . bad factory conditions, long hours and poor health conditions are characteristic of capitalistic oppression.[9]

Moreover, Dewey's association with a group of liberal thinkers on the faculty—educators such as Albion Small and W. I. Thomas of the Department of Sociology; Edward W. Bemis and Thorstein Veblen of the Department of Political Economy; Frederick Starr in anthropology; and Tufts and Mead from his own department—added to his growing awareness of the need to find some means for practical social reform. It was from his experience at Hull House and his discussions with liberal faculty members that Dewey came to look upon the school as a social lever for the improvement of America's democratic society.

The key for a positive reconstruction of a democratic society that would become more humane and in which all would share the benefits, Dewey felt, would be the utilization of the schools as a medium for social exchange. According to Dewey, the failure of the present school system was that it was incapable of teaching students real life experience.

From the standpoint of the child, the great waste in the school comes from his inability to utilize the experiences he gets outside the school in any complete and free way within the school itself; while, on the other hand, he is unable to apply in daily life what he is learning at school. That is the isolation of the school—its isolation from life.

What needed to be done, Dewey claimed, was for the school to become a miniature community that would, in effect, reflect the habits and attitudes of its members. In Dewey's opinion, an individual was a product of his own environment. His attitudes, dispositions, prejudices, and habits were a direct result of his own social upbringing. It was the environmental factors which directly influenced the way one thought.

The idea of evolution has made familiar the notion that mind cannot be regarded as an individual, monopolistic possession, but represents the outworkings of the endeavor and thought of humanity; that it is developed in an environment which is social as well as physical, and that social needs and aims have been most potent in shaping it—and the chief difference between savagery and civilization is not in the naked nature which each faces, but the social heredity and social medium.[10]

By teaching young children the realities of life, Dewey hoped to give them a better understanding of the way people act so that from such experience they would learn how to correct the persistent problems plaguing modern society. His primary objective was to enable children to see for themselves life as it actually is. He felt that a first-hand observation of the way people react in various situations would make a lasting impression upon the child. It was his belief that the young mind, when in its formative stage, would readily perceive for itself the difference between social abuse and social justice. That was the key, Dewey maintained, for achieving the end of social democracy.[11]

Dewey's tenure at Chicago lasted until 1904. During that time he became a leading critic of the classical methods of teaching, established his own experimental school which advocated the theory of child-centered education, and assumed the role of academic spokesman for social reform. Clearly, the Chicago years were a time of intellectual growth for Dewey. But if they were years of academic achievement, they also proved to be years of pedagogical controversy.

The controversy centered around Dewey's own concern for and active involvement with the Laboratory School at the University of Chicago. The Laboratory School, an outgrowth of Dewey's philosophy of progressive education, was objected to by many of the university's more conservative-minded professors. Dewey had hoped that the school would provide a new method whereby the child would, through his own experiences, become funded with the information and skills for dealing with new problems in a more intelligent way. The emphasis upon the child learning from his own experiences instead of being taught by rote was central to Dewey's conception of progressive education. In 1899, for instance, he wrote in *The School and Society* that the basic problem facing educators was "how to retain these advantages [industrial advances], and yet introduce into the school something representing the other side of life—occupations which exact personal responsibilities and which train the child in relation to the physical realities of life."[12] It was not so much that Dewey wished to abandon all forms of classical learning as it was that he was angered by the unwillingness of many educators to apply those theories to real life experiences. Yet, there were many educators who viewed Dewey's theories on education as radical and nontraditional. His experimental school came under heavy pressure from many of his colleagues at the university. The leading critic of Dewey's views on progressive education was Wilbur S. Jackman, who at that time was the dean of the School of Education. In 1903 the dispute between Dewey and Jackman finally came to a head when Jackman demanded more administrative control over the Laboratory School and in the process attempted to undermine Dewey's influence. The following year, disgusted with bureaucratic interference and internal squabbles, Dewey resigned from his position as chairman of the Department of Philosophy. That summer he headed for Columbia University.

From 1904 to 1914 Dewey developed his interest in research and publication in his new academic home. Teaching both at Teachers College and in the philosophy department made his early years at Columbia University immensely pleasurable and productive. He managed to publish *Ethics* in 1908, on which he collaborated with his old colleague from the University of Chicago James Hayden Tufts, *Moral Principles in Education* in 1909, *The Influence of Darwin on Philosophy* in 1910, and *How We Think* also in 1910. These years were relatively peaceful ones in the life of John Dewey. They were not marred by any of the bitterness and pedagogical rivalries that he had experienced while at the University of Chicago. He appeared more relaxed and seemed to enjoy his work more than even he himself would have cared to admit. But if this period seemed to him to be one of contentment and happiness, the years immediately ahead would not prove so generous.

CHAPTER TWO

DISAPPOINTMENT

> We all jump to conclusions; we all fail to examine and test our ideas because of our personal attitudes. When we generalize we tend to make sweeping assertions; that is from one or only a few facts we make a generalization covering a wide field.
>
> Dewey, *How We Think*

> That the gallant fight for democracy and civilization fought on the soil of France is not our fight is a thing not to be realized without pangs and qualms.
>
> Dewey, *Characters and Events*

> I have been a thorough and complete sympathizer with the part played by this country in this war, and I have wished to see the resources of this country used for its successful prosecution.
>
> Dewey, "Democracy and Loyalty in the Schools"

Perhaps the only thing one can be absolutely sure of when discussing the tumultuous events of 1914–18 is that they marked a major turning point in the life of John Dewey. The relatively peaceful and quiet years which he spent in the classroom at Columbia University pursuing elusive truth were suddenly interrupted by the firing of a single shot from the pistol of an Austrian Serb. But the gallant fight for democracy, with which Dewey readily identified himself, proved not so chivalrous in the form of the realities of actual warfare. No one event proved more traumatic to Dewey than the clash of armies on the battlefields of central Europe that resulted from this "shot heard round the world." Dragged from a relatively secure position in academia, Dewey was forced to take a stand when the time finally arrived for America to assume her role in world affairs. The choice was not an easy one. Yet his decision, no matter how realistic it may have seemed to him at the time, brought him untold misery and dissatisfaction. His support for the war, which catapulted him into the public limelight, later dimmed and almost destroyed his reputation. Unfortunately for Dewey, under the impact of the war he had jumped to conclusions without being able to test all his ideas.

Prior to World War I Dewey had been working on redefining and improving his instrumentalist or experimental approach to social affairs. A product of the spirit of progressivism then dominant in the United States, Dewey looked for ways of relating his social philosophy to the improvement of America's democratic society. The quest for some form of "socialized democracy" which became the rallying cry for all progressives concerned with the issues of peace and social justice, Dewey neatly incorporated into his own philosophical writings and educational teachings. The urgent need to "uplift" the masses and minimize social and international conflict Dewey viewed as the most important task confronting his pragmatic philosophy.

Dewey's pragmatism contained elements of pacifist thinking. Although he did not become a pacifist until after World War I, Dewey's philosophy was nonetheless a curious mixture of moralism and pacifism that had as its goal the creation of a democratic society. In almost all of his earlier writings one can find evidence of his deep concern for developing the proper mental and moral attitudes necessary for establishing useful social relationships. In *Psychology,* for example, which was written in 1886, Dewey pointed out that "moral feeling is the only explicit social feeling. In moral feeling man feels his true self to be one which comprehends possible relations to all men. . . ." A few years later in *Outlines of a Critical Theory of Ethics,* he elaborated further by arguing that

> the moral end must . . . include the ends of various agents who make up society. It must be capable of constituting a social system out of the acts of various agents, as well as an individual system out of the various acts of one agent; or, more simply, the moral end must be not only the good for all the particular acts of an individual, but must be a *common good*—a good which in satisfying one, satisfies others.

And in *Ethics,* written during the height of the Progressive era, Dewey lashed out against the immoral, nonthinking nationalist, whose sympathies ran counter to the spirit of democracy:

> The stranger, alien, foreigner, has always, for psychological reasons, tended to be an object of dread to all but the most enlightened. The growth of national states carried this feeling over from individuals and small groups

and concentrated it upon other states. The self-interest of the dynamic and military class persistently keeps the spark of fear and animosity alive in order that it may, upon occasion, be fanned into the flames of war. A definite technique has grown by which the mass of citizens are led to identify love of one's own country with readiness to regard other nations as enemies.

An enlightened public opinion was the means, Dewey maintained, by which to extinguish the flames of nationalistic jealousy and animosity. His writings sustained the established conviction that social cooperation rested upon understanding, not fear.[1]

The quest for moral understanding and peaceful cooperation was a dominant theme in Dewey's pragmatic philosophy. In keeping with his own instrumentalist technique, which combined empirical observation with the formulation and testing of tentative plans that would be reappraised and revaluated in the light of observed results, Dewey hoped that the progressive forces of the social sciences would establish a medium whereby the human environment would be geared toward socialism rather than toward the concept of laissez faire individualism. His pragmatic formula, therefore, consisted of the transformation of intelligence and moral ideals, backed by scientific experimentation, into useful vehicles for social reform. This formula, according to Dewey, supplied the means that would illuminate the way to a peaceful reordering of society. For it was the means more than anything else that mattered to a pragmatist like Dewey. Thus, the analogy between a surgeon performing an operation and Dewey's philosophy, which Mr. Joseph Ratner made years later, appears particularly helpful.

The surgeon [Mr. Ratner said] must remove the tumor, that is certainly clear; but the *method* he uses, *how* he removes it, is equally important, for the removal and the method of removal cannot be separated; they continually interact and it is the consequences of their interaction that determine the life and health of the patient.

So, too, with Dewey's philosophy the method used to achieve a particular goal depended upon one important factor: the creation of a civilized integration of intelligent life. And the attainment of that goal, he always emphasized, should be reached through nonviolent means.[2]

Even in terms of his educational views, Dewey's approach to social change was analogous to that of a pacifist. The aim of education, he continually stressed, was to fulfill the notion of a democratic society in which all shared the fruits of productivity while at the same time contributing to the welfare of all. For Dewey, education was supposed to be both a moralistic renaissance enabling all individuals to learn to live together peacefully and a practical application of life's everyday experiences to the body of common knowledge already acquired. Education was the key to social cooperation and peace. In *My Pedagogic Creed,* which was originally published in 1897, Dewey let it be known that "moral education centers upon this conception of the school as a mode of social life, that the best and deepest moral training is precisely that which one gets through having to enter into proper relations with others in a unity of work and thought." No doubt, Dewey entertained further thoughts on this subject when he pointed out in *The School and Society* that "a society is a number of people held together because they are working along common lines, in a common spirit, and with reference to common aims. The common needs and aims demand a growing interchange of thought and growing unity of sympathetic feeling." Equally important, in *Moral Principles in Education,* Dewey assailed the educational system in America for its promotion of philistine ethical habits.

> The social work of the school is often limited to training for citizenship and citizenship is then interpreted in a narrow sense as meaning capacity to vote intelligently, disposition to obey laws, etc. But it is futile to contract and cramp the ethical responsibility of the school in this way.

Too often in the past, Dewey claimed, education had been used for narrow and nationalistic purposes. Instead of creating an atmosphere of social harmony, education had degenerated, in his opinion, into a meaningless exercise in chauvinism. Education, as a mode of social life that offers the best and deepest moral training, was, according to Dewey, the only kind of learning conducive to a democratic way of life.[3]

Dewey's concern for social democracy—a democracy best characterized as a form of communal participation without strict governmental control—as well as for the relationship between the "philosopher" and the "public man" was remarkably borne out in his earlier writings on democracy and progressive education. Such writings as *The Ethics of Democracy, Psychology, Outlines of a Critical Theory of Ethics, The School and Society, My Pedagogic Creed, The Child and the Curriculum, Ethics, Moral Principles in Education* and *How We Think* amply demonstrated Dewey's overriding concern for rethinking and redefining issues as well as suggesting new ideas for solving social, economic, and political problems through the use of intelligence and the scientific method. In all of his writings prior to the start of the war, Dewey envisioned his democratic ideals as part of a moralistic-educational crusade that attempted to inculcate in the American mind the values of reason and understanding as opposed to those of armed force and violence. Industrial ills, war, open class conflict, imperialism, and poverty, he believed, could be eliminated through the democratic processes of social cooperation and human understanding. In no way did he encourage the use of armed force to abrogate social injustices. Reason was his primary, and only, weapon. To him, militant force was incompatible with the ethical dictates of democracy. Like Sir Thomas More's, Dewey's utopia was a quest for peace and social harmony.

The issue of war, however, was a topic Dewey paid very little attention to before 1914. Quite clearly, Dewey's entire philosophy had constantly pointed out the desirable qualities of a peaceful and intelligent solution of problems. The justification for the use of force or violence to bring about social change Dewey dismissed as incompatible with his pragmatism. In fact, Dewey's pragmatism, as it was related to public issues, had always emphasized a nonviolent approach to social conflicts. He viewed war (or the deliberate misuse of force and violence) as an irrational method for dealing with human problems. At no time—prior to 1914—did he consider resort to war a viable or intelligent method for establishing the kind of democratic world community which he envisioned. War itself, he argued, was a problem, not a solution. Thus, he was most sympathetic with those intellectuals who opposed America's policy of imperialism during the Spanish-American War in 1898, claiming that imperialism was a lapse in our moral responsibilities for the creation of a peaceful democratic world order. Further, he proudly boasted, at the start of the Progressive era, that "the times were so ripe" that the peace "movement hardly had to be pushed." And later, during the height of Theodore Roosevelt's popularity, he remarked in typical Jamesian fashion:

> The argument for the necessity (short of the attainment of a federated international state with universal authority and policing of the seas) of preparing in peace by enlarged armies and navies for the possibility of war, must be offset at least by the recognition that the position of irresponsible power is always a direct temptation to its irresponsible use. The argument that war is necessary to prevent moral degeneration of individuals may under present conditions, where every day brings its fresh challenge to civic initiative, courage, and vigor, be dismissed as unmitigated nonsense.

At no period before the World War was he sympathetic with the militant Darwinism of Roosevelt and his followers. More could be accomplished through learning and social reconstruction, he urged, than by waging a war in the interests of physical supremacy.[4]

Interestingly enough, however, Dewey did not publicly claim to be a devout pacifist during this period. Although he opposed war as being incompatible with his pragmatic approach to social problems, he said nothing with regard to the concept of pacifism. Since Dewey's pragmatic values were based on a peaceful and intelligent solution of conflicts, it may be assumed that Dewey had no reason to question his philosophical position on the issue of war. The resort to armed force as a means, he had argued, led to its irresponsible use. It would seem reasonable to conclude, therefore, that Dewey felt it was unnecessary for him to claim he was a pacifist simply because he believed that his pragmatic philosophy had clearly defined his position. In his mind no further qualifications or clarifications were needed.

Yet, with the outbreak of hostilities in 1914, Dewey began to change his position regarding the "unmitigated nonsense" of military force. As it became increasingly apparent that Germany's militaristic ambitions were also tied in with her philosophical conception of the state, Dewey underwent a change in his attitude toward war. Earlier, as a graduate student at Johns Hopkins, he had rejected the absolutist philosophy of the German idealists. Now, with German idealist philosophy gradually being transformed into a rationalization of German war aims, Dewey saw a golden opportunity to argue for the use of armed force as a means for bringing about lasting peace. Hoping that the American people would see the virtues of a democratic world order, Dewey went about preparing to explain why German nationalism was a basic threat to world peace and democratic understanding. The emotional appeal for war to offset the evils of German militaristic nationalism and at the same time to end war once and for all was so great that Dewey himself abandoned his earlier argument against the use of military force in international relations. So strong was this emotional appeal that Dewey allowed his own pragmatic idealism to be captured by an irrational motive. Little did he realize at this time how disastrous the consequences would be. Thus, he openly attacked the German war aims, arguing in effect, that they were part of a ceaseless and agelong striving to realize the national will embodied in the German people. By 1915, therefore, he became increasingly critical of both German philosophy and politics, arguing that "patriotism, national feeling and national consciousness . . . have been transformed by deliberate nature into a mystic cult." This mystic cult surrounding militarism, Dewey now believed, had become the moral embodiment of the Prussian state. Like his former colleague at the University of Chicago and the New School, Thorstein Veblen, who pointed out that "the German ideal of statesmanship is . . . to make all the resources of the nation converge on military strength," Dewey no longer accepted the romantic notion he once held of the desirability of German idealism. In a letter to Scudder Klyce, an eccentric friend and critic, he spoke of the deep emotional strain he had undergone while writing *German Philosophy and Politics.* He also expressed a tremendous feeling of relief over the fact that "I was discharging my long-accumulating bile." Admitting that he "had the devil of a time freeing myself" from the mystic cult of German idealism, Dewey now managed to argue that the German mind was quite incompatible with the American mind. "To be in an unsympathetic land, a land which does not understand," he reasoned, "is a stimulus to the most tense kind of Romantic fancy."[5]

Throughout 1916 Dewey began formulating a philosophical rationale with which to sustain the basic values of American democracy against the militaristic policies of the Prussian state. Although very early in the year he signed an appeal to socialists, along with John Reed, Henrietta Rodman, Franklin Gidding, and Carlton Hayes, urging them to continue their support for Wilson in the fall presidential election because "he had kept us out of war," the submarine attacks on American shipping and the reluctance by the German High Command to halt its aggressive policies caused Dewey to reconsider his views on the war. This was a relatively uneasy period for Dewey. The pragmatic method—a philosophy of social reconstruction based on action—had never before been challenged by the threat of world war. It was up to him, he now felt, to come forward with a philosophical justification for the use of military force as an acceptable and intelligent means for bringing about that progressive conception of an international community based on democratic ideals which he prized. His immediate purpose and first inclination was to convince the American public that if armed force was to be applied it should be done in an intelligent and rational fashion. If such force was applied intelligently, it might assist in the creation of a world order based on equality and peace. Thus, in two of Dewey's articles, "Force and Coercion" and "Force, Violence and Law," which were published in the early months of 1916, he contended that coercive force and war could not be separated from the system of power politics in international diplomacy. In true pragmatic fashion Dewey reasoned that the war could not be dissociated from the ends it sought to achieve. The question, as he saw it, was one of clarifying the dynamics of social change: on the one hand there was force, on the other, violence. Because of the fact that law was the use of efficient force, legal force in the form of military enforcement could thus be considered a legitimate lever of social change; violence, however, was a wasteful force and therefore to be spurned. As he arrived at this hypothesis, he began questioning it more seriously. Realizing that his philosophy called for action, Dewey believed that it was possible for him to argue that the intelligent use of armed force was the only legitimate means with which to establish lasting peace while at the same time countering the irrational forces of hyperpatriotism.

Dewey realized, however, that his pragmatic-instrumentalist support for war would be questioned by many of his friends and intellectual admirers. He was also aware that many of his pacifist contemporaries would be upset with his decision. Yet he believed that some form of action was needed. He was convinced that, although pacifism as an ideal was both worthy and admirable, it was, given the present circumstances, simply unrealistic. For Dewey, pacifism became a negative concept; it implied withdrawal. In terms of his own philosophy which continually stressed action, the pacifists' method, he now emphasized, "is like trying to avoid conflict in the use of the road by telling men to love one another, instead of by instituting a rule of the road." The pacifists' lack of awareness as to the seriousness of the matter thus led Dewey to inform his readers in the *New Republic* that "at the very worst most of these young people appear to me victims of a moral innocency and an inexpertness" which can only be overcome by realizing the possibilities of "intellectualizing" the use of force. Like the famous trial lawyer Clarence Darrow, Dewey discovered that pacifism is probably a good doctrine in time of peace, but of no value in wartime. Pacifism, Dewey was now convinced, shared a lack of faith in constructive, inventive intelligence.[6]

When it appeared early in 1917 that American military participation had become inevitable, Dewey converted his energies toward "employing force economically and efficiently, so as to get results with the least waste." Bolstered in his support of the war by the fact that his oldest son, Frederick Archibald Dewey, was commissioned an officer in the United States Army, Dewey emotionally called upon all Americans to join the war effort and work for the construction of a postwar world designed to perpetuate peace. Dewey sincerely believed that if the war was intelligently directed it might be used to achieve worthwhile ends beyond the defeat of Germany. The real problem was making the people understand this fact before they were overwhelmed by a chauvinistic patriotism.[7]

Dewey's hope for American participation was answered on April 2, 1917. After two years of intense negotiations, President Wilson succumbed to the pressures of patriotic loyalty and national honor. Throughout 1915 and 1916 Wilson had sought to stave off American involvement in the war. His own reelection campaign had been geared to assuring the American public that Europe could settle her own domestic squabbles without any help from us. But the refusal of the German Imperial Government to change its submarine policy as well as its covert activities in Mexico on the part of German Foreign Secretary Alfred Zimmermann, left Wilson with little room in which to operate. By March 1, 1917, with the release of the Zimmermann note being made public, American sentiment for military involvement had reached its peak. A month later America was at war.

Wilson's war message to Congress, which was passed by a vote of 82 to 6 in the Senate and 373 to 50 in the House, renewed Dewey's faith in America's democratic mission. If there was a war to be fought in the name of self-righteous ideals and unselfish principles, World War I, Dewey felt, was just such a war. The phrases Wilson echoed such as "the world must be made safe for democracy," "a war to end all wars," and "peace without victory" were pleasing to Dewey's ear. His faith in war as a progressive vehicle for social reconstruction undoubtedly had been reaffirmed by Wilson's solemn message. Perhaps the war, he thought to himself, might not be such a bad adventure after all.

By June, 1917 Dewey was America's leading academic spokesman for the war effort. Technique had now replaced cooperation while reason gave way to emotion. A month earlier he had written an article in *Seven Arts* magazine which carried further his justification of America's commitment across the Atlantic while also criticizing Germany for starting the war. His distaste for the militaristic aspects of the German state was clearly evident in this article. The war against Germany, he pointed out, was not to be directed against its people but rather its philosophy—a philosophy that glorified the state and idealized militarism. It was America's mission, he declared, to see that our ideals should also be realized by our Allies. To Dewey, the mission consisted of an Allied victory which in turn might guarantee and insure the creation of a new world order based on peace and democracy. Over and over again he would emphasize this theme. It was his primary reason for supporting war in the first place. His support for United States involvement, therefore, was based upon a pragmatic argument which justified the use of military force as a means for bringing about peace. Dewey's optimism was so strong that his philosophic support for World War I failed to deal effectively with the more troublesome aspects of a nation at war. So concerned was he about the ends that he completely miscalculated the rationality and effectiveness of the means. Moreover, by insisting that American ideals should be forced upon our allies—the war should be fought for what we thought was right—he was contradicting his own criticisms of German idealism and nationalism which he had developed earlier in *German Philosophy and Politics.* It was his conviction, nevertheless, that the submarine and airplane might "do more to displace war than all the moralizing in existence"; that "air navigation alone would obliterate national frontiers," and that the "social mobilization of science" would "initiate a new type of democracy."[8]

During the months of July, August, and September, 1917, Dewey published four articles in the *New Republic.* "Conscience and Compulsion," "The Future of Pacifism," "What America Will Fight For," and "Conscription of Thought" all illustrated Dewey's attempt to unify the country behind a program of socialized democracy for "binding up the wounds that had rent the body politic and putting an end to years of aimless drift." It was his initial disposition to believe that war might strengthen American democracy at home and international progressivism abroad. Thus, he felt compelled to show that the method of intelligence did not exclude the use of force in international relations. The net result of these four articles was a conscious effort on the part of Dewey to demonstrate the fundamental compatibility between pragmatism and war.[9]

Dewey seems to have overcome, at this point, his preoccupation with American indecisiveness. The shift from "hesitation" and "aimless drift" to criticizing the conscience of pacifists is clearly evident in his summer articles. Having long ago cast aside his own uncertainties, he now turned to those who still had "doubts, qualms, clouds of bewilderment" about America's entry into the war. To counteract what he regarded as "muddled thinking" on the part of the pacifists and to help expedite the war effort, Dewey called for more attention to the means of its prosecution. In "Conscience and Compulsion" the question, he decided, was not one of being overwhelmed by the forces of compulsion but rather one of allowing the conscience to develop "the machinery, the specific, concrete social arrangements . . . for maintaining peace . . . ." In "The Future of Pacifism" Dewey called upon "those who still think of themselves as fundamentally pacifists in spite of the fact that they believed our entrance into the war a needed thing" and urged them to try to convert the aims of the war to agree with Wilson's ideals. In "What Will America Fight For" he stressed the need for a practical "business-like psychology" that would perceive the ends to be accomplished and make an "effective selection and orderly arrangement of means for their execution." He also spoke of pragmatism's help in enabling people to understand better the progressive social possibilities of the war. The extensive use of science for communal purposes and the creation of a world organization which "crosses nationalistic boundaries and interests" added to his conviction that the use of armed or coercive force might bring about his desired program of socialized democracy. And finally, in "Conscription of Thought" Dewey "hauled up his heaviest technical apparatus" to prove that pragmatism was no ally of pacifism at this time, and that "American participation should consist not in money nor in men, but in the final determination of peace policies which is made possible by the contribution of men and money." Here—in these four articles—was the pragmatic manifesto of Dewey's philosophy placed at the service of the country at war.[10]

Although Dewey was firmly committed to an Allied victory, he did not believe that the improvement of the world should customarily be furthered through international conflict. The paradoxical thing about his wartime writings is that throughout all of them a pacifist theme was most pronounced. Despite Dewey's argument for activism and engagement, one fact remains clear: the theme of world peace was clearly evident in both his thinking and his writings. Indeed, while telling Americans that commitment to our overseas adventure was necessary, he did not forget to remind them that "a task has to be accomplished to abate an international nuisance, but in the accomplishing there is the prospect of a world organization and the beginnings of a public control which crosses nationalistic boundaries and interests." Even though "these aims are not as yet immediate actualities. . . ," he went on to argue, "it is ridiculous to say that they are mere idealistic glosses, sugar-coatings of the bitter pill of war. They present genuine possibilities, objects of a fair adventure."[11] The hope of the world lies within the recognition that "the peculiarity of our nationalism is its internationalism."[12] In order to avoid enmity and division, the world would have to agree to the possibilities of international cooperation. Without it, Dewey explained, the effort to secure unity would result in failure.

A spirit of international progressivism can easily be detected in Dewey's wartime writings. A compulsive urge for social and international reconstruction based on democratic ideals best accounts for Dewey's pragmatic justification for war. Although Dewey had overlooked such examples of American self-interest as insurance of the security of loans to allies, safety of American ships and cargoes traveling to and from the war zone, the search for new markets, and the growing predominance of the United States in world affairs, it can be pointed out that his primary goal had been the achievement of world peace on a permanent basis. If Dewey must be labeled a hawk, it should be done with certain reservations. A distinct air of dovishness appeared in all his articles.

From Dewey's pragmatic point of view, moreover, the war was simply a realistic means for enabling him to draw up a plan for world peace and domestic reconstruction. In no way was the martial spirit his guiding light. In "A League of Nations and Economic Freedom," for example, Dewey urged that the free-trade provisions of Wilson's proposed Fourteen Points be employed to encourage the "haves" to give credit and raw materials to the "have-nots" at low interest rates and cheap prices. Equality of trade conditions, Dewey believed, was a prerequisite for curing nations of the impulse to make war. In the long run, Dewey pointed out, it would be in the best interests of wealthy nations to perform such charitable acts. Not only would they be working for peace but also building up more prosperous markets for the future. Borrowing a page from Norman Angell's *The Great Illusion,* Dewey sought to transform economic avarice into international shareholding.[13] Furthermore, in "Internal Social Reorganization after the War," Dewey proposed that domestic social reconstruction was necessary in order to guarantee world peace. Unlike Edward Bellamy's plan for the creation of an industrial army or William James's proposal for a domestic reconstruction corps, Dewey urged the creation of government agencies for the purpose of securing steady and useful employment as well as combating industrial oppression. It was Dewey's firm belief that if government agencies could effectively organize a nation for war, they could also work toward upgrading the scale of living by fighting a war against industrial abuse and capitalistic oppression. He saw the war as a unique opportunity to foster social reconstruction at home. The greatest benefit resulting from the war, Dewey maintained, would be a new social consciousness that would provide

> greater ability on the part of the workers in any particular trade or occupation to control that industry, instead of working under . . . conditions of external control where they have no interest, no insight into what they are doing, and no social outlook upon the consequences and meaning of what they are doing.[14]

In both articles Dewey's primary concern was for the creation of a lasting and durable peace. If at times it appeared as though the means he chose proved mistaken, the ideals, nevertheless, were worthy of some consideration.

Dewey's plan for world peace and domestic reconstruction was too vague to be given serious consideration by statesmen and world leaders. He was well aware, however, that it was somewhat vague to begin with. Yet, it was characteristic of his own instrumentalist philosophy to offer incomplete programs that he hoped would be tested and revaluated later on in the light of accumulated evidence. The plan he sketched, therefore, indicated a direction needed to be taken, and would assume a more concrete form as experimental steps were taken to implement it. The problem, unfortunately, was that it was excessively optimistic in view of the hostile environment in which it was proposed. The method of intelligence was no challenge to the forces of ultranationalism and hyperpatriotism. Just how economic parity could be achieved, given the contemporary atmosphere of international animosity, or how government agencies could establish social justice in light of domestic intolerance, Dewey's plan failed to answer adequately. Furthermore, his argument that the war might enhance the cause of domestic and international democracy became politically incapacitated by the virulent war psychology. Instead of democracy serving the cause of world peace, it became the rallying cry for America's most militant hawks. Ironically, democracy became not an international ideal or domestic social lever but an expression of national value and patriotic fervor. Optimism rather than the war itself proved to be Dewey's biggest adversary.

But if there was one tangible motive behind Dewey's support for the war, it was his belief in the practical possibilities of a world organization in support of peace. While continuing to work out his philosophical justifications for American military involvement, he also became an ardent supporter of President Wilson's call for a League of Nations. If Dewey's pragmatic idealism had one goal, it was to see the war bring about a new world order. The Wilsonian rhetoric for a "war to end all wars" and a crusade to "make the world safe for democracy" made a strong impact on

Dewey. Perhaps it would be only proper to conclude that Dewey shared with Wilson the progressives' dream of a world based on international cooperation and democratic understanding. In an article entitled "What Are We Fighting For?" he argued that "if we are to have a world safe *for* democracy *and* a world *in* which democracy is safely anchored, the solution will be in the direction of a federated world government and a variety of freely experimenting and freely cooperating self-governing local, cultural, and industrial groups." This, according to Dewey, "is the ultimate sanction of democracy, for which we are fighting."[15]

When the possibility of a League of Nations came under critical discussion and debate in the closing weeks of the war, Dewey readily offered his views. In a series of four articles published in the *Dial* magazine during November and December of 1918, Dewey called upon the leaders of the world to generate a new type of international diplomacy that "would stimulate the tendency to use the intellectual power generated in modern industry and commerce for something besides personal advantage."[16] The four articles, "The Approach to a League of Nations," "The League of Nations and the New Diplomacy," "The Fourteen Points and the League of Nations," and "A League of Nations and Economic Freedom," were solidly behind the fourteen conditions of peace set forth by Wilson. Interestingly enough, they called for greater cooperation among people by stressing the ethical possibilities of human understanding along with equalization of economic conditions. "The resources and abilities are at hand if we choose to use them," Dewey told his readers. "The question is as to the depth and endurance of our desire."[17]

Despite this rather optimistic appraisal supporting a pragmatic justification for military force, there was another side to the war, one which was less pleasant. When Dewey asked his readers in the *New Republic* to accept his philosophical explanation for the war, he did not expect their patriotic zeal and intolerance to reach the unreasonable proportions that it soon achieved. Stunned by the adverse effects of the massive propaganda campaign launched by George Creel's Committee on Public Information, Dewey watched helplessly as the growth of a negative nationalistic spirit ran counter to his own pragmatic idealism. The illiberal nature of war was a factor he was aware of but failed to assess precisely. If he had taken the time to consult Wilson's war message to Congress, which stated that "if there should be disloyalty, it will be dealt with with a firm hand of stern repression. . . ," Dewey might not have been so badly misled.[18] As events were to show, Dewey's optimism blinded him to a proper understanding of the war mentality, and, even more important, his pragmatic philosophy was ineffective when faced with this new predicament.

While Dewey was preparing to send off a completed manuscript to

Herbert Croly—editor of the *New Republic*—in the early months of 1917, he was struck by the unwillingness of a colleague and fellow department chairman at Columbia to allow the son of the late Russian novelist and pacifist Count Leo Tolstoy to lecture at the university. When Dewey questioned Professor John D. Prince, head of the Department of Slavonic Languages, about his refusal to allow the guest to deliver his lecture, he found to his dismay that Prince was afraid the young count might belittle patriotism. Prince's reasoning, quite naturally, proved unsatisfactory to Dewey. In a letter to the *New York Times,* Dewey criticized Prince's position, arguing that the right to free speech was a basic part of the American democratic system. In addition, as Dewey pointed out, academic freedom should not be eroded by a chauvinistic patriotism that had already shown its worst side among the European nations. Democratic liberty and academic freedom were virtues, Dewey claimed, that had to be guaranteed as well as protected.[19]

Yet academic illiberalism did become part of the very nature of war's intolerance, and Dewey, quite clearly, had reason for concern. Indeed, the problem of academic freedom became further compounded when in the fall of that year Professors Henry Dana and James McKeen Cattell were dismissed by the Board of Trustees—with the approval of President Nicholas Murray Butler—for their alleged "unpatriotic" disapproval of the war. Dewey's immediate reaction to the dismissals was one of dismay. Annoyed by the authoritarian tactics of President Butler and the Columbia Board of Trustees, Dewey, along with two other professors, James Harvey Robinson and John Reed Powell, wrote a letter to Professor A. A. Young of Cornell University. Young, chairman of the Committee on Academic Freedom and Tenure of the American Association of University Professors, was requested by Dewey and the others to investigate the case "in order to protect the name of the University in case the procedure of dismissal was justifiable and to protect not only the repute of these men but others against arbitrary action in case the action in substance or form was unjustified."[20] Unfortunately, the investigation never materialized.

The dismissals of Dana and Cattell, however, were not the last by the Board of Trustees. No sooner had the furor died down at Morningside Heights than another situation arose, more explosive than the first one. Leon Fraser, a young political scientist, had just completed an article soon to be published in the *New Republic* criticizing the military training camp at Plattsburgh, New York. The article so inflamed the patriotic President Butler that he demanded Fraser's resignation. When the young professor refused to resign under pressure, Butler summoned the Board of Trustees, which immediately dismissed him. Fraser's dismissal sent shock waves vibrating throughout the academic community and also brought forth a sharp response and warning from Dewey's friend and colleague in the Department of Political Science, Charles A. Beard. Unfortunately, the board would not retract its decision; this caused Beard to resign. The resignation greatly affected Dewey. As he told a *New York Times* reporter: "I regard the action of Professor Beard as the natural consequence of the degrading action of the trustees last week. I personally regret the loss to the university of such a scholarly man and teacher of such rare power."[21] This incident revealed a side of the nature of war that he had hoped would not occur. Unfortunately, Dewey remained in his soft academic cushion at Columbia decrying the excesses of war yet refusing to abandon his original commitment.

Academic intolerance, however, was not confined to the college campus in 1917. In December of the same year three teachers–Samuel Schmalhausen, Thomas Mufson, and A. Henry Schneer–were dismissed from their teaching positions at De Witt Clinton High School in New York City. They were discharged, according to the City Board of Education, for "holding views subversive of good discipline and [*sic*] undermining good citizenship in the schools."[22] Fearing the rise of Prussianism at home, Dewey lashed out at the board by calling them "self-righteous patriots" who impugned other people's loyalty. He also stated that the three teachers were treated unfairly in being "charged with a lack of that active or aggressive loyalty which the state has a right to demand, in war time particularly, from its paid servants."[23] What was most discouraging to Dewey, however, was the fact that chauvinistic patriotism had filtered into the academic community. Education–that citadel of democracy–was being corrupted by its own excessive zeal to back the war effort.

Public vindictiveness toward those who opposed the war could not easily be abated. Many of the "opponents of war" underwent severe hardships–even the threat of death at the hands of their fellow Americans. Criticism of conscientious objectors became so severe at one point, during the summer of 1917, that Dewey argued that "such young people deserve something better than accusations, varying from pro-Germanism and the crime of Socialism to traitorous disloyalty, which the newspapers so readily 'hurl' at them–to borrow their own language." But public reaction to dissent was strong. The Espionage Acts made it doubly difficult for anyone who wished to disagree or express disappointment with the conduct of the war. As Dewey began to recognize that his hopes for understanding throughout the world would no longer prove feasible even at home, he remarked sadly: "Treason is every opinion and belief which irritates the majority of loyal citizens. For the time being the conservative upholders of the constitution are on the side of moral mob rule and and psychological lynch law." This "explanation of our lapse" proved to be a rude awakening for Dewey. Yet, having tied his whole philosophy to the war effort, he was incapable of finding a cathartic remedy for domestic intolerance. Miscalculating the power of intelligence, all Dewey could say now was that "the appeal is no longer to reason; it is to the event."[24]

Both Jane Addams and Norman Thomas could sympathize with Dewey's rational judgment that domestic intolerance is a dangerous thing. But their sense of appreciation had been diminished by the fact that Dewey himself had abandoned their ranks. Dewey's defection had increased their despair. It was a difficult period, Jane Addams recounted, when "every student of our time had become more or less a disciple of pragmatism and its great teachers in the United States had come out for the war. . . ."[25] It was even more difficult for her to recall the days at Hull House when John Dewey spent a great deal of time teaching the values of human cooperation and understanding. Norman Thomas also found it hard to accept the logic of Professor Dewey's article "Conscience and Compulsion." Thomas, indeed, could not believe his eyes when he read the article in the *New Republic.* So incensed was he by Dewey's remarks, that he made his own plea for "War's Heretics." Castigating Dewey for his unreasonableness in toying with man's conscience, Thomas went on to argue that "it cannot be too strongly insisted that the majority of conscientious objectors . . . believe that the same course of action which keeps oneself 'unspotted from within' will ultimately prove the only safe means for establishing a worthy social system."[26] To both Jane Addams and Norman Thomas it was a sad fact that Dewey's pragmatism, which had served as a symbol of intelligent humanitarianism in the past, could so easily adjust itself to the dictates of war.

But if there was one person who in any way caused Dewey to reconsider his position, it was Randolph Bourne. As a former student, Bourne was a sympathetic admirer of Dewey's pragmatic philosophy. Bourne enthusiastically accepted Dewey's philosophy of progressive education and was himself instrumental in spreading his ideas on the subject. It was a major disappointment to Bourne when Dewey began arguing for American military participation in Europe. Dewey's support for the war, therefore, came as a shock to Bourne, who saw it as a direct contradiction to all the values he had stood for.

Bourne's criticisms centered around Dewey's argument that war might be guided to a constructive conclusion. It was not so much the pragmatic method of intelligence that irritated Bourne as it was the abandonment of moral values central to Dewey's philosophy. Such values as nonviolence, social justice, communal cooperation, and human understanding were being cast aside in the win-the-war rush for democratic internationalism. What Dewey failed to see, according to Bourne, was that his pragmatic idealism had caused him to miscalculate the irrational forces of war. More importantly,

Dewey's emphasis on utility afforded him no specific program to counteract the predominant trend of "vagueness" and "impracticality." To Bourne it was obvious that Dewey had no concrete plan in mind as to the specific working-out of his democratic desires, either nationally or internationally, once the war had ended. A philosophy of adjustment, Bourne felt, was no philosophy at all.

His first attack appeared in an article entitled "Conscience and Intelligence in War." Objecting to Dewey's position, Bourne argued that war was an uncontrollable force which could offer no international benefits. In obvious contrast to Dewey's argument that "if we entered the war intelligently we would choose the ends which the war technique might serve," Bourne began by saying that "war is just that absolute situation which is its own end and its own means, and which speedily outstrips the power of intelligence and creative control." Was not Dewey's pragmatism placing technique above values, Bourne asked? Was not war a failure of the power of intelligence? Ending on a bitter note, therefore, Bourne severely chastized Dewey by saying that "it is perhaps better to be a martyr than a hypocrite. And if pragmatists like Mr. Dewey are going to accept 'inevitables,' you at least have an equal right to choose what shall seem inevitable to you." His article was such a devastating criticism of the pragmatic position on war that Jane Addams felt compelled to write Bourne to tell him how much she had enjoyed reading it.[27]

Bourne's most telling criticism, however, appeared in an article under the caption "Twilight of Idols," published in the *Seven Arts,* in October, 1917. Here Bourne maintained that Dewey's naive belief that war might serve a useful purpose "pointed to two defects in his philosophy." One was his attitude of optimism, which led him to misinterpret the influence of intelligence in wartime. The other was his relation of thought to action, in which he "overly stressed technique at the expense of value." Both these views, Bourne contended, were based on a method of expediency. In his denunciation of Dewey, Bourne developed his own pragmatic evaluation of Dewey's philosophy, concluding that pragmatism was not geared for emergencies. Linking pragmatism to opportunism, Bourne further excoriated the way in which the pragmatists accepted the war by referring to it as "a scientific method applied to uplift." But perhaps more serious was Bourne's charge that the pragmatist intellectuals' insistence—with Professor Dewey at the helm—on reason and education for peaceful transition was now being converted to support the war effort. The distinction between means and ends, Bourne emphasized, could no longer be evaluated by a pragmatic method in response to war. Understandably, the disappointed Bourne thought of pragmatism as a philosophy of technique, "a philosophy which tells you how to accomplish your ends once the ends have been established."

And although he admitted that Dewey hoped to develop his technique along with vision—a capacity for framing ideals and ends—he felt that Dewey and his disciples had become completely technique-conscious and morally blind. In a letter to his literary companion Van Wyck Brooks, Bourne sadly reflected: "No intellectual leader has cared to think. The defection of Dewey is typical."[28]

It would appear that Randolph Bourne did much to discredit the pragmatists' support for the first World War. So effective was Bourne's attack upon Dewey and his disciples that Dewey himself never completely forgave the "literary wit" from Bloomfield, New Jersey. In January, 1919, when Dr. Frederick Matthias Alexander's *Man's Supreme Inheritance*—with an introduction by Dewey—was harshly reviewed by Bourne (Bourne wrote the review shortly before his death in the fall of 1918, but it did not appear in public until January of the following year), Dewey declared he would no longer write for the *New Republic* if the editors of the magazine continued to print any of Bourne's unpublished material. And later, while on a train traveling to the Trotsky hearings in Mexico in 1937, the novelist James T. Farrell pressed Dewey on the subject of Randolph Bourne. Finding it hard to receive much information from the usually quiet Dewey, Farrell nevertheless did manage to get Dewey to say that "Bourne was extremely clever and gifted, but he did not have depth."[29] It was obvious, however, that Bourne did have a great impact on Dewey, if in no other way than to point out that the eminent philosopher's support for war was based on an "unanalyzable feeling" that this was a war which had to be. To accept such a position, Bourne reasoned, was clearly an abandonment of what pragmatism actually stood for. To accept the means at hand without the ability to predict the ends was unquestionably a gross philosophical misconception of what thinking is all about. Dewey's generalizations and sweeping assertions, Bourne contended, were completely out of line with his philosophical reasoning. Such an attack clearly demonstrated how "empty-handed" Dewey's pragmatism really was when challenged by the irrational forces of war.

But if Bourne's attack was galling to Dewey, it nonetheless provided him with a new insight into his own philosophical methodology. In a direct way, Randolph Bourne's criticisms opened the door for Dewey to carefully reexamine his own pragmatic beliefs and predispositions. Although Bourne himself may have been guilty of falsely accusing Dewey for abandoning all values—Dewey's basic goal was to achieve world peace—he was indeed correct in arguing that Dewey's support for war was morally wrong. Bourne's moral argument gave Dewey something to think about. By pointing out that the pragmatic method was in fact an instrument for peaceful social change that relied more upon moral reason than blind emotion, Bourne had initiated a whole new trend in Dewey's way of thinking when it came to the issue of war and peace. Perhaps most of all, Bourne brought back to life Dewey's earlier assumptions and beliefs regarding the peaceful aspects of his pragmatic method. Accordingly, the war and its tragic aftermath convinced Dewey that violence was not only immoral but also unpragmatic. The emotional impact of war had proved to be more compelling than any appeals to reason and understanding. Thus, later on he would write:

We have depended upon the clash of war, the stress of revolution, the emergence of heroic individuals, the impact of migrations generated by war and famine, the incoming of barbarians, to change established institutions. Instead of constantly utilizing unused impulse to effect continuous reconstruction, we have waited till an accumulation of stresses suddenly breaks through the dikes of custom.[30]

Adjustment to past habits would now have to give way to a conscious reordering of society.

Clearly [Dewey noted in *Experience and Nature*], we have not carried the plane of conscious control, the direction of action by perception of connections, far enough. We cannot separate organic life and mind from physical nature without also separating nature from life and mind. The separation has reached a point where intelligent persons are asking whether the end is to be catastrophe, the subjection of man to the industrial and military machines he has created.[31]

Bourne's emphasis on nonviolence and reason produced Dewey's conversion to pacifism. Bourne's criticisms were so telling that Dewey was compelled to write later that "what is needed is that the more rational and social conduct should itself be valued as good and so be chosen and sought. . . ." The importance of such a need, he also maintained, "is . . . to remake social conditions so that they will almost automatically support fuller and more enduring values and will reduce those social habits which favor free play of impulse unordered by thought, or which make men satisfied to fall into mere routine and convention." The means he chose to employ for accomplishing this noble task were those of a pacifist:

The justification of the moral non-conformist is that when he denies the rightfulness of a particular claim [i.e., right to wage wars] he is doing so not for the sake of private advantage, but for the sake of an object which will serve more amply and consistently the welfare of all.[32]

Indeed, this statement is a far cry from his "business-like" opposition to the conscientious objector of World War I. He was now willing to bite the bullet, and he did!

The criticisms by Randolph Bourne, the dismissals of Henry Dana, James M. Cattell, and Leon Fraser at Columbia University, the firing of the three teachers at De Witt Clinton High School in New York, and the public's intolerance of conscientious objectors all began to weight heavily on Dewey's conscience. An inner struggle for balance developed. Torn between his hopes for a better world and his increasing disillusionment with the way events were turning out, Dewey appeared extremely depressed. A growing conflict between the quiet and reserved professional academician and the outspoken archangel in support of American war aims quickly manifested itself in the form of his general reluctance to visit friends. Quite clearly, a feeling of loneliness and abandonment set in. The sobering experience of the war quickly started to take its toll on Dewey. So upset was he by the dissolution of the prewar progressive consensus that he had always identified himself with, as well as by the never-ending criticism he was receiving from some of his long-time personal friends, that, as Max Eastman recalls, "he got into a state of tension that in most people would have been an illness."[33] Perhaps the greatest shock to Dewey came in the form of rejection by his close friends and admirers. It was to prove difficult enough for him to witness the failure of his democratic hopes and desires, but it was to prove even more discouraging to him to have to hear those who in the past had been his staunchest supporters now denounce him as a misguided child. What the war managed to accomplish, Dewey's detractors angrily noted, was not the encouragement of progressive enlightenment but its dissolution. Consequently, not only did Dewey become alienated from Bourne's intellectual circle but also somewhat from himself. This great personal strain and psychological torment led Dewey to seek treatments for a back ailment which he claimed was quite painful, from an unconventional physician by the name of Frederick Matthias Alexander. If for no other reason than to seek solace, Dewey now longed for understanding. Whether or not the treatments were purely physical remains a question of considerable speculation.

Ironically, Dewey's romantic hope had been partially fulfilled, but it also was soon to be completely forgotten. The war, the bloodiest in history up to that time, recorded tremendous casualties (American losses totaled 48,000 killed in action, 2,900 missing in action, and 56,000 dead of disease, while Russia counted 1,700,000 battle deaths, Germany 1,800,000, France 1,385,000, Britain 947,000, and Austria-Hungary 1,200,000). The mental anguish resulting from this experience equalled the number of casualties on the field of battle. The resulting joy that accompanied the signing of the armistice at three o'clock in the morning of Monday, November 11, 1918, was suddenly silenced by the thoughts for those who had sacrificed their lives in combat. Happiness was mixed with grief, joy with despair. And as people had time to think, bitterness began to replace compassion. The hope for a just settlement had been lost during the war. The trauma of destruction proved more effective than any willingness to reconstruct a new world order along the lines of peace and understanding. Retribution rather than cooperation greeted President Wilson as he sailed for France in December, 1918.

The Paris Peace Conference, or the Treaty of Versailles, proved abortive from the start. As Wilson sat and consulted with Lloyd George of Great Britain, Clemenceau of France, and Orlando of Italy, it became painfully clear that patriotism, nationalistic jealousies, and revenge were more important than a League of Nations and world peace. "Peace without Victory" was bargained away on the conference table–understanding negotiated away for retaliation. Huge reparations, the seizure from Germany of the mineral-rich territory of Alsace-Lorraine, and a "war guilt" clause proved offensive to those supporting the doctrine of a "just peace." Like the Christians who were fed to the lions, Germany was sacrificed at Versailles. Perhaps for these reasons Dewey could no longer share any of Wilson's optimism for peace. His retreat from idealism to pessimism was now in full swing.

By the early months of 1919, therefore, Dewey was voicing his own disillusionment with the prospects for international peace. His attitude underwent a drastic metamorphosis characterized by despair and uncertainty. In marked contrast to his wartime beliefs, he now reasoned that the war had failed to bring about either a regeneration of the nation or a lasting advance toward international peace. The four-year struggle had been so destructive and widespread that the mere prospect of a future war evoked an overwhelming sense of dread. Yet, far from ensuring a permanent world peace, the Treaty of Versailles, he honestly feared, would lay the groundwork for future wars; it was for all intents and purposes the negotiated establishment of inequality. Almost a year after the armistice with Germany was signed, Dewey published his own interpretation of the work at the Paris Peace Conference under the caption "The Discrediting of Idealism." Writing as one of those who, though "strongly opposed to war in general broke with the pacifists because they saw in this war a means of realizing pacific ideals," Dewey surprisingly added his own apologia to that of his wartime critics: "The defeat of idealistic aims has been, without exaggeration, enormous. The consistent pacifist has much to urge now in his own justification; he is entitled to his flourish of private triumphings." The peace had been abortive, he added, because intelligence had not been used. The defeat of idealism, he sadly concluded, was due to a failure of intelligence: an optimistic belief that physical energy in unison with morals and ideals could have a self-propelling and self-executing capacity.[34]

The principal blame for the catastrophe at Versailles, in Dewey's opinion, rested upon the shoulders of the "American people who revelled in emotionalism and who grovelled in sacrifice of its liberties. . . ."[35] More importantly, the Versailles tragedy also demonstrated, he believed, the American people's lack of faith in the intelligent use of armed force. "If the principle of [military] force to the limit had been in operation in behalf of our ideals," Dewey firmly insisted, "the professed aims of the United States might have been achieved." In practice, he reflected, the United States should have insisted on the terms of its entry before going into the war on the side of the Allies. But just how this could have been done, or how military force was to be directed by intelligence, Dewey did not say. Little did he realize at the time that he himself had contributed to the illusion of coercive force and therefore was partly to blame for the failure of American idealism.[36]

Dewey even rejected his earlier support for the League of Nations because he was convinced that it represented both structurally and functionally an implementation of a no longer relevant, undemocratic nationalistic philosophy and set of assumptions. Agreeing with the editorialist Walter Lippmann, who also had supported Wilson's war aims, that "the results are so little like the promises," Dewey concluded that there was very little hope for the extension of government beyond national boundaries.[37] The results of this "Carthaginian Peace" convinced Dewey that the peacemakers had devoted their attention not to an international organization dedicated to achieving a permanent peace but rather to "details of economic advantage distributed in proportion to physical power to create future disturbances."[38] He now feared even more the corruption of democracy by outside influences while, at the same time, realizing the need for international cooperation. His article "Our National Dilemma" printed in the *New Republic* on March 24, 1920, pictured the country as faced with the dilemma that isolation is impossible and participation perilous. Having discredited his own idealism, Dewey now maintained that the foreign policies of France and England were completely "non-democratic" and bent upon the destruction of Germany. The United States had an obligation, Dewey vigorously warned, "not to engage too much or too readily with them until there is assurance that we shall not make themselves or ourselves worse, rather than better, by what is called sharing the common burdens of the world."[39] Quite clearly, this line of reasoning or argumentation would have been more appropriate to the pragmatist argument at the beginning of the war than at its completion.

Yet, if there was one question Dewey asked himself as he prepared for a postwar trip to the Far East, it was this: Had the pacifists been right in the first place? Perhaps he would have conceded many points to his erstwhile opponents; but generally speaking, he believed that the realists had been right in using the war as a means for carrying forward the ideal of international progressivism. His support for war, he earnestly believed, was consistent with the realists' understanding of power politics in world affairs. If armed force had been employed intelligently, he argued, miracles might have been performed. Unfortunately, war is not a good magician.

The inability to bring the war to a just conclusion and the birth of an intense and explosive nationalistic spirit was convincing proof of how excessively optimistic Dewey's understanding of the progressive possibilities of war had been. In later years Dewey would disavow the utilization of military force, sanctions, or economic boycotts as a rational and intelligent means for solving the problem of world peace. His rejection of the League of Nations after 1919, his reluctance to cooperate with Old World politics, and his general desire to avoid European entanglements merely point out how far he went in the opposite direction. Thus, his acceptance of pacifism as an intelligent means for achieving world peace became a newly discovered aspect of his own pragmatic philosophy. The war and its attendant consequences, therefore, brought to Dewey's attention a part of his philosophy he had never before realized or even seriously considered. Moreover, if anything, Dewey's pragmatism after the war once again became more value-conscious and less technique-minded. His pragmatic ideals now, in fact, were more in line with his newly acquired pacifist thinking.

CHAPTER THREE

DEMOCRACY'S AMBASSADOR TO THE FAR EAST

> The commercial open door is needed. But the need is greater that the door be opened to light, to knowledge and understanding.
>
> Dewey, *China, Japan and the U. S. A.*

The Great Crusade for world peace and international democracy ended in dismal failure. An atmosphere of increasing disillusionment and intense revulsion against war characterized the American scene after November, 1918. Never had the spirit of optimism turned so quickly into an aura of pessimism. The Progressive renaissance for Dewey and those of like mind was now over. The tragedy of the Treaty of Versailles, the economic and political chaos in Europe as a result of the war, the refusal of the United States to join the League of Nations, the harsh reality of domestic intolerance and brutality, and America's repudiation of the ideal of internationalism all added to the conviction that there was no immediate hope of realizing President Wilson's noble aims. The war with all its idealistic fanfare and progressive spirit was now regarded simply as a horrible mistake. No one was more aware of this than John Dewey himself.

The failure of intelligence to democratize the world and guarantee lasting peace was a tremendous blow to his previous philosophical support for war. Instead of the war furthering the goals of internationalism, as he had hoped, it allowed intolerant nationalism and superpatriotism to assume the dominant role in people's lives. Moreover, instead of the war serving as an educational experiment by which to achieve the higher values of peace and understanding, it had merely degenerated into a technique of hatred and despair. For all Dewey's hopes and aspirations that this war would be a war to end all wars, the ultimate conclusion was one of tragic proportions. Not only had this war degenerated into the most bloody of all times, but it also demonstrated to mankind that world peace was a long way off. So misinformed had Dewey been about the pragmatic aspects of war that he rarely wished to engage in debate about the matter. The means he chose to support failed miserably to bring about the end he originally hoped for.

The end of the war, nevertheless, brought Dewey an unexpected opportunity to break away from the routine of his daily concerns. In the summer of 1918 he received an invitation from the University of California at Berkeley to lecture during the fall semester. The timing of the invitation could not have been more perfect. During the winter and spring months Dewey had been searching for a way out of his dilemma. The popularity of Randolph Bourne's criticisms, the rapid increase in domestic intolerance, his wife's physical illness, and his own mental fatigue and conscience-ridden doubts over his position on the war, added to Dewey's conviction that a trip away from New York was desperately needed. Indeed, it was obvious to those close to him that his state of mind was in need of repair. In early August, after having requested and received a sabbatical leave for the academic year 1918–19, Dewey and his wife departed for the west coast.

The stay at Berkeley was an enjoyable change of pace for the Deweys. Away from the hectic pace of city living, they found the majestic beauty of northern California admirably suited to their leisurely way of life. Neither Dewey nor his wife was a city person at heart. In fact, Dewey's own easygoing mien may be attributed to his boyhood years in the small city of Burlington, Vermont. So agreeable was their stay at Berkeley that they both seemed much more healthy. In addition, Dewey also appeared to be regaining some of his confidence which he felt he had lost as a result of his wartime position. Indeed, it was, they happily agreed, merely the start of a long-awaited vacation.

Yet, it was while he was lecturing at Berkeley that the seeds were planted for a journey to the Far East. Since he was scheduled to lecture only for the fall semester, Dewey had time to think about what he would do during the remainder of his sabbatical. The nearness to the Far East convinced him that he and his wife should continue their westward journey and head for Japan. They were anxious to expand their cultural horizons. Both thus agreed that Japan would be a pleasant place to visit.

Aside from merely enjoying the pleasures of vacationing in the Far East, Dewey saw immense political advantages from such a visit. He somewhat shrewdly looked upon a trip to the Far East as a golden opportunity to regain some of the prestige he had lost as a result of his support for the war. In his letters to his children while he was in the Far East, one can find sufficient evidence that before his journey to the Orient he had already entertained the possibility of publicizing his views on democracy as a means for redressing past grievances. He looked upon himself as a new Messiah preaching the word of democracy as the panacea for war. Democracy was for him the most important weapon in his arsenal for world peace. An overriding passion to get back into the good graces of the more "value-minded" of his liberal opponents led Dewey happily to inform an old friend of his that "Mrs. Dewey and I have decided that we may never again get as near Japan as we are now and that as the years are passing, it is now or never with us." And so on January 22, 1919, the Deweys boarded the Japanese liner *Shunyu Maru* and headed for the land of the rising sun.[1]

Upon learning of Dewey's planned visit, Dr. Ono Eijiro cabled Dewey and invited him to give a series of lectures at the Imperial University in Tokyo. Ono, a leading banker in Japan, had met Dewey while he was studying for his Ph.D. degree in political science at the University of Michigan. Dewey, who was also fond of Ono, more than welcomed the opportunity to lecture in Japan. In a rather optimistic fashion he hoped that the lectures might help to bring about closer relations between Japan and the United States. Here was the opportunity he had been looking for. Already Japan had displayed her expansive desires in the area of foreign affairs when she placed her Twenty-one Demands on the doorstep of the Chinese embassy in 1915. Dewey now recognized the immense advantages he could gain by calling for the Japanese government to adopt a more peaceful and democratic policy in the realm of international relations. The lectures, he believed, would serve as a vehicle for communicating his own ideas for world peace. Furthermore, he saw the lectures as a means for bringing him back into the good graces of his wartime critics. Thus, while sailing across the Pacific, he wired to Ono expressing his delight with the proposal. Arrangements were then made for Dewey to deliver a series of eight lectures at the university. The lectures were to be given on Tuesday and Friday afternoons at 3:30 P.M., beginning on February 25 and lasting until March 21. On February 9, 1919, the Deweys set foot on the Japanese mainland.

The general theme of his talks dealt mainly with the problem of reconstructing moral and social thinking and the benefits to be derived from a democratic way of life. Throughout the eight lectures Dewey referred to the problems resulting from the war and the general need for all peoples to reconsider their traditional habits of thought. The audiences were generally polite and attentive as the American philosopher pointed out that philosophy had to be reconstructed along the lines of contemporary democratic thought. Philosophy could no longer afford to remain static or tied to the past. The need was for developing new ways to create a world society based on democratic principles. The failure to avoid the tragedy of the last four years, he constantly reemphasized, was primarily due to the inability to adapt to modern ways of collective thinking. That was the key, Dewey felt, which was needed for reconstructing philosophy. The lectures appeared in book form in 1921 under the title *Reconstruction in Philosophy.*

The lectures were an important key in understanding Dewey's new attitude toward the issues of war and peace. They mark a turning point in Dewey's acceptance of pacifist values. The justification of the use of military force was no longer acceptable to him. In its place the instrument of democracy would serve as the vehicle for achieving international peace and cooperation. Not only would democracy serve as a social, economic, and political force but it would also serve as an ideal helping mankind to reorganize its thinking. It was around this theme that Dewey later developed the lectures which he so forcefully delivered to the Chinese nation.

While in Japan, Dewey continued to notice the increasing amount of emphasis being placed on armaments by the Japanese. This fact, coupled with Japanese bitterness at west coast American racism, made him feel a bit uneasy. However, he was more worried about the growth of a Japanese military state comparable to that which had existed in Germany before the war. Aware of what had occurred in the last few years, Dewey directly appealed to the Japanese liberals. He hoped that they would accept his democratic ideals and utilize them to counteract the growing influence of the military and industrial classes. He made a special plea to the academicians, who, he believed, were the spokesmen for liberalism and democratic understanding. His lectures, which were directed more toward building a bridge for closer relations between the United States and Japan than for any new discoveries in the field of philosophy, also contained appeals for international peace. The threat of a powerful Japanese military state in the Far East, he ardently contended, would destroy the delicate efforts then being made to secure world peace. Unfortunately, the Japanese government largely reflected the wishes of its army. With the continuous rise of peasants into the officers' ranks—an upward social mobility which was jealously guarded and protected from liberal criticism—it became even more difficult for Dewey to convey his democratic message. Consequently, his influence was confined largely to academic circles.

Dewey's Far Eastern adventure was surprisingly extended when—while still lecturing at the Imperial University in Tokyo—he received yet another invitation. This time the invitation was to lecture at the National University in Peking, during the academic year beginning in June, 1919 and ending in March, 1920. The invitation came from a group of Dewey's former Chinese students at Columbia led by the leading Chinese pragmatist and educator Hu Shih.[2] Dewey was delighted at the opportunity to visit China, and he immediately informed Columbia University of his decision to stay on in the

Far East. Upon completing his lectures in Tokyo, Dewey and his wife boarded the next boat and headed for China, arriving in Shanghai on April 30, 1919.

Dewey's stay in China was highlighted by the fact that the country at that particular time was experiencing an internal social and political revolution. During the latter half of the nineteenth century, China was opened increasingly to foreign commercial exploitation. It was not until 1911, however, that a revolution finally took place which overthrew the feudalistic Manchu dynasty and established in its place a republican form of government. Yet, despite this political advance, little had been accomplished in the way of renovating the decaying and archaic social institutions which retarded China's economic growth. The government in Peking, unfortunately, was more a government in name than in reality. China's economic problems, along with student unrest over the decision at Versailles to leave in Japanese hands the former German concessions in Shantung, culminated in a long protest movement which began only four days after the Deweys set foot upon Chinese soil. The May Day Movement, as it is now referred to, marked the beginning of a long and bitter conflict between Chinese nationalists and Chinese communists that eventually resulted in the establishment of Red China after World War II. Thus, the situation at that time appeared so confusing and complex that, in a letter to his Columbia colleague John Jacob Coss, Dewey candidly remarked: "China remains a massive blank and impenetrable wall when it comes to judgment."[3] So many things were happening during his first six months in China that even Dewey admitted it was increasingly difficult to keep abreast of the day's events.

His main concern while in China was to offer the people his own views of a democratic society. Aware of a unique opportunity because of China's internal social and political problems, Dewey was more than eager to fulfill his wishes for a democratic China. Thus, the kind of democratic community he had in mind was one in which ". . . there would be opportunities for individual development, opportunities for free communication of feeling, knowing, and thinking." Such a foundation could be established, he felt, by "free participation" and a "willing contribution" on the part of each member of the society. So convinced was he that the Chinese had an instinctive attraction for a democratic political order and that they saw in America "a projection of China's democratic hopes for herself," that Dewey traveled up and down the coastal cities lecturing and giving talks on the virtues and benefits of a democratic way of life.[4]

His lectures–recently published in the English language by Robert W. Clopton and Tsuin-Chen-Ou–provide a clear understanding of what Dewey considered to be his mission while in China. All the lectures emphasized the need for a democratic social, political, and economic order. All related back to the theme of the recent war and its effects upon society. All of them also stressed the urgent need to update the methods of philosophical thinking, a theme he had earlier made public while lecturing in Japan. Equally important, his lectures attempted to point out that the doctrines of nineteenth-century rugged individualism and Marxist communism would not be China's answer for the future. Perhaps Dewey underestimated the telling impact communist ideology would have on the Chinese people in subsequent years. All in all, the lectures amounted to a ringing defense of the democratic way of life, with a special plea to the Chinese people to adapt to modern ways of thinking–a theme he would later expand in *Individualism Old and New.*

Two problems especially bothered Dewey during his stay in China. One was China's inability to overthrow her rigid adherence to past philosophical conceptions. The influences of feudalism and Confucianism were deeply rooted in the Chinese mind. In a letter to a friend Dewey quixotically remarked, "Whether I am accomplishing anything as well as getting a great deal is another matter . . . . I think Chinese civilization is so thick and self-centered that no foreign influence presented via a foreigner even scratches the surface."[5] This dogmatic adherence to past customs, Dewey reasoned, was a stumbling block toward future reforms. He strongly believed that it made it increasingly difficult for the Chinese people to adapt to Western ideas of modernization. In order for democracy to become a working ideal in China, Dewey judged, modern methods of social improvement had to be developed. Moreover, China's inability to relate to modern conditions made her easy prey for industrialized nations like Japan. It was this factor which caused Dewey to express his concern over China's fate in the face of imperialistic predators.

The other problem was the growing threat of Chinese Bolshevism. In three of his lectures, "Communication and Associated Living," "Economic and Social Philosophy," and "Nationalism and Internationalism," Dewey emphasized his distaste for political theories of authoritarianism. The difference between authoritarianism and democracy, he pointed out, was that "the nations that are suffering the most acute internal disorder are those that have had authoritarian governments, such as Russia and Germany . . . . In the democratic nations, on the other hand, reasonable order prevails. But this is order which is not and has not been maintained by force."[6] The contrast between a society which is based on peace and mutual understanding and one that is based upon the use of coercive force was now uppermost in Dewey's mind:

> Authoritarian political theory and democratic political theory are diametrically opposed. The essence of democratic political theory is that it

> promotes social communication, cooperation, and interaction among individuals. A democratic society depends for its stability and development not on force, but on consensus. In such a society each member is entitled to develop his abilities, pursue his own interests, and seek to achieve his own purposes. An authoritarian society, on the other hand, because it inhibits initiative and discourages cooperation, and because it resorts to force to suppress dissent, can never be stable in any true and lasting sense.[7]

What worried Dewey was that China's feudalistic economic order—or lack of it—made her easily susceptible to the influences of communist rhetoric. The Bolshevist appeal for a quick solution—Dewey's philosophy of pragmatism never propounded quick solutions—to the peasants' economic ills, Dewey cautiously observed, made communism a serious threat to the democratic principles he had been attempting to get across to the Chinese people.

Although Dewey did not believe the threat of communism or Bolshevism in the Orient to be an immediate one, he was worried about future prospects. Despite the unofficial nature of his trip to China, Dewey was sufficiently concerned to approach the Military Intelligence Bureau of the U. S. army, which at that time had been keeping a close eye on Chinese political developments. Dewey's association with the Military Intelligence Bureau stemmed from a report he wrote for the bureau in August, 1918, on Polish support in America for the war.[8] Now, after talks with Chinese nationalist leader Chiang Kai-shek, Dewey wrote a letter to Colonel Drysdale of the bureau and cautiously informed him that for the time being

> the sum of the whole matter is that the intellectual class is radical in its beliefs and much interested in all plans of social reform. But it is a small class . . . with little influence and not concerned to organize itself to get more. The whole social and economic background of Bolshevism as a practical going concern is lacking.

An immediate take-over by the Bolshevist forces, Dewey believed, was highly unlikely. His prescience, nevertheless, led him to conclude in his report to Drysdale that if changes were not made to guide China toward accepting Western science and technology, it would not be long before the Chinese people would be forced to resort to radical measures. This was where, Dewey felt, Bolshevism would pose its most serious threat.[9]

Yet, it would be unfair to conclude that Dewey's anticommunist stand was correct. For all practical purposes, Dewey's opposition to Marxian dialectical materialism stemmed from his own philosophical predisposition against the use of radical measures as a means for social uplift. What Dewey failed to realize was the unique ideology behind Marxism that called for social and economic equality based on action. Rather than remaining an intellectual tool, Marxism held out its hands to the peasants and offered them a concrete plan for social amelioration. So defensive was Dewey about the method of democracy that he actually forgot to implement a plan whereby its ideology could be carried out. It was Dewey's failure to take democracy out of the intellectual realm which proved so tragic. Had he been able to do so, the fate of China might have been much different.

But perhaps more important was Dewey's overall concern with the problem of foreign relations. China's inability to cope with the imperialistic ambitions of foreign powers, as well as Dewey's own disappointment with the diplomatic machinations then taking place at Versailles, caused him to write in his letters to his children that "I'm coming to the opinion that it might be well worth while to reject the treaty on the ground that it involved the recognition of secret treaties and secret diplomacy."[10] Throughout these letters and the subsequent articles that he wrote for the *New Republic,* one senses that Dewey was sadly disappointed with the Paris Peace Conference. Little had been done in the way of helping China. Somehow, he felt, China was being shortchanged. The handing over of Shantung to Japan only added to his previous conviction that "all of our hopes of permanent peace and internationalism having been disappointed at Paris . . . has shown that might still makes right, and that the strong nations get what they want at the expense of the weak . . . ."[11] Even the Open Door Policy, he now came to believe, was in reality a pathway to economic imperialism. China was suffering, and he made it clear to his readers in the *New Republic* that "the key to peace in the Far East exists at the present time in America."[12] Our economic superiority should be generated for peaceful purposes. It was up to the United States, he maintained, to break the "Far Eastern deadlock." And the first move toward breaking that deadlock, Dewey insisted, was for the United States "to obliterate the treaties connected with Japan's Twenty-one Demands" and restore economic self-sufficiency to China.[13] Only by allowing China to develop on her own, Dewey was sure, could peace be restored to the Far East. If knowledge and understanding "will not create a public opinion which will in time secure a lasting and just settlement of other problems," he said, "there is no recourse save despair of civilization."[14] The task was a formidable one. All Dewey could really hope for was a sense of moderation and understanding on the part of the other major powers. But moderation and understanding were in short supply. They were being checked by nationalistic intransigence.

The remainder of Dewey's stay in China was devoted to delivering lectures at National Peking University, National Peking Teachers College, and National Nanking Teachers College. Having been granted an extended leave by Columbia University, Dewey remained in China until July, 1921. Overall, the Deweys spent twenty-six months in China, developing in the process a great amount of respect for the Chinese people. Finally on July 11, 1921, the Deweys departed with many fond memories and saddened by the fact that they would be leaving behind many close friends. Yet, they also looked forward anxiously to their return home.

Once back in the United States, the Deweys immediately headed for New York. Within three weeks Dewey was at his desk at Columbia University. But China's economic and political future was a subject with which he remained deeply concerned. Aware that industrialism, war, and commercial rivalry had shattered China's long tradition of isolationism, Dewey longed for the day when China would become modernized and able to stand on her own two feet without the fear of being overwhelmed by the more powerful nations of the world. His hopes for international peace were aroused when he heard of Congressional talk about the possibility of a naval armaments conference to be held in the nation's capital within the coming weeks.

During the month of December, 1920, Senator William E. Borah, the gray-haired, theatrical orator from Idaho, presented a joint resolution from both houses of Congress requesting that the newly elected president, Warren G. Harding, confer in Washington with the governments of Great Britain and Japan concerning agreement to lessen naval strength. The basic reason for this request was the fear of another arms race. Tensions over the Far East and the build-up of naval armaments had been in progress for some time. Great Britain was especially anxious to negotiate some form of naval agreement, if only to maintain her own naval superiority over the United States. Realizing, however, that the prospects of another armaments race would be not only costly but also financially disastrous, His Majesty's government seemed more than willing to settle on an equal footing with America. The United States government was also willing to come to the conference table. Growing concern over Far Eastern problems, accompanied by the rise of a powerful Japanese military state, prompted the State Department to request Japan's presence at Washington. Ever since the Paris Peace Conference, it had appeared that Japan and the United States were headed for a shootout. Japanese bitterness over America's racial policy as well as Wilson's opposition at Paris to Japanese control over the former German-owned islands in the Pacific irritated the Imperial government to the point where the Diet in 1920 authorized a construction program to give the empire a force of twenty-five capital ships by 1927. The United States, on the other hand, upset by Japan's Twenty-one Demands on China and her continuous abuse of the Open Door Policy, which when drawn up in 1899–1900 had specifically guaranteed and protected the commercial, territorial, and administrative integrity of China, initiated plans to enlarge naval bases in Hawaii and the Philippines and to fortify Guam in order to counteract Japan's military moves in the western Pacific. Fearful of another

World War, the Congress of the United States looked upon the proposed Washington Conference as a way out of the dilemma.

Harding, upon assuming the office of president in March, 1921, was anxious to sidetrack League supporters–"We do not mean to be entangled," he declared in his inaugural address–while at the same time putting the United States in a favorable light among peace advocates throughout the world.[15] Although he realized the need for such a conference, Harding's motive appears to have been more political than humanitarian. He resented Borah's initiative and secretly tried to squelch the move. But both press and public enthusiastically supported the idea of a tri-power disarmament conference. Pressured on all sides, therefore, he readily agreed to the Congressional request and assigned Secretary of State Charles Evans Hughes to begin making formal preparations as early as July, 1921.

The language of the State Department's invitations was phrased to please those nations that desired complete disarmament at once. Its broad inclusiveness spoke of "limitation of Armament, in connection with which Pacific and Far Eastern questions should be discussed."[16] This was a point that Dewey was most happy to see appear in the invitations. The requests were first addressed to Great Britain, France, Italy, and Japan which, with the United States, had made up the Big Five at Versailles. A special invitation was also sent to China. Later in the autumn Belgium, the Netherlands, and Portugal were extended invitations to join the other six nations in a broadened program designed to cover "such common understandings . . . as may serve to promote enduring friendship."[17] Secretary of State Hughes was designated, as head of the American delegation, to preside over an agendum which included naval limitation, new weapons, land armament, and such Far Eastern questions as China, Siberia, and the mandated islands. With much dignified optimism but very little concrete assurance, the Washington Conference convened on November 12, 1921, exactly three years and one day after the signing of the armistice ending World War I.

Reaction to the conference was mixed. Oswald Garrison Villard, liberal editor of the *Nation* and leading pacifist during the war, was enthusiastic about the prospects of the conference. He pointed out to his readers that "I cannot sympathize with the radicals who scoff at the whole thing. A tremendous public education is going on, a vast public opinion is being created."[18] Others, like Nathaniel Peffer, a Washington news columnist, were more cynical. With Versailles fresh in his memory, Peffer went on to argue: "And now it is proposed to sanctify the whole cynical procedure by an exchange of treaties which may or may not be interpreted as a new and more sinister alliance . . . . What else than a fiasco and a hoax to befool a world longing for surcease of slaughter?"[19] Indeed, the prospects were not encouraging to those who had witnessed the art of diplomatic chicanery two years earlier. Sober realists like Peffer were perhaps in a much better position to judge than optimists like Villard.

But when the conference convened as scheduled, Dewey, like Villard, was more than elated with its prospects. A month before, he had addressed a body of Chinese students, who were celebrating the tenth anniversary of the founding of the Republic of China, at Columbia. "The disarmament conference," Dewey declared, ". . . will be a real parting of the ways for the United States, which is on trial as to the sincerity of its good will and to its honesty and intelligence."[20] In typical pragmatic fashion, Dewey looked upon the conference as a means, not an end. More than anything else, it was the prospect of arousing public opinion, rather than disarmament, that would lead directly to world peace. Here was an opportunity, he believed, to gain a better understanding of and appreciation for the Far East, regardless of the direct results of the conference. Like Villard, he too was of the opinion that a tremendous public education was in the offing. "It is possible that a by-product of the Conference may be more valuable than any direct results which will be obtained. I mean by this a better understanding, a greater knowledge of the conditions which exist in the Far East."[21] Dewey also believed that a new type of liberal and international thought—somewhat analogous to America's democratic tradition—could be influential in shaping the foreign policy of every nation. The "peace of the world in the future," he noted, "can be guaranteed only by substituting people-to-people diplomacy for government-to-government diplomacy."[22] Thus, more than a commercial open door was needed. An "opened door of open diplomacy" free from propaganda was the key to opening the door "to light, to knowledge and understanding."[23] At least, this was his message in a pamphlet the *New Republic* published in 1921 entitled, *China, Japan and the U. S. A.: Present-day Conditions in the Far East and Their Bearing on the Washington Conference.*

The strength of Dewey's conviction that the Washington Conference would serve a useful measure in helping China as well as in aiding the interests of world peace can be found in a series of articles that he wrote for the *Baltimore Sun* during the period the conference was in session. The first three articles, "Causes of International Friction," "The Anglo-Japanese Alliance and the United States," and "China's Interests" indicated Dewey's support for the abolition of the Anglo-Japanese naval agreement—an alliance originally aimed at Germany and Russia, both of whom were now rendered helpless by war and revolution—as well as his encouragement to the diplomats at Washington to allow China to sustain her own socio-economic self-development. "Suggested Measures," the last in Dewey's series of seven weekly articles, contained his own proposals.

The crux of the problem, according to Dewey, was "to minimize international supervision and control of China while proposing the maximum of practicable international supervision and control of individual nations' activities toward China."[24] It was time to stop treating China as a sick patient. The conference, he added, should establish a permanent international commission for Far Eastern affairs. Control and regulation of economic activity was Dewey's game plan. This he believed could be accomplished by formulating a kind of constitution to govern the conduct of the commission. It was around this commission that Dewey put forth his "suggested measures." These proposals, as he recounted them, dealt mainly with the economic reorganization of China's development. It was this factor which took precedence over the reduction of armaments. By attempting to solve the economic problems, he emphasized, the conference would also be working toward guaranteeing a lasting measure for world peace. "Put a stop to the piecemeal partition of China and the alienation of its resources from without; put a stop to the building of warships; and the problems of the Far East will gradually present themselves in a proper perspective."[25]

In subsequent weeks Dewey continued to write for the *Baltimore Sun*. He constantly reemphasized his themes of a commercial open door and an opened diplomacy.[26] Realizing the serious threat which Japanese militarism presented to China as well as to world peace, and aware of the failures at Versailles, Dewey was more than ever vigilant in calling for mutual trust of nations "in one another's good faith and good will."[27] It was extremely difficult for him not to caution the United States on her own role. Thus, he urged that the United States abandon all talk about the prospects of constructing a naval base on the Pacific island of Guam. It would be unfair, he thought, if, while we were encouraging international cooperation at Washington, we secretly harbored imperialistic ambitions in the western Pacific. The presence of a naval base at Guam, Dewey believed, would only increase Japanese fears and wreck any chance of bringing lasting peace to the Far East. Unfortunately, Dewey's influence in countering the objectives of the War Department was less than successful.

On December 13, 1921, the Four-Power Treaty was signed. After prolonged haggling, the signatories—Britain, Japan, America, and France—agreed to respect one another's rights in the Pacific, and to refer future disputes in the Far East to a joint conference. Of equal significance, the Four-Power pact specifically abrogated the Anglo-Japanese Alliance. It provided the United States with some breathing room in which to operate in the Pacific while at the same time enabling Britain to withdraw from an embarrassing commitment.

In addition to the Four-Power Treaty, two other pacts were signed simultaneously on February 6, 1922. The first, the Five-Power Naval Treaty of Washington, stated that the major powers would agree to limit navies and maintain capital ships (warships over 10,000 tons) in a ratio of 5:5:3 for England, the United States, and Japan and 1.67 for France and Italy. The treaty was to remain effective until 1936, when any one of the signatories might give a two-year notice of termination. A ten-year holiday in the building of new capital ships was also included in the treaty. The second pact, the Nine-Power Treaty, pledged the consenting nations to respect the independence of China and its territorial and administrative integrity; to provide full opportunity for the development of an effective Chinese government; and, above all, to maintain the principle of equal opportunity for the commerce of all nations within China. As a result of the Nine-Power Treaty, the Open Door was given a new, although limited, lease on life and "the Sick Man of the Far East" was at last administered some medication.

The results of the treaties were certainly favorable to the United States. Secretary Hughes's stunning proposals, which marked the opening of the conference and set the tone for amicable relations, were happily received and overwhelmingly endorsed. A combination of idealism with what was perhaps the only sound solution for success–graduated disarmament on the high seas–enabled Hughes to receive everything he had asked for, including restoration of full Chinese sovereignty over Shantung and sale by Japan of the valuable and strategic Shantung Railroad. Thus, in a decade marked by strife, uncertainty, disillusionment, and insecurity the Washington Conference proved to be a landmark in history. It remained the only peace conference of the twenties–and there were many–where mutual agreement replaced distrust, and understanding, fear. It was also the most successful.

But notable as the results of the Washington Naval Conference were, they failed to reconcile or even make clear the basic clash between the Open Door and Japan's special claim to interests in China.[28] Japan's unwillingness to give up her imperialistic ambitions in the Far East, especially in China, was clearly in evidence during the course of the conference. Her intransigence made it increasingly difficult to achieve any worthwhile results. The diplomatic game of having your adversary concede as much as possible did not end at Versailles. But Japan is not entirely to blame. The failure of the conference to take notice of Dewey's "suggested measures" and to allow China to assume responsibility for her own economic reorganization in no way alleviated the serious problem of imperialism on the part of the rest of the industrialized nations. The principle of democratic equality, Dewey now came to realize, was merely a cover for imperialistic machinations.

Although Dewey hailed the naval disarmament conference as one more step in the direction of world peace, he was less than satisfied with the economic provisions of the treaty regarding the independence of China. To him it appeared an anomaly that the nations attending the Washington Conference could pledge themselves to respect the independence of China while they at the same time insisted on protecting their own imperialistic ambitions. The economic stranglehold over China, he pointed out, was still in effect. China, in reality, was not free. And so long as the commercial Open Door of economic exploitation remained in existence, Dewey argued, the problems of imperialism and war would not be solved:

> The common belief at the present time that the Pacific is to be the scene of the next great world catastrophe, the fatalistic belief that conflict between the white and the yellow race is predestined, are really expressions of a sense of a deep, underlying cleft that makes mutual understanding impossible. But instead of trying to lessen the cleft by effort to understand each other, we talk about an irrespressible conflict of forces beyond human control, or else about the competition for control of the natural resources of China and the tropics. I would not minimize the danger in this competition, but it is ridiculous to suppose that it is so great as to make the Pacific the scene of an inevitable war. If we succeed in really understanding each other, some way of cooperation for common ends can be found.[29]

Once again Dewey could only lament that the door to open diplomacy remained shut when it came to genuine understanding and good faith.

In subsequent years Dewey continued to write and talk about China. He was saddened, however, by the actions of Congress when in 1924 it passed the National Origins Act. The act, which fixed a total annual immigration quota and required that national quotas be calculated on the basis of the proportion of descendants of each nationality living in the United States in 1920, also forbade all Oriental immigration. Enraged by the nativist attitudes then prevailing in the United States, Dewey saw the passage of the act as a direct slap in the face of our Oriental friends and foes alike. Not overlooked as discriminatory, this insult proved especially appalling to the Japanese, who greeted it with a day of national mourning. The undemocratic nature of the act and its passage by the United States government, Dewey believed, provided Japan with a needed excuse with which to carry on her militaristic ambitions.

Dewey was appalled, moreover, by America's own imperialistic desires. It appeared to him that during this period of rising prosperity America deliberately chose to ignore China's plight for fear of a conflict with her own predatory interests. Dewey's hope that the beacon of American democracy would shine forth as a symbol for mutual cooperation and international understanding was rudely shattered when he saw how the American government itself placed economic superiority above world peace. "The doctrine of the Open Door, of maintaining the territorial integrity of China," Dewey informed his readers in *Survey*, "ran counter with our own interests."[30] Out role was merely paternalistic, Dewey claimed. According to Dewey, the Open Door policy in China, which originated from the pen of Secretary of State John Hay around the turn of the century in order to offset the "spheres-of-influence" policy practiced by other nations, was deliberately being abused by the very country that initiated the idea. "Is China a Nation or a Market?" he asked his readers in the *New Republic*. Indeed, the pecuniary interests of American manufacturers, merchants, and exporters led Dewey to ask: "Do we wish China to be treated as a free and self-respecting people should be treated or as a market upon which to dump goods for the pecuniary profit of a small number?"[31] And in a response to Major General William Crozier's article "What Hope for China?" Dewey scoffed at the general's idea "of a union of great and imperialistic Powers having the sole purpose of assisting another nation. . . ." Such intervention, Dewey maintained was a serious challenge to Chinese nationalism. Writing the words a pacifist would have used, Dewey persuasively argued that "it will take time for China to make the transition. . . . But it must come by patience, sympathy and educative effort, and the slow processes of commerce and exchange of ideas, not by a foreign rule imposed by military force."[32] So forceful was Dewey in his line of reasoning—an approach along pacifist lines—that General Crozier refused to write a rejoinder to his argument.

Dewey's activities in the Far East and his later concern with United States foreign policy in the Orient demonstrated his continuing interest in the establishment of a democratic world order along peaceful lines. Throughout the 1920s Dewey, as a peaceful publicist, constantly reminded his listeners and readers that the Far East was a serious sore spot in international affairs. But the people refused to heed his advice. Their isolationist attitude proved admirably suited to the pecuniary dictates of the day, namely, conspicuous consumption and conspicuous waste. Most Americans living in the twenties, it would seem, were too concerned about their own prosperity to express any interest in China's fate along with the basic problems of imperialistic expansionism. Thus, Dewey, wavering between optimism and annoyance, realized that a permanent settlement to Far Eastern problems was a long way off. He knew only too well that American selfishness and ignorance would remain, as they had in the past, barriers to mutual cooperation and international understanding.

CHAPTER FOUR

EDUCATION FOR PEACE AND DEMOCRACY

> We may desire abolition of war, industrial justice, greater equality of opportunity for all. But no amount of preaching good will or the golden rule or cultivation of sentiments of love and equity will accomplish the results. There must be change in the objective arrangements and institutions. We must work on the environment, not merely on the hearts of men.
>
> * * * * * * * * * * * *
>
> The world war is a bitter commentary on the nineteenth-century misconception of moral achievement—a misconception, however, which it only inherited from the traditional theory of fixed ends, attempting to bolster up that doctrine with aid from the "scientific" theory of evolution. The doctrine of progress is not yet bankrupt. The bankruptcy of the notion of fixed goods to be attained and stably possessed may possibly be the means of turning the mind of man to a tenable theory of progress—to attention to present troubles and possibilities.
>
> Dewey, *Human Nature and Conduct*

When Dewey returned to the United States in the fall of 1921, he devoted a great deal of time to his growing interest in educational peace research. His university lectures in Japan and China, his talks to the Chinese people in the provinces, and the many articles he wrote for the *New Republic* and *Asia* clearly illustrated Dewey's overriding concern for the establishment of a world order based on peace and democracy. His quiet refusal to accept the Order of the Rising Sun, the highest honor the Japanese government could bestow on a foreigner, during his educational mission to Japan, was convincing proof of his allegiance to the democratic way of life. Moreover, he was strongly of the opinion that education, based on democratic principles, should play a predominant role in bringing about world peace. His intense and abiding interest in formal education, therefore, was a natural consequence of his philosophical position.

Even though Dewey believed that such social institutions as the home, local government, and church, rather than the school, were the basic force in shaping minds, he did not agree with the opinion of more conservative-minded educators that the school must passively accommodate itself to external exigencies. He envisioned the school as a basis for dynamic change. He argued that the school could indeed become a dynamic instead of a reflexive agency—one that would search out and reenforce concrete patterns to remake society while at the same time enabling each individual to realize his full potentiality in the process of change. According to Dewey, the sad fact was that

> while our educational leaders are talking of culture, the development of personality, etc., as the end and aim of education, the great majority of those who pass under the tuition of the school regard it only as a narrowly practical tool with which to get bread and butter enough to eke out a restricted life.

Such a philistine outlook had to be discarded. The aim of education had to be conceived in a less exclusive way. "If we were to introduce into educational processes the activities which appeal to those whose dominant interest is to do and make," he said, "we should find the hold of the school upon its members to be more vital, more prolonged, containing more of culture." Education was more than a process of adjustment. It was a creative encounter between man and his environment which called for innovation and reform. To Dewey, education represented the most intelligent means for achieving his goal of a peaceful democratic world order. No longer would he attempt to use the discredited argument of armed force as a legitimate lever for social change.[1]

Dewey's lectures at Columbia during the 1920s provide a useful insight into his concern for the philosophical and educational perplexities of social cooperation and human understanding. Whether it was in the educational courses he taught at Teachers College or in those of a more technical nature in the philosophy department, Dewey constantly stressed the need for "shared experience," "cooperative culture," "communication," and "communal participation."[2] Perhaps it would be only fair to conclude that Dewey looked upon his classroom lectures as vehicles for social engineering. At least he had hoped that his students would interpret them in such fashion.

Although it must have been disconcerting for students to sit in class and watch Dewey constantly stare out the window, speaking in a low monotone while crumbling his notes into a paper ball—all at the same time—they were, nevertheless, clearly interested in hearing what he had to say about such perplexing and disturbing problems as modern technology, war and social cooperation. Two of his former students, Irwin Edman, an eminent philosopher in his own right, and Harold F. Clark, a noted banker and leading economist, have testified that what Dewey had to say was of considerable importance even though it may have needed certain clarification. As a teacher, Edman readily admits, Dewey was not exactly stimulating.

> I admit the first lecture was quite a shock, a shock of dullness and confusion, if that can be said. It was at any rate a disappointment. I had not found Dewey's prose easy, but I had learned that its difficulty lay for the most part in its intellectual honesty, which led him to qualify an idea in one sentence half a page long. In part also it lay in the fact that this profoundly original philosopher was struggling to find a vocabulary to say what had never been said in philosophy before, to find a diction that would express with exactness the reality of change and novelty, philosophical words having been used for centuries to express the absolute and the *fixed.*[3]

Edman's opinion was shared by Clark, who, like most young, energetic, enthusiastic, and emotionally aroused students entering the classroom for the first time, typified that academic trait of inquisitiveness and sweet innocence.

> What he was talking about—and he was not the most brilliant lecturer—was stimulating [Clark remembers], but he usually said it in not the simplest and clearest ways. He would usually have trouble finding his notes and straightening them out. But when he finally got around to saying what he had to say, it was always extremely important and it would stand thinking over for a long time.[4]

Such statements by two former students must necessarily lead to some speculation as to Dewey's effectiveness as a teacher. If it were simply a matter of style, Dewey would certainly have to be classified a failure. Yet, perhaps Dewey's saving grace as a teacher and lecturer was his constant preoccupation with the dual roles of philosophy and education in the twentieth century. The stimulation students derived from his lectures was due primarily to his deep concern for present-day social and intellectual problems. A relativistic theme was most noticeable in all his lectures. Like Carl Becker's history, Dewey's philosophy searched for the "heavenly city" right here in the twentieth century. His desire to make philosophy both understandable and meaningful, despite his own oratorical style, was based primarily on his own efforts to unite social experience with learning.

But perhaps more important was Dewey's attempt to make his lectures guideposts for developing effective and efficient techniques for social engineering. "Social philosophy," Dewey wrote in the syllabus to one of his courses, "is a technique for clarifying the judgments which are constantly passed of necessity upon social customs, institutions, laws, arrangements, actual and projected."[5] For Dewey, the relationship between his public views and his philosophy was perhaps best expressed when, during one of his lectures in his course on social and political philosophy, he informed his students that the process of thought is, in actuality, a method for conscious social planning.

> No man knows what the morrow may bring forth. Yet *what is wise today depends largely upon what is going to happen tomorrow.* Consider how much of our thinking is really an act of prevision in forming some kind of idea of what the sequence of events is going to be. In other words how much of our thinking takes the form of planning, arranging what is now under our control with regard to future conditions and eventuality. This forecasting, anticipating, expecting, and planning for the future is one form of introducing continuity into experience.[6]

Quite clearly, Dewey was a social philosopher. The primary function of philosophy, in his view, was "to find an intelligent substitute for blind custom and blind impulse to habit and conduct."[7] It was his unique ability to make his philosophy "socially conscious" in the eyes of his students that gained him the admiration and respect of people like Edman and Clark. As a teacher he believed that it was his duty to clarify students' thinking on society's problems. His lectures are a monument to that belief; they are an ample demonstration of his sincere conviction that philosophy and education served no useful purpose in life unless they attempted to reconstruct one's thinking processes while at the same time aiding in the improvement of one's social conditions.

Aside from his immediate academic concerns at Columbia in the twenties, Dewey became more and more interested in the possibilities of educational peace research. His initial interest in peace research was sparked in the spring of 1917 by an interdisciplinary war issues course at Columbia University. The war issues course opened up new vistas for Dewey. It convinced him that the method of intelligence–a process whereby thought is socially organized, cooperative, experimental and concerned with the solution of concrete problems as attested to in experience–was capable of incorporating different disciplines into an organic conception of society. Such a process he pointed out, would thus allow people to identify causal relationships or patterns of events, conditions, and behavior that produce violent conflict and from such recognition to devise strategies for preventing them. The sterile or philistine academic approach had to give way to a more comprehensive, all-encompassing effort of interdisciplinary cooperation. Moreover, since Dewey equated peace with democracy and argued that a democratic society was inherently compatible with human cooperation and understanding, the course added to his initial disposition that in order to work on the international system itself, major changes in our domestic institutions would also have to be accomplished. Perhaps the basic point made in this lecture series was that the ancient proposition upholding the doctrine of the nation state, as a guarded and sacred institution, remained the major barrier to world peace. A powerful nation state was a threat to democracy, as evidenced by the German experience. The key to conflict control, in his opinion, was to deflate the emotions and values attached to nationalism and substitute in their place a world order based on international law and governmental organization. Clearly, the course proved immensely profitable to Dewey. It gave him the initiative and desire to see to it that education would focus all its attention and energies on the individual as the creator of worldwide social change. The school, quite obviously, became his arsenal of peace.

For years Dewey had been attempting to make the school a peaceful and active lever for social change within the community. The function of the school fitted neatly into his philosophical position on the use of intelligence. Enlightenment was the way to combat chauvinism. Time and time again Dewey stressed the importance of the school as a means for cultural enlightenment and human understanding. As far back as 1897 in *My Pedagogic Creed*, Dewey argued that "all education proceeds by the participation of the individual in the social consciousness of the race." In *The School and Society*, which he wrote at the turn of the century, Dewey pointed out that the school and education represented the best "means of seeing the progress of the human race." Furthermore, in *Moral Principles in Education*, a book he wrote during the middle of the Progressive era, he flatly stated: "Apart from participating in social life, the school has no moral end nor aim." And in his classic work on the subject of education, *Democracy and Education*, Dewey contended that "it is the business of the school environment to eliminate, so far as possible, the unworthy features of the existing environment from influence upon mental habitudes. It establishes a purified medium of action. Selection aims not only at simplifying but at weeding out what is undesirable." Obviously, war was one medium of action that Dewey hoped would be eliminated. Yet, somewhat ironically, World War I had diverted Dewey's attention from the function of education in favor of a more physical and violent solution for achieving social change. He had, as described earlier, been corrupted by the war fervor—so corrupted, in fact, that the war proved a personal disaster. Thus, after the war Dewey made another right-about turn and once again urged the use of education as a peaceful means for achieving social democracy.[8]

While in China, Dewey had time to define more precisely his views for obtaining peace through the schools. In one particular lecture, "The Cultural Heritage and Social Reconstruction," Dewey laid down three ground rules that were necessary if the schools were to create a feeling of democratic cooperation and world citizenship. The first rule and basic aim of education was for the school to create good citizens. When asked by the Chinese students to define what he meant by "good citizen," Dewey responded by listing four qualifications: (1) a "good citizen," had to be a good neighbor, a good friend; (2) a "good citizen" had to be as able to contribute to others as to benefit from other's contributions; (3) a "good citizen," in the economic sense, had to be one who produced rather than one who merely shared in the production of others; and lastly, (4) a "good citizen" also had to be a good consumer. According to Dewey's humanitarian and socially conscious outlook on life a "good citizen" was a person who contributed to the well being of society. Above all, a "good citizen" was also one who appreciated the values of peaceful living by contributing to and sharing with his fellow citizens the fruits of society. Dewey's second rule encouraged educators to create an atmosphere of harmony and friendliness whereby a feeling of world citizenship could be generated through the schools by making "students want to fulfill their duties to society, not from compulsion, but by curiosity and willingness, and out of love for their fellow men." But perhaps the most important rule was his last one, which directed its attention to the general desire to acquaint students with the nature of social life and to the needs of society, as well as to their preparation for meeting these needs. A knowledge of one's environment and a willingness to eliminate its unworthy features, Dewey reasoned, was the main source of educational inspiration for the student. Social reconstruction, he believed, required more than sentiment. It demanded a general understanding of the nature of the problem and a willingness to adapt to new ways of thinking. In each case, therefore, Dewey impressed upon his Chinese students the necessity for education to work upon cultivating the social, political, economic, and cultural institutions of a democratic society. "The school is the instrument," he concluded, "by which a new society can be built, and through which the unworthy features of the existing society can be modified."[9]

Dewey's goal for achieving world citizenship and lasting peace was based upon a social science approach to education. To Dewey, history and geography were the essential subjects that were necessary for alleviating the existing social ills in the world. In *The School and Society* he argued that "to study history and geography is not to amass information, but to use information in constructing a vivid picture of how and why men did thus and so; achieved their successes and came to their failures." In a like manner, Dewey emphasized in *Democracy and Education* that "the segregation which kills the vitality of history and geography is divorce from present modes and concerns of social life." According to Dewey, the use of "geography and history for cultivating a socialized intelligence constitutes its moral significance." It came as no surprise, therefore, that during Dewey's disillusioned state of mind after the war he concentrated on the social sciences as the best approach to education for peace.[10]

During his stay in China and later while serving out his remaining years at Columbia, he elaborated upon his earlier themes of the social functions of geography and history. The study of geography, he now maintained, must devote its attention to social and political problems. By that Dewey meant that geography would have to take into consideration the various peoples, their cultures, their habits, their occupations, their art, and their contributions to the development of culture in general. History as well would have to divorce itself from its past emphasis on dates, heroes, and battles. More study, Dewey maintained, would have to be centered upon the social meaning of history. Thus, in his lectures to the Chinese and his students at Columbia, he suggested that

> before starting with history as such it would be a good idea to identify the important problems of present-day society—problems in politics, social problems, economic problems, problems in diplomacy, and others. Then explore each of these problems in its historical setting; try to determine the origin of the problem; examine past efforts to deal with the problem; find out what sort of situation caused it to become a problem.[11]

An excellent illustration of this type of approach occurred in the spring semester of 1923 when Dewey, while teaching one of his standard courses at Columbia entitled "Social and political philosophy," discussed in class his recent article "Ethics and International Relations," which he had written as part of his lecture series on the issue of war and peace.[12]

Dewey had always been interested in applying his scientific methodology to the study of the humanities, but his concern with the establishment of a social science program in the schools as a means for developing domestic tolerance, racial harmony, and international friendship reached a more active stage upon his return from China. In 1923 he sponsored a school program designed to promote international cooperation. Applying the social science approach of James Harvey Robinson's "New History" to education, as well as carrying over the seeds from an argument he raised in an earlier article entitled "Nationalizing Education," Dewey proposed that the chauvinistic patriotism found in current textbooks be eliminated.[13] He charged that the textbooks then being used in history courses throughout the United States, for example, were designed to promote a "blind love for one's country." He also argued that the use of such texts in the classroom not only diminished the possibilities for creating an atmosphere of international understanding but also increased the chances for domestic intolerance as well. Dewey's program was designed, therefore, to do two things: namely, counter the government's determined policy of isolationism as well as overcome the attitude of militant nationalism on the part of One Hundred Per Centers then prevalent in America. In addition, the program focused its attention primarily upon the need for a new kind of curriculum which would explore the theme of nationalism within an international context. What this curriculum should develop and encourage, he contended, is an attitude of world patriotism, not chauvinistic nationalism.

> We need a curriculum in history, literature and geography [he told his students at Teachers College and readers in the *Journal of Social Forces*], which will make it more difficult for the flames of hatred and suspicion to sweep over this country in the future, which indeed will make this impossible, because when children's minds are in the formative period we shall have fixed in them through the medium of the schools, feelings of respect and friendliness for the other nations and peoples of the world.[14]

Thus, through a combination of progressive ideals and pragmatic theories Dewey hoped that the school would be the primary means for developing social consciousness and social ideals in children.

Dewey's reason for believing that education might be the means for transcending nationalistic boundaries was found in the important and positive role it had played in the consolidation and unification of the German-speaking peoples during the nineteenth century. What interested Dewey most was how the German leaders had used education to nationalize the people. Although in Germany, national interests captured education for narrow and exclusive purposes, mainly for the perpetuation of the political state, Dewey, nevertheless, saw a beneficial side to this experience. Since education had been captured by and made instrumental to nationalism, is it therefore not possible, Dewey asked, to initiate a new program whereby education would enable all peoples to transcend their own national boundaries? Already, Dewey pointed out, science, art, and commerce were compelling factors making it possible for peoples living in different countries to cooperate with each other, thus making the world more interdependent. This recent development led Dewey to call for "a new movement in education to preserve what was socially most useful in the national heritage and to meet the issues of the emerging international society."[15] The identification of patriotism with "national interests," which inevitably leads to exclusiveness, suspicion, jealousy, and hatred of other nations, Dewey argued, would now have to be abandoned as well as subordinated to the broader conceptions of human welfare. Therefore, in teaching history and the social sciences it was Dewey's primary goal to emphasize

> whatever binds people together in cooperative human pursuits and results, apart from geographical limitations. The secondary and provisional character of national sovereignty in respect to the fuller, freer, and more fruit-

ful association and intercourse of all human beings with one another must be instilled as a working disposition of mind.[16]

This was indeed an ambitious task that Dewey set for himself and his colleagues. Yet aside from this early proposal, Dewey did not attempt to elaborate any further on how the school plan could be implemented, simply because most Americans showed little interest in the scheme at that time. The 1920's, it must be remembered, were a decade marked by political conservatism and economic prosperity. Such an atmosphere was not receptive to Dewey's idea. A business and middle-class point of view dominated the thinking of the American public. Throughout the twenties big business and the federal government worked hand in hand. It was not the in the best interests of the country, Republican leaders warned their constituents, to encourage government regulation over the economic activities of major corporations. The government's function was not to be an economic watchdog. President Harding argued that Americans desired "a period. . . with less government in Business and more Business in government." His successor, Calvin Coolidge, reflected the same sentiments: "The business of America is business." Coolidge, it also should be pointed out, was admirably suited for the job. His truism "When more and more people are thrown out of work, unemployment results" remains a classic example of how the intellectual powers of the presidency succumbed to unthinking supporters of the status quo. President Hoover, as well, supported his predecessor's program and the prevailing doctrine of normalcy when he declared that Alexander Hamilton "well comprehended the necessities of Federal Government activity in support of commerce and industry." But the business of America turned out to be a lot more than just business and economic prosperity. It was, so to speak, to protect the vested interests and maintain the status quo. The apparent "endless prosperity" that marked this period gave rise to a conservative spirit that sought consolidation of gains and maintained vigorous opposition to dissent. In contrast to the widespread faith in reform characterizing the Progressive period, a harsh, narrowminded satisfaction with American institutions distinguished the postwar decade. The revival of the Ku Klux Klan, the initiation of newer and tougher immigration laws, the rebirth of racial and religious discrimination more severe than in past decades, and the arrival of Prohibition as the manifestation of rural suspicion and class oppression, were stunning examples of an America that sought change in order to counteract reform.

Any movement which called for change or a reordering of priorities was looked upon with scorn and derision. Dewey's education for peace proposals met just such opposition. Like his predecessors Horace Mann and Theodore Parker, Dewey appeared trapped by the reactionary conservatism of his own time. His emphasis on developing peaceful attitudes toward other peoples ran counter to the prevailing atmosphere of censorious patriotism and conspicuous consumption. The business ethic was intertwined with domestic intolerance. Do not tamper with the system when things are going so well, was the motto. Thus, although he could fully account for the reasons behind the opposition to his plan, he was unsuccessful in overcoming the emotional ties in support of such resistance. Perhaps if he had offered his program during a different period, things might have proved more promising. At least partial acceptance would surely have been guaranteed. Unfortunately, his increasing involvement with the outlawry of war movement and his own reluctance to expound his school program in the face of growing domestic intolerance account for Dewey's lack of success with educational peace research during the late twenties.[17]

Besides his academic duties at Columbia in the 1920s, Dewey also spoke out in opposition to the virulent nationalism then going on in America. The country's pecuniary prosperity, political conservatism, and general dissatisfaction over World War I resulted in a sudden intensification of American patriotism. The effects of the war, he believed, still left scars on the body politic. He was extremely perplexed by the rise of public intolerance—especially in a democratic country like America. In a series of meetings held as part of a faculty-student conference entitled "Philosophers and Fascism," which took place at the home of Columbia University philosopher Herbert W. Schneider in the late 1920s, Dewey began to develop a pessimistic view toward government control over civil liberties.[18] Government propaganda, spurred on by the war, was, according to Dewey, becoming a serious threat to democratic liberties. Aware of how domestic intolerance—fed by the sinister designs of the Committee on Public Information—had gotten out of hand during the late war, Dewey was convinced that now more than ever was the time for education to create an atmosphere of "discriminating intelligence." What proved equally distressing to Dewey was the pragmatic efficiency with which government was now using public information to manipulate the people. Arguing along the same lines as Randolph Bourne before the war, Dewey now encouraged colleges and schools throughout the country to develop liberal ideals and values with which to counteract the techniques of governmental propaganda.[19]

But education proved unsuccessful in its attempt to stem the rising tide of intolerance and chauvinistic patriotism. Americans, concerned mainly with finding ways of spending their new-found wealth, condoned the stifling of dissent. Consequently, Dewey became increasingly angry at the noticeable increase in attitudes of apathy and conservatism in the United States. He also lamented the prevailing belief that most people didn't care. What proved particularly distressing to Dewey was that this feeling took hold of the American mind so soon after the war. The war, Dewey believed, should have taught us a lesson. But what Dewey suddenly came to realize was that most Americans were simply determined to forget the war and its accompanying disillusionment. This was indeed a sick world, Dewey cynically remarked to his readers in the *New Republic*. It has always been a sick world, he sensitively observed, but "it may be doubted if the consciousness of sickness was ever so widespread as it is today. Our optimism of the cheery word, of sunshine and prosperity is a little too assertive. . . ."[20] No doubt, Dewey wondered whether appeals to emotion had not now definitely outweighed those of reason.

By 1927, three years before his retirement from Columbia University, Dewey was convinced that reactionary conservatism was a basic part of the American society. The spillover from the Red Scare of 1919, characterized by hysteria and midnight witchhunts led by Attorney General A. Mitchell Palmer, lingered on in the consciousness of many Americans. Redbaiting was still a favorite pastime in many parts of the country. In early April, for instance, Dewey was sharply critical of an American Legion post in Philadelphia for its part in demanding the dismissal of two professors at the West Chester State Normal School. The charges, which were vague to say the least, accused the two educators of alleged sympathy for political radicalism. The accusations lacked both substance and fact. The Columbia experience of 1917, he now feared, was happening all over again. The real danger to American liberties, Dewey loudly proclaimed to a group of liberals gathered in the City of Brotherly Love, comes from those "superpatriots" who are afraid of free discussion and exchange of opinion. "Who is the better citizen," Dewey asked, "he who criticizes what he cannot agree with or he who only nods yes?" The "hush, hush boys," Dewey sadly lamented, "are the greatest danger in our life at present."[21] Yet his anger became more noticeable when nearly seven months later Nicola Sacco and Bartolomeo Vanzetti—two Italian aliens and admitted anarchists who were accused of a payroll robbery and murder at South Braintree, Massachusetts, in April 1920—were executed. To Dewey, the trial and its eventual outcome were products of the war psychology. So annoyed was Dewey by these "senseless" executions that he personally saw them as a direct attack on his own libéral-democratic educational principles.[22] Indeed, Dewey's own views toward society became more radicalized as a result of the executions of Sacco and Vanzetti.

All that he had been teaching, Dewey now came to realize, had been discarded for a philistine patriotism, a patriotism that breeds intolerance and hatred toward others. No wonder war exists, he explained to his readers in the *World Tomorrow*, when "patriotism, national honor, national interests and national sovereignty are the four foundation stones upon which the structure of the National State is erected." No wonder, he continued, "that the windows of such a building are closed to the light of heaven; that its inmates are fear, jealousy, suspicion, and that War issues regularly from its portals."[23] Unfortunately, no one paid much attention to his warnings.

Throughout his entire educational career Dewey firmly believed in the social function of education. For Dewey, education was always the means that could achieve the end: namely, democratic society. As he once wrote: "Democracy had to be born anew every generation and education is the midwife."[24] His writings in the twenties further explored this point of view. Thus, for example, in *Reconstruction in Philosophy* (1921), *Human Nature and Conduct* (1922), *The Public and Its Problems* (1927), and *The Quest for Certainty* (1929), Dewey took pains to explain to his readers that education was the instrument for subordinating the more harmful nationalistic sentiments to broader conceptions of human welfare. In addition, despite the atmosphere of harsh reaction and bitter disillusionment which existed in the twenties, this "untired radical" continued to demonstrate that undaunted progressive spirit of unlimited optimism in his application of education to social problems.

Yet, given the extraordinary climate of reaction against idealism and reform in the United States during the 1920s, just how successful was Dewey's program for accomplishing international peace through the schools? How effective were Dewey's educational theories when it came to combating the pernicious ideologies of racism and patriotic chauvinism? In each case, it appeared as though Dewey was headed in the right direction. Literature, history, and geography were essential components in his educational scheme for changing the cultural matrix of society. Thus, by allowing students the opportunity to explore their world through the interaction of history, literature, and geography—via the medium of the social sciences—Dewey had hoped that new questions would be raised and a more thoroughgoing examination of social problems undertaken. Moreover, the possibility that these subjects could be stripped of their archaic functions in the classroom while at the same time enabling students to draw the distinction between peoples and institutions had been a major objective of Dewey's theories on progressive education. But somehow his ideals fell far short of their expected goal. Perhaps Dewey was too optimistic over the chances of education bringing about a lasting peace so soon after the war. Perhaps, too, he failed to calculate accurately the long-term effects of domestic intolerance which resulted from the war. Obviously, America was not yet ready or prepared for change!

Dewey's views on educational peace research were an important by-product of his pragmatic approach to world affairs. An informed public opinion, he always urged, was the most realistic and efficient means for attaining lasting peace. Yet, public opinion, for the most part, remained unenlightened during the 1920s. Consequently, it is not so much that Dewey found solutions to the world's problems. Rather, his importance lies in his determination to raise new ideas in the hope of answering old questions. Such ideas as the role of the school in creating an attitude of international cordiality, the function and meaning of world patriotism, the role of the social sciences as a bridge for understanding other cultures, and most importantly, the job of the educator to teach the values of peace and nonviolence to his students, were uppermost in Dewey's mind. And even though his ideals remained unfulfilled or incapable of being tested at that time, he nevertheless was correct in suggesting that the key to world peace still lies within the realm of education. To Dewey, that was our only hope.

CHAPTER FIVE

EDUCATION FOR UNDERSTANDING, NOT FOR WAR

> Peoples do not become militaristic or imperialistic because they deliberately choose so to do. . . . They become militaristic gradually and unconsciously in response to conditions of which militarism is the final consequence. Education of youth and the reflex of that education on parents and friends is an important part of the forces which have militarization for their consequence.
>
> Dewey, introduction to Barnes, *Militarizing Our Youth*

During his remaining years at Columbia and throughout the 1930s, Dewey was an outspoken critic of militarism in colleges and schools. If there was one consistent policy which Dewey adhered to throughout his entire life, it was his opposition to any form of military training in an academic environment. Why did Dewey oppose militarism on campus? What exactly were his basic objections? How is it that a leading supporter of World War I could be so dogmatic in his refusal to support a program of militarism in education?

Two factors may account for Dewey's policy. One was his own individualistic strain of nineteenth-century democratic libertarianism. Born during a period in American history when the vast open spaces of western America dictated a style of life marked by Jeffersonian ideals and rugged individualism, Dewey continually practiced the democratic virtue of libertarianism. Freedom of conscience, self-confidence, and unlimited progress were characteristics of a democratic society Dewey came to love and admire. Democracy, moreover, symbolized for Dewey a living ethic for all Americans. For Dewey, democracy was the embodiment of man's own individual social and moral growth. Democratic liberty and individualism, according to Dewey, were synonymous terms. It is no wonder, therefore, that Dewey would strongly object to any system which stressed discipline and conformity at the expense of one's individual liberties.

The other factor—perhaps somewhat more noteworthy—was his firm belief that discipline was unsuited to classroom purposes. He opposed the authoritarian practices of military training as well as the emphasis on rigid conformity to drill. Such techniques, he believed, were monotonous and boring. To Dewey, education was a creative and self-developmental process; any form of strict discipline ran counter to his views on progressive education. Rigid uniformity was unacceptable to Dewey. "Under the name of discipline and good order," he pointed out in *How We Think*, "school conditions are often made to approximate as nearly as possible to monotony and uniformity. Desks and chairs are in set positions; pupils are regimented with military precision." Education, he argued, must allow for creativity. An education with "its passivity of attitude, its mechanical massing of children, its uniformity of curriculum and method" ran contrary to the spirit of Dewey's views on progressive education.[1] A sense of libertarian values plus a belief in a self-developmental form of education, accounted for Dewey's consistent opposition to militarism in education.

As far back as 1877 when Dewey was a student at the University of Vermont, one can find evidence of his distaste for military drill on campus. In the minutes of the faculty for that year, there appears a disciplinary note on John Dewey indicating that he was penalized "for taking part in a concerted absence from military drill."[2] Dewey was considered to be an excellent student. But his refusal to demonstrate enthusiasm for, or actively participate in, militia drills proved upsetting to many of his teachers and fellow students. It was not so much that Dewey was unpatriotic. Rather, he found very little educative value from such training. It was this particular point of view which Dewey maintained throughout his entire professional career.

While teaching at the University of Chicago, Dewey continued to oppose any form of militarism on campus. He was aided in his opposition by the fact that the university's president, William Rainey Harper, was a sympathetic student of Count Leo Tolstoy's works and a convinced pacifist. In addition, Dewey's association at Hull House with Jane Addams, who in 1896 visited Tolstoy during her trip to Russia, was further incentive on his part to keep the schools a lever for peaceful social change. Moreover, the establishment of the experimental school in 1896, which emphasized self-learning and social cooperation, fitted neatly into Dewey's conception of democratic liberalism. In order for the school to function effectively as a social instrument, Dewey believed, it had to remain free from the restraining hand of martial conformity and patriotic obedience.

Education, Dewey argued, was a medium for harmonious social exchange, not blind intolerance.

It was not until the outbreak of the first World War, however, that Dewey had a chance to express publicly his opinions in opposition to military training in the schools and colleges. Throughout the debate over preparedness in the three years immediately preceding United States involvement in the war, Dewey joined such liberal opponents of war as Jane Addams, Lillian Wald, Oswald Garrison Villard, Norman Thomas, and President Alexander Meiklejohn of Amherst College in opposing military training. As early as 1915 pacifists and leading educators were quoting John Dewey as saying that military drill had no educational value and that it was "undemocratic, barbaric and scholastically wholly unwise." In the following year, moreover, Dewey expressed his dissent from the rising military preparedness movement in America. In an article entitled "Our Educational Ideal in Wartime," Dewey warned his readers that "the habit of mind thus formed is as incompatible with democracy as is sheer militarism. . . ." The threat of militarists imposing their values on students Dewey saw as a serious danger to democratic liberty.[3]

In April, 1916, Dewey expressed his disapproval of a plan by Major General Leonard Wood to nationalize all immigrants by military training. Dewey argued that the plan was ludicrous and undemocratic. "If authentic America is not to be a cross-fertilization of our various strains," Dewey remarked, "it had better be a juxtaposition of alien elements than an amalgam of the barracks, an amalgam whose uniformity would hardly go deeper than the uniforms of the soldiers." To assume that military training could become an efficient tool of public education, Dewey pointed out, was a deplorable self-deception. To Dewey, "military service is the remedy of despair—despair of the power of intelligence." But Dewey's criticisms did not stop with General Wood. A week after his reply to Wood, Dewey responded to Rear Adm. Caspar F. Goodrich's proposal for compulsory service for native youth by saying that "the argument seems to be born of the feelings rather than of intelligence." And toward the latter part of 1916, when the preparedness advocates began gaining strength, Dewey continued his plea that militarists leave the schools alone. The possibility that state legislatures might initiate plans whereby two or three hours a week of drill exercise would be compulsory led Dewey to write: "A different way of teaching American history is an infinitely greater factor in national preparedness than a few hours of perfunctory drill by boys whose minds are on their own hour of release." The dogmatic conformity and lack of critical intelligence being perpetrated within educational circles was extremely upsetting to Dewey. The ability of the preparedness people to demand complete obedience to the majority's wishes, Dewey saw as a serious threat to democratic liberty.[4]

Dewey, however, did not side with the Addamses, Bournes, Thomases, and Villards when it came to opposing American military participation overseas. In fact, as stated earlier, Dewey became the leading spokesman among intellectuals who supported the war. Nevertheless, Dewey remained steadfast in his belief that militarism be kept out of the schools and off the campuses. With the exception of his pamphlet *Enlistment for the Farm*, which was part of the Columbia University War Series, Dewey did not encourage any association between the war and the function of the schools.[5] Even this pamphlet was merely part of a propaganda campaign to encourage farm students to help increase crop production. In no way did the pamphlet imply that the schools were to become breeding grounds for the military establishment. Unfortunately, Dewey's stand on the war offered no consolation to those who, like Randolph Bourne, held consistently to their pacifist values.

Although Dewey supported the policy of conscription once the United States entered the war, he was, nonetheless, appalled by the tactics of the superpatriots within his own university. The rigid stance assumed by Columbia's president, Nicholas Murray Butler, the dismissals of Professors Dana, Cattell, and Fraser in the fall of 1917 by the board of trustees, and the demands put upon the faculty members to get behind the war effort proved particularly distressing to Dewey. There was, moreover, considerable mutual antagonism between Butler and Dewey. As William Heard Kilpatrick remembers, Butler was very critical of John Dewey's philosophy. Butler himself was a philosopher and disliked Dewey's influence at Teachers College. Dewey, on the other hand, did not appreciate what he considered to be Butler's stronghanded and authoritarian practices, and he was also extremely upset over the way Butler turned out Cattell.[6] It was bad enough that this war had to be fought with the blood of American soldiers, Dewey reasoned, but when it affected the entire liberal framework within the academic community, it proved to be that much more destructive. The inability of faculty members to express their dissent, the militant cry of excessive patriotism, and the general atmosphere of intolerance within the university environment strongly convinced Dewey that the academic world was no place for the martial spirit.

Dewey's recent experience with the damaging aspects of wartime intolerance added to his conviction of the urgent need to divorce militarism from education. Early in January 1918, only three months after the dismissal of three professors at Columbia University, Dewey offered his own moral equivalent for war and universal military training. In the spirit of William James, whom Dewey admired and whose article "The Moral Equivalent of War" he praised in *Human Nature and Conduct,* Dewey called for a universal training for social service. The only effective kind of universal training, he informed his listeners at a meeting of the Educational Association of the Middle West in Chicago, is one not for military purposes. Borrowing a page from James's essay, Dewey stressed four factors which would be necessary for the training of youth in the area of social service. These factors, which included physical labor, economic efficiency, social competency, and consumption of goods, had as their primary goal the reconstruction of society along the lines of peaceful cooperation and nonviolent service to the community. In many respects Dewey's plan was a combination of James's psychological approach to human behavior and Randolph Bourne's sociological plea for an improvement in the quality of life.[7]

When the war ended, the Department of the Army moved to establish a Reserve Officers Training Corps on college campuses. This attempt to inaugurate a new era in civilian-military relations—a result of the war psychology—culminated in the National Defense Act of 1920. The act itself, an ambitious plan for bolstering the nation's military might in the hopes of not being caught off guard if the threat of war should once again become a reality, provided for the establishment of over three hundred ROTC units with about 125,000 students participating in the program on college campuses throughout the country. In addition to the creation of the ROTC program, another provision of the act provided for the construction of summer training camps for youths—a carry-over plan from General Leonard Wood's prewar Plattsburgh movement. The plan, optimistically referred to as Universal Military Training (UMT), opened its doors to prospective recruits in 1922, offering a combination of military and civic instruction to 10,000 young men for a thirty-day period.

Dewey was strongly opposed to the National Defense Act's plan for the establishment of ROTC units on college campuses. The existence of militarism in schools Dewey viewed as incompatible with his philosophy of education, a philosophy which sought to encourage the potentialities of the individual and the well-being of society. The appeals to becoming a man, to demonstrating one's physical abilities, and to love for one's country which the United States Army and veterans' organizations traditionally made, Dewey argued, were "a lot of bunk." The development of the mind was more important to Dewey than any Darwinian entreaties for physical vigor. Intelligence was a higher priority, he believed, than masculinity. But, with the growth and legalization of militarism on many college compuses, Dewey began searching for new alternatives to offset what he considered to be a dangerous influence upon democratic liberties. He therefore heartily endorsed the plan for the formation of a Committee on Militarism in Education.

The Committee on Militarism in Education, (CME) was organized in 1926. Its leaders were Frederick Libby, Kirby Page, John Nevin Sayre, and Oswald Garrison Villard. Its membership was composed mainly of pacifists, religious leaders, and liberal educators. Its primary purpose was to act as a lobbying group seeking legislation to prohibit the use of federal funds for compulsory military training courses in ROTC units on campus. A secondary function, though equally important, was its role as an educational propaganda agency. In the numerous pamphlets—usually written by leading educators and noted pacifists—that were distributed throughout the colleges and universities in the United States, the CME deliberately tried to counteract the military influence then being generated by the ROTC units on campus.

Dewey's initial reaction to the CME was one of enthusiasm. He readily signed an endorsement—along with fifty-four other prominent citizens including Jane Addams, Senator William E. Borah, Carrie Catt, Oswald Garrison Villard, and Senator Robert La Follette—to Winthrop D. Lane's pamphlet *Military Training in Schools and Colleges of the United States.* The pamphlet, which appeared in March, 1926 was a detailed and documented attack upon the War Department's efforts to encourage military training through the use of ROTC units and the Citizen's Military Training Camps. The War Department, however, in its own report scoffed at the Lane pamphlet, accusing those who signed it of being unpatriotic. Dewey was outraged by the War Department's document, which was written by the military departments in American universities and colleges. In response he accused the War Department of a "a deliberate attempt to cast discredit, by name, on more than fifty representative men and women of America" whose only "crime is that they are interested in developing the spirit of peace and international cooperation in this country and opposing the Prussianizing of American institutions, particularly our schools." The atmosphere of military training within the academic community, Dewey argued, was not the kind of environment conducive to work along the lines requiring free thought. Higher education, he maintained, ought to exist for the encouragement of independent thinking and not for chauvinism.[8]

Dewey now continued his own campaign against the militarists. He wrote an introduction to Roswell P. Barnes's *Militarizing Our Youth: The Significance of the Reserve Officers Training Corps in our Schools and Colleges*, a pamphlet which appeared in the spring of 1927. Here Dewey responded to the charges of the War Department, stating that the military brass were "certainly long on venom and fury, but short on facts and figures—except figures of speech." In a more serious manner Dewey invoked his reader's attention by asking him:

> Is the reader aware that there is in existence in this country a well-organized movement to militarize the tone and temper of our national life? . . . Is he aware that the effort of this vested interest to militarize this country is operating deliberately and knowingly through the medium of our schools and colleges?

In an effort to enlighten his readers as to the seriousness of the problem, Dewey pointed out that the ability of the academic community to criticize the government and maintain a liberal posture was being deliberately undermined by a concerted endeavor on the part of the military leaders in the United States. "Nothing will be as fatal to the success of the militaristic attempt," Dewey concluded, "as knowledge of the facts. To suppress the dissemination of this knowledge is the logical course for the militaristic interest to pursue."[9]

In later years, especially during the thirties when it appeared as though another world war was likely, Dewey continued to pursue his interest in freeing the academic world from the cloak of militarism. In 1930, he signed a pledge to a manifesto issued by the Joint Peace Council, which on October 12, 1930, called for the abolition of military training of youths. "Military training," the Council declared, "is the education of the mind and body in the technique of killing. It is education for war. It is the perpetuation of the war mentality. It thwarts the growth of man's will for peace." Other notables signing the pledge included Albert Einstein, Jane Addams, Upton Sinclair, Sigmund Freud, H. G. Wells, and Bertrand Russell. In addition to signing his name to pledges calling for the abolition of militarism in education, Dewey also spoke out against the growing threat of government censorship. In a speech delivered at the annual meeting of the American Association for the Advancement of Science, held at New Orleans in early February, 1932, Dewey criticized the "organized efforts of persons connected with the War Department to prevent speakers suspected of pacifism from getting a hearing by students." Equally appalling had been the War Department's effort to discredit Americans who placed peace above armaments. Thus, in a February 22 speech before the Department of Supervisors and Teachers of Home Economics of the National Education Association in Washington, D. C., Dewey called the audience's attention to a recently published statement by the branch of the War Department responsible for military training in colleges which referred to Jane Addams as the "most dangerous woman in America." How was it possible, Dewey asked, to develop humanitarian values in the schools when the War Department insisted upon making a fetish of a narrow patriotism?[10]

Dewey remained firm in his opposition to military training in schools and colleges despite the rise of dictatorships in Europe. In a number of articles which appeared in the educational journal *Social Frontier* during the thirties, Dewey criticized the propaganda techniques of the War Department as well as those of other advocates of a new preparedness program.[11] Throughout his writings it is quite clear that Dewey believed that the only way to prevent what was happening in Europe from occurring in the United States was for Americans to create an atmosphere conducive to critical intelligence. Dewey's concern now was not the threat of another military engagement across the Atlantic, even though he expressed apprehension over such a possibility. Rather, his main interest was his fear that democracy might be destroyed from within without the firing of a single shot. If the War Department and preparedness propagandists had their way, Dewey believed, totalitarianism would exist in America as it did in Germany, Italy, and Russia. "War propaganda and the situation in Hitlerized Germany," Dewey observed, "prove that unless the schools create a popular intelligence that is critically discriminating, there is no limit to the prejudices and inflamed emotion that will result."[12] Appeals to nationalism under the guise of a philistine patriotism were for Dewey, the major threat to academic freedom. Without the freedom of inquiry and ability to criticize, Dewey argued, the habits of intellectual action that are necessary for the orderly development of society can not be created.

Dewey continued his arguments against militarism in schools and colleges right up until American entrance into the second World War. In 1940, with the threat of American involvement in another war clearly on the horizon, Dewey rejected the War Department's appeal for universal military service. Departing from his position in World War I, in which he had supported a wartime draft, Dewey now entirely opposed any form of military conscription. He looked upon the policy of conscription as part of a conspiracy by the Roosevelt administration to divert the people's attention away from domestic economic problems in favor of American military involvement overseas. He argued therefore that a universal draft not only would affect the moral fiber of the academic community but also was nothing more than a prelude to United States intervention in another war. In July, 1940, for example, he signed another peace pledge—this one sponsored by the Committee on Militarism in Education. The pledge, which appeared on July 9, 1940, in the *New York Times,* was signed by 240 educators, writers, religious leaders, and professional business men and women, including such distinguished people as Oswald Garrison Villard, Howard K. Beale, Merle Curti, William Heard Kilpatrick (who was at that time the president of the CME), John Haynes Holmes, and A. J. Muste. The declaration, a response to the Selective Service bill then being sponsored in Congress by Senator Edward R. Burke of Nebraska and Representative James W. Wadsworth of New York, called the proposed peacetime drafting of manpower for military duties "transparent sophistry" and declared that "involuntary military service is undemocratic" and "smacks of totalitarianism."[13] Unfortunately, from Dewey's standpoint, the Declaration against Conscription proved unable to stem passage of the bill. Once again, Dewey reflected, the appeal was to the emotions rather than to reason.

CHAPTER SIX

OUTLAWRY OF WAR: A NEW APPROACH TO WORLD PEACE

> My claim is precisely that an idea of what is to be done and moral theory are identical.
>
> * * * * * * * * * * * * *
>
> Ideas . . . whether they be humble guesses or dignified theories are anticipations of some continuity or connection of an activity and a consequence which has not as yet shown itself. . . . They are intermediate in learning, not final.
>
> *The Early Works of John Dewey*

The conversion of John Dewey to pacifist values and his concern for international peace during the postwar period was highlighted by his participation in the outlawry of war crusade. What exactly was the movement to outlaw war? How did it originate? Who were its leaders? What did it hope to accomplish? How successful was it, given the world situation after 1919? And lastly, why did America's leading pragmatist support a cause which many, if not most, historians have labeled unworkable and utopian?[1]

The outlawry of war crusade was primarily a moralistic-legalistic approach to international diplomacy. Relying on a simplistic appeal to grassroots moral sentiment, the outlawrists looked back to a time when progressive ideals had captured the heart of the average American. They rested their case on the tragedy of Versailles by arguing that European politics was corrupt. They offered what they considered to be a "purely" American peace plan—as opposed to the League plan already in existence—which would do three things: (1) outlaw war as a legal method of settling international disputes; (2) establish a code of international law which all nations would adhere to; and (3) create a court of justice similar to the United States Supreme Court which would encourage each nation to surrender its own war criminals—no matter how influential—to this international tribunal. The outlawrists also opposed the League of Nations because of its advocacy of the use of sanctions; paradoxically, however, they did not claim to be a pacifist organization. But perhaps most important, the outlawrists embarked upon a vigorous educational campaign which sought moral support from the American people. The advocates of outlawry were firmly convinced that it was up to the people and not the politicians to make world peace a working reality. Disillusioned by the clandestine activities which took place at Versailles in 1919, they remained skeptical of any and all forms of conventional political and diplomatic activity.

The driving force behind the outlawry of war crusade was a rich Chicago lawyer by the name of Salmon O. Levinson, who was once characterized by British MP Lord Robert Cecil as "energetic but annoying."[2] Levinson, who had graduated from Yale Law School in 1888 after attending the University of Chicago, had been a very successful corporation lawyer. His interest in peace had been initiated by the war's adverse effects on the stock market—obviously not to his own pecuniary interests. Originally a staunch supporter of Wilson's plan for a League of Nations, Levinson gradually became disillusioned by what took place at Versailles. His increasing disenchantment after 1919 led to his own conclusion that the use of sanctions against a nation was the equivalent of war and that it was ludicrous to attempt to outlaw and abrogate war while at the same time keeping it as a means of enforcement. As a result of his disappointment with the peace treaty, Levinson abandoned his support for the League and began propagating his own ideas of delegalizing war.

Yet, as his official biographer points out, Levinson encountered many difficult problems when it came to clarifying the goals of the outlawry crusade—problems which he was unable to resolve even in his own mind. One problem, for instance, was Levinson's insistence on the necessity of "legal equality of all states" while at the same time he opposed any definition of an aggressor because some major power like England "might be found to come under it." Such reasoning aroused the doubts of League supporters such as James T. Shotwell, who questioned Levinson's conceptual approach to international politics. Another problem Levinson encountered was his refusal to support the use of force in international affairs while at the same time paradoxically claiming in no uncertain terms that his organization was not a pacifist movement. The logic behind his reasoning was so contradictory that leading peace advocates like Kirby Page found it difficult to understand. But perhaps the biggest problem Levinson faced was his inability to distinguish between self-defense and defensive war.

When questioned at one point in the mid-twenties by James G. McDonald, chairman of the Foreign Policy Association, about self-defense, Levinson responded by stating that "it is conceivable that some nation may run amuck and if so any involved nation that might be attacked would have the God-given right to defend itself. . . ." Levinson's reply to McDonald's question clearly indicates the outlawry chief's lack of commitment to the doctrine of nonviolence that his movement advocated. Such inconsistencies on Levinson's part made it extremely difficult for realists to consider seriously his proposals. Despite these inherent difficulties, however, no one could deny that the guiding spirit behind the movement was its founder, Salmon O. Levinson. After all, he personally spent $15,000 a year to publicize the idea of making war illegal!

Levinson recruited a number of important people besides John Dewey. Among the more notable figures was Senator William E. Borah of Idaho, of whom Walter Lippmann once wrote: "Like the universe and like the weather the only thing to do about Borah is to accept him."[3] Borah, who maintained a firm stand against entangling alliances and an unwavering skepticism of all things European, was the political spokesman for Levinson's crusade. His vigorous opposition to the League of Nations–Borah was one of the Senate "irreconcilables" opposed to Wilson's plan for a world organization to maintain peace–also endeared him to Levinson's heart. Yet it appears likely that Borah used the outlawry movement to enhance his own political prestige. In many respects, Borah, being the staunch isolationist that he was, did little in the way of encouraging his contemporaries in Congress to embark upon a bold foreign policy dedicated to peace. Rather, he simply reflected the temper of his time and used the crusade as a springboard to support his own presidential ambitions.

Another leading figure in the movement was Raymond Robins, affectionately called the Colonel by his close friends. Robins, who was noted for his oratorical ability, was once described by *New Republic* editorialist William Hard as possessing "enormous physical fighting vigor" which is "always the same, always in violent emotion, always at white heat."[4] Robins's support for the outlawry idea derived from his hatred of Woodrow Wilson (Wilson disapproved of Robins's support for the Russian Revolution while the latter was serving with the Red Cross in Russia during the war), his firm conviction of America's national mission, and his disdain for Old World politics. He was every bit the supporter of nonconventional causes. He loved the political battlefield and enjoyed the oratorical clashes which he normally encountered. In later years his enthusiasm for radical causes waned. A bout with a mental disability instead of a forensic encounter ended his oratorical career.

Charles Clayton Morrison, a Protestant minister from Chicago, was another leading figure in the crusade. Morrison, who in his book *The Outlawry of War* suggested that anyone who spoke of peace without having read Charles Sumner's "True Grandeur of Nations" be sentenced to the city library for half a day and made to read it as punishment, was editor of *Christian Century Magazine*. He was totally dedicated to the cause and spent numerous hours writing and speaking in its behalf. He shared the nineteenth-century religious pacifist view that man was created in the image of his maker and therefore was inherently good. He was extremely distrustful of European politics and believed that the only way to secure world peace was through the plighted word of nations. He was recruited by Levinson primarily because of his popularity and broad influence within orthodox Protestant circles. Being the editor of an influential magazine also helped.

John Haynes Holmes was also an important leader in the crusade. As pastor of New York's Community Church on Park Avenue and Thirty-fourth Street, Holmes possessed considerable influence. He was dynamic He was articulate. And he was extremely gracious. His audiences were always captivated by his powerful voice and sense of logic. He knew when and how to reach his listeners. His congregation loved him not only for his religious principles but also for the liberal causes which he supported. During World War I Holmes distinguished himself when he opposed American involvement in the war. While in the pulpit, he put forth his reasons for siding with the pacifists. In his argument Holmes pointed out that violence would only result in more violence; that the means would determine the end; and that, therefore, fighting could not fulfill the high ideals of the prowar liberals. His plea for nonresistance endeared him to the hearts of pacifists and liberals alike who opposed the war. He shared something of Randolph Bourne's distrust of the pragmatic argument that the means employed would guarantee a constructive end. He sought to make the concept of pacifism both realistic and active. His reputation among pacifists and liberal clerics, as well as the fact that he was the editor of a Christian periodical, *Unity*, was all the more reason why Levinson actively sought his help.

Dewey, perhaps the chief theoretician and defender of the outlawry idea, was drawn to Levinson's plan because of its unique simplicity; or so it seemed to him if not to others![5] His attraction to the crusade was based on a genuine desire to unite Levinson's legalistic approach to peace with his own moralistic appeal to mankind's ethical sentiments. He believed that a "a re-organization of international relations would serve to harmonize the ethics of nations with those of individuals and thus help to civilize international life."[6] He was committed, moreover, to the belief that a community of enlightened members could actively participate in their own self-creation. Outlawry of war, as both a social instrumentality and diplomatic weapon, was one means, indeed the only realistic means, Dewey maintained, whereby the people could demonstrate their willingness to make world peace an actuality.

The basic premise as well as pragmatic argument in back of Dewey's support for the outlawry plan rested upon his assumption that the means proposed to implement this new idea—an educated public opinion which recognizes the need for internationalism and cooperation among nations—was also to function as the means for making a treaty outlawing war when signed and the Code of Law and Supreme Court when created, effective and enduring instruments of international peace. At no time did Dewey contemplate the "chimerical possibility" of successfully outlawing war by a mere juristic declaration or by legal excommunication. The function and effectiveness of a World Supreme Court, in Dewey's opinion, rested not upon enforcement of sanctions but upon the educated moral sentiments—the means—of mankind.

It was the earnest desire on the part of Dewey to provide a method whereby, before the politicians engaged in serious negotiations, the real and permanent groundwork—that is, the educational groundwork—would already have been completed among the peoples of the world. Although Dewey and the outlawrists offered no specific plan by which to enforce the goal of the delegalization of war (they opposed the use of traditional measures such as military sanctions and boycotts), they did, nonetheless, propose an educational alternative. It was Dewey's primary intention to see to it that reason would take precedence over emotion; outlawry was just the first step in the legal battle against war. The objective of the program was to work on the minds and dispositions of the people. If more people were taught that war was a crime against humanity, Dewey reasoned, then coercive measures to prevent its recurrence would no longer be needed. Understanding would replace fear, and agreement distrust. Quite clearly, the problem, as Dewey so realistically pointed out on numerous occasions, was not what reprisals a nation must fear for considering acts of blatant aggression but the moral incompatibility in undertaking such a course. If the internationalism of the modern world, in both its economic and psychological, and its scientific and artistic aspects, was to be truly liberated and made articulate, outlawry of war was the most realistic, indeed the only realistic, means for firmly establishing "an international mind to function effectively in the control of the world's practical affairs."[7] Thus, it would appear that Dewey's identification, association, allegiance, and participation in the outlawry of war crusade was in complete agreement with his pragmatic approach to international peace. In no way was it an idealistic or utopian fancy of Dewey's, as many of his detractors would like to have us believe. Perhaps Merle Curti put it best when he wrote:

> If Dewey's dedicated devotion to this program seemed naively idealistic to some of his contemporaries as well as to historians, it was nevertheless an important testimony to his conviction that war might be eliminated if the world stopped thinking in terms of war and that an unlimited national sovereignty contradicted both common sense and social and human needs.[8]

His initial interest in the plan, however, dates as far back as the early months of 1918. How did it all begin?

In early February, 1918, Dewey received a letter from an old friend in Chicago. The letter was from Salmon O. Levinson whose wife, the former Nellie B. Haire, had been a student of Dewey's and a classmate and close friend of his wife during his teaching days at the University of Michigan. Levinson's letter was simply a request that Dewey contact Herbert Croly, editor of the *New Republic*, to ask him if he would be willing to print an article he had just written. Attached to the letter was an article entitled "The Legal Status of War." Upon reading the article, Dewey wrote back to Levinson promising him that he would contact Croly as soon as he could. On March 9, Levinson's "The Legal Status of War" appeared in the pages of the *New Republic.*[9]

The article, an interesting brief on the jurisprudence of war, pointed out that under international law all wars were considered legal. Carrying one step further Hugo Grotius' seventeenth-century treatise on the law of war and peace (*De Jure Belli et Pacis*, published in 1625 at Paris), Levinson called for the delegalization of war and gave as an example the abrogation of duelling as a practical step toward achieving this goal on an international scale. "As long as international law continues to legalize war," Levinson argued, "all nations are moral accessories before the fact to 'collective murder.' " What Levinson proposed, in effect, was that war be made a crime. But what was most significant about Levinson's plan was his proposal for outlawing war by a written code of nations backed by the decrees of an international tribunal. The idea of actually declaring war an illegal institution struck a new chord in international politics.[10]

Dewey, quite clearly, was interested in the Levinson scheme. The plan which suggested that the people participate in outlawing the existing institution of war fitted neatly into Dewey's outlook on world peace. Levinson's plan, moreover, was compatible with his own instrumentalist approach to philosophy. As Dewey reflected upon the possibility of its success, he reasoned that the process for outlawing war would depend primarily upon educating the people as to their moral responsibilities in the world. This would require, Dewey believed, changing the existing thinking on war, which considered it a legitimate institution. A code of law and a court–

as both a means and an end–coincided with his pragmatic approach to world politics. Thus, the means–the moral sentiment to create a court–could be interconnected with the end–the moral sentiment to back the court's decisions. Outlawing war added a new twist to Dewey's pragmatic idealism.

Shortly after Levinson's article appeared in the *New Republic*, Dewey expressed his own support for the Outlawry of War plan in an article entitled "Morals and Conduct of Statesmen." Praising Levinson for his bold new plan, Dewey urged his *New Republic* readers to think seriously about reorganizing the world along the principles of outlawry of war. Too often in the past, Dewey asserted, war had been considered a legitimate method of settling international disputes. The fact that war was considered legal as well as being recognized as an institution, Dewey said, was one reason why wars continued to exist. "War to put a stop to war," Dewey stated, "is no new thing. History shows a multitude of wars which have been professedly waged in order that a future war should not arrive." It was now incumbent upon all Americans, Dewey pointed out, to support a new type of social-political organization, one of "compelling moral import."[11]

Dewey's interest in the outlawry idea grew during his trip to the Far East. His conversion to pacifist ideals and his skepticism regarding the Treaty of Versailles and the League of Nations had already increased considerably when he received a letter from Salmon O. Levinson prior to his departure from San Francisco. "I'm so afraid that the Versailles conference will end," Levinson wrote, "in some twentieth century rhetoric. . . ."[12] These particular words weighed on Dewey's thoughts during his journey to the Orient. Upon arriving in Shanghai–after a six weeks stay in Japan–Dewey saw all the more reason why Levinson's admonition was indeed correct. The surrender of the Shantung peninsula to Japan was a blow to Dewey's hope the Western powers might help liberate China from her feudalistic bonds. As weeks and then months passed, Dewey found himself secretly hoping that the Chinese would reject the treaty. As it turned out, China declined to sign the Treaty of Versailles in protest over Japan's right to govern the Shantung peninsula. By late 1919 Dewey, upset by the results of the treaty, was no longer willing to support the League of Nations.

Dewey's enthusiasm for the outlawry plan as an alternative peace measure to the League of Nations developed while he was lecturing to the Chinese students at the National University in Peking. In one particular lecture entitled "Nationalism and Internationalism," Dewey informed his students that "such international law as now exists has neither a tribunal to render judgments nor an executive authority to give effect to such judgments. When the world is at peace, international law works fairly well, but as soon as trouble erupts it loses its effectiveness." The first step necessary for peace, Dewey urged, was the development of cooperation within the framework of law between the various governments. But how was this to be accomplished, he asked? His answer was simple. For Dewey peace was determined by public opinion. "People must take an interest in, become informed about, and demand to have a voice in the foreign policies of their government. . . . " A truly democratic foreign policy, he maintained, relied upon the consent of the people. Yet it was somewhat unrealistic of Dewey to expect all people to become international diplomats. Nevertheless, it is quite clear that at this point in time, Dewey was moving from his earlier support of the League of Nations into the outlawry camp. His appeal to the people to assume a more active and vigilant role in world politics indicated how far he was now willing to go in embracing Levinson's proposal. Throughout his entire stay in China his appeals were directed to the people rather than the diplomats! The message was quite clear. "I hope to see a growing demand on the part of the public," he concluded, "that it have an effective voice in determination of the foreign policies of its government."[13]

Upon returning to the United States in 1921, Dewey was more than ever convinced that outlawry was the most effective peace plan available for reaching the common people. No sooner was he back teaching at Columbia than his old friend Salmon O. Levinson wrote that "after five years of effort . . . I cannot but feel gratified at the many friends who are supporting the cause and the gripping way it seems to take hold of 'common people everywhere.' " Buoyed by Levinson's optimism that "we have been making great progress on Outlawry since I last communicated with you," Dewey took it upon himself to write to Senator William E. Borah suggesting that the senator put himself at the head of the movement to outlaw war. "The man who first takes the leadership in a constructive movement at the present time," Dewey informed the senator, "will put himself in a position to go as far in politics as he may care to, even to the presidency, and . . . you are far better situated to lead this movement than anyone else." Obviously Dewey's effusive entreaty pleased Senator Borah, who wrote back to Dewey indicating his own sympathies for Dewey's sentiments with regard to a grass roots peace movement. "The difficulty with the whole situation," Borah told Dewey, "is that all the plans and schemes for peace are either made by those who do not believe in peace, or if not actually made by them dominated in vital particulars by them." Borah's viewpoint, like Dewey's, was that the people, rather than the politicians, should have a greater say in questions concerning war and peace. "I have no faith in any scheme of peace, Dr. Dewey, which does not reach back to the people and give greater and controlling power to the masses over the questions of peace and war." Dewey, encouraged by Borah's response, began making plans for an all-out campaign to educate the people to the benefits that could be derived from outlawing war.[14]

The greater part of 1922, however, Dewey devoted to completing his manuscript on *Human Nature and Conduct* as well as to getting readjusted to the rigorous demands of academic life. He was, nevertheless, still concerned about the prospects of outlawry and continued to urge Levinson to spend more time developing his financial resources as well as building a sound organizational base. Yet lack of appropriate funds and organizational difficulties plagued the outlawry crusade throughout most of 1922.

At the outset of 1923 the outlawry machinery did begin to gain momentum. As early as February 14 Senator Borah introduced his resolution for an "international law of peace." Senate Resolution 441 contained three major proposals. First, a universal treaty was proposed declaring war "a public crime under the law of nations." Included within that treaty, according to Borah, would be a "solemn agreement" by which each nation would "indict and punish its own international war breeders or instigators. . . ." Second, there was to be "created and adopted . . . a code of international law of peace based upon equality and justice between nations. . . ." And third, there was to be established "a judicial substitute for war" modeled after the Supreme Court of the United States, "which would exercise between nations a power similar to the authority of the U. S. court in disputes between the states." In addition, Borah was most emphatic in pointing out to his Senate colleagues that this authority did not "include in theory or fact the right to use force in executing decisions but rested on the compelling power of enlightened public opinion." The resolution, as everyone expected, was a big boon to the Levinson peace faction. By appealing to the moral sentiments of the American community, Borah's resolution represented a program which most Americans could feel at ease with. Clearly, Senate Resolution 441 presented a "purely" American peace plan, one not associated with the corrupt politics of the Old World.[15]

Levinson was extremely pleased with the resolution. Aware that public support was increasing for the outlawry plan, he continued to urge Dewey to devote his full intellectual powers to the cause. In one letter in early February 1923, he informed Dewey that "we three [Levinson, Borah, and Robins] expect you to wield your mighty pen right along in championship of the cause." In the following month Levinson flattered Dewey by writing him: "You know I am most grateful for your invaluable aid in our common cause." Throughout the many letters Levinson wrote Dewey, he continually played upon Dewey's ego, constantly telling him how important he was to the cause and what a great job he was doing. Yet, beneath Levinson's fulsome praise for Dewey one can detect a "domineering personality" in his letters. Consumed by his overriding passion for the outlawry crusade, Levinson became adamant in demanding total allegiance. At times he tended to forget that his followers had other matters to deal with. If it had not been for their close friendship, one wonders how long it would have been before Dewey admonished Levinson.[16]

By early March, with the Borah resolution now public, Dewey began "wielding his mighty pen" for the cause. Convinced beyond a doubt that the League–because of its advocacy of the use of sanctions–was no longer a feasible means for guaranteeing world peace, Dewey rejected an invitation by Arthur Dunn, chairman of the People's Committee of One Thousand of the Pro League of Nations, to join his organization. Dewey, reflecting an attitude many isolationists would agree with, sardonically replied to Dunn's request by asking him: "Do you expect the United States to go to war against all Europe in order to force them to reduce armaments and balance budgets? Why should they do it after we get entangled in their affairs on their own terms when they won't do it on their own account?" Any scheme, Dewey thought, which made use of the sanctions of physical force against recalcitrant nations was "inherently undesirable."[17]

Yet why did Dewey, whose support for World War I had been based on a favorable assessment of the use of force, decide to move in the opposite direction? Would it not have been more consistent with his pragmatic-instrumentalist philosophy (he always claimed that his pragmatic ideals were a "connection of an activity" already in existence) to support the use of sanctions and a League established for peace already in operation? The answer would seem to be that, having discredited his own justification for supporting World War I, he now found it easier to accept what he considered to be a stronger pacifist position–one which he felt was available to him in the outlawry of war crusade. Moreover, unlike that of his fellow outlawrist, S. O. Levinson, Dewey's pacifism would not permit him to support the doctrine of self-defense. He believed that once war had been outlawed, such concepts as self-defense and defensive war would become obsolete in international diplomacy. In addition, his opposition to the League of Nations was based in part on his distrust of European politics and in part on his disavowal of the use of sanctions. His philosophic reasoning no longer allowed him to advocate the use of armed force to counter military aggression. In his opinion there did not exist any intelligent means for the employment of military force. Sanctions, he now argued, were a method of force which would hinder rather than help the peace-making process. Thus, what was most noticeable regarding Dewey's philosophical position after the war was his retreat from his earlier support for the use of coercive force to a more pragmatic point of view consistent with pacifist beliefs and values, a position Randolph Bourne would have heartily approved, had he still been alive.

Dewey's support for outlawry was matched by his strong opposition to the League and World Court. In an article entitled "Shall We Join the League?" Dewey stated that

> it is hard to find any evidence of readiness to cooperate in any definite systematic way, much less to tie ourselves up with that League of governments which embodies all the forces which have brought the world to its present pass. . . . The notion that we have only to offer ourselves as universal arbiter–and paymaster–and all will be well is childish in the extreme.

But Dewey's remarks did not go unchallenged. League supporters such as Arthur O. Lovejoy–a philosopher and cofounder with Dewey of the American Association of University Professors–responded to Dewey's charges by vigorously proclaiming that the outlawrists were nothing more than a group of utopianists who failed to see the reality in back of world politics. In reply, Dewey explained his view that the League was inextricably tied up with the corrupt politics of the Old World. As Dewey commented to Lovejoy: "The League is *not* honestly named. It is a League of governments pure and simple." Even Levinson was proud of Dewey's rejoinder, telling him that "you are certainly doing the most heroic work for Outlawry of anybody. You have delivered smashing blows in all directions. From the viewpoint of Lovejoy, you should be called 'Killjoy.' "[18]

Yet his offensive against the League supporters did not stop with Lovejoy. During the months of March and April, 1923, Dewey continued to castigate the League in the pages of the *New Republic*. In two particular articles, "Political Combination or Legal Cooperation" and "If War Were Outlawed," Dewey called his readers' attention to the advances the outlawry crusade had made during the past six years. Demonstrating his sympathies for pacifist ideology–a position he had objected to during the war– Dewey now argued that when war becomes a crime, the pacifist will be the "active patriot-loyal citizen, instead of an objector, a nuisance and a menace, or a passive obstructionist." In obvious contrast to his earlier beliefs, Dewey argued that the League with its use of sanctions would never be able to create an atmosphere which would allow the pacifist to become a loyal citizen. A tremendous education was in the offing, Dewey pointed out, and it was up to the people to become "peace patriots" rather than "intolerant chauvinists."[19]

In addition to writing, Dewey gave public addresses on the outlawry subject. In a letter to Levinson, Dewey informed him that he spoke "to two or three hundred students here [Columbia University] on the topic." Apparently his speech was convincing, for he was requested by a woman's club on international affairs and the Newark Lawyers Club to present formal addresses on the "Outlaw topic." Levinson, obviously pleased by Dewey's showing, encouraged him "to lecture more or less widely, particularly at the universities. . . ." Even Dewey himself was enthusiastic about the progress that was being made and began making plans for organizing a New York Committee for the Outlawry of War to cooperate with the main office in Chicago.[20]

The meetings of the new branch were held at the home of Mrs. Willard Straight, whose late husband had been the founder and owner of the *New Republic*. An organizing committee was set up, with Mr. Reuben Clark as chairman; it also included the following committee members: Mrs. Willard Straight of Manhattan, Mrs. Adeline E. Post, a prominent socialite from New York City, Mrs. Theodore Dreiser of Brooklyn, Mr. Frank A. Munsey of the *New York Herald,* and a Mr. Christopher P. Connolly from East Orange, New Jersey. Dewey, quite naturally was elected honorary chairman of the New York branch. Unfortunately, little is known about the activities of the New York Committee for the Outlawry of War. At this point it is uncertain whether the committee actually went beyond the planning stage. The chances are that it did not. The only clue which may substantiate this point of view was a remark Dewey made in one of his letters to Levinson indicating that the committee had been "making slow progress."[21] In all probability, lack of funds and strong opposition from the well-established League organizations in cities along the east coast may have prevented the New York committee from gaining the public support that it desperately needed.

At the same time that Dewey was attempting to organize a branch of the outlawry of war crusade in New York, he traveled to Boston for a debate with Manley O. Hudson. This debate, sponsored by the Unitarian Laymen's League, was held on the evening of May 21, 1923, to consider the topic: "Shall the United States Join the World Court?"

Hudson, Professor of International Law at Harvard University, was a skilled speaker. Two months earlier he had successfully debated both Raymond Robins and Salmon O. Levinson at a Foreign Policy Association luncheon at the Hotel Astor in New York City. Now debating in his own backyard, Hudson called upon American support for the Harding-Coolidge proposal for joining the World Court by arguing: "I see no hope for progress in our time toward the escape from war except as we will develop these international institutions that are today at hand." He scoffed at the outlawrists in their argument that if the United States gave its support to the Court it would in effect be supporting the League of Nations. Dewey, however, vehemently objected to Hudson's line of reasoning, pointing out that "international law at present is based on the principle that war is a legitimate final appeal for the settlement of disputes, and that the present international machinery is in reality a war system." Moreover, he added, "a court to abolish war which is maintained by war would defeat its own purposes." But what Dewey seemed most concerned about were the political difficulties involved in establishing international peace. For Dewey, people, rather than the diplomats, were the prime movers in creating peace. The League, according to Dewey, was the embodiment of twentieth-century diplomatic rhetoric. Outlawry, on the other hand, he believed, represented a people's movement. "Just think what a difference it makes," he told his audience, "whether you begin with the people and end with the politicians or begin with the politicians and end by putting something over on the people."[22]

When the debate had ended, both men answered questions from the audience. The tension had eased somewhat after each speaker had spoken approximately fifty minutes. Hudson appeared firm and defensive about his position; he refused to accept any of Dewey's views on the outlawing of war. Dewey, however, seemed more sympathetic to some of Hudson's views, telling his questioners that no matter which position they supported they should all nonetheless get behind the drive for world peace. When asked a particular question about his own feelings regarding the debate that evening, Dewey concluded humorously:

> There is some question as to whether there is any real antagonism between the views of Professor Hudson and myself, or whether it is possible for anybody to favor both. Well, as I said, I am in favor of any means to help remove war. You may remember the very old, somewhat vulgar story of the man who received a telegraphic message of the death of an obnoxious relative, and it said: "Shall we embalm, bury or cremate?" And he replied: "Embalm, bury and cremate; take no chances." And that is the way I feel about this.[23]

A loud applause and much laughter echoed throughout the auditorium.

Levinson, meanwhile, was worried about the concerted effort then being undertaken by League supporters to sidetrack his organization. Fearful that they would divert attention from the outlawry crusade, Levinson explained to Dewey his feelings regarding the danger "of our plan being swallowed up in the terrific efforts now being made to force us into the League of Nations." Outlawry had to be made more appealing to the American people. "We do not want to occupy a corner of a program," he related to Dewey, "ours must be the cornerstone."[24] Yet despite the remarkable gains their cause had made by mid-1923, both Levinson and Dewey viewed with alarm and suspicion the organized attempts being made to discredit the outlawrists' position.

For, although progress had been made, the movement did suffer some setbacks. In a letter to Dewey, Edwin M. Borchard, Professor of International Law at Yale University, declined to accept Dewey's offer to join the New York Branch of the American Committee for the Outlawry of War, informing him that "it is well known to all of you that the chances of realizing such a worthy objective are quite remote. . . ." Albert Bushnell Hart, Professor of History at Harvard, sarcastically referred to the movement to outlaw war as "amateur diplomacy." Robert Lansing, former secretary of state under Woodrow Wilson, criticized the crusade as an absurdity which appealed to unthinking and unrealistic pacifists, "who ignore real conditions and the application to them of logic and reason, and loudly clamor for something which common sense and rational thought perceive to be as impracticable as it is vain." But perhaps the most telling criticism leveled at the outlawry crusade came from the biting pen of Walter Lippmann in late August.[25]

In an essay entitled "The Outlawry of War," Lippmann called to his *Atlantic Monthly* readers' attention the significance of the outlawry crusade while at the same time criticizing the program as too idealistic. "What they are relying upon fundamentally," Lippmann remarked, "is not their court and their code, but the treaty 'outlawing war.' They believe that this slogan has the power to arouse and then to crystallize mankind's abhorrence of war." The central fallacy in their argument, he continued,

> is this refusal to acknowledge the necessity of diplomacy for just those war-breeding disputes which are not within the competence of their code and their court. For, if diplomacy is a necessary method of maintaining peace, then no plan which does not provide for it can be an effective plan to abolish war.

Lippmann, it seems, struck at the very heart of the outlawry plan. Their failure to consider the role of diplomacy in international politics Lippmann viewed as a serious mistake, one which could only be classified as unrealistic. But what proved to be most irritating to Lippmann was that the outlawrists were advocating an idealistic plan at the expense of one that was–for Lippmann and those of like mind–very realistic; namely, the League of Nations and the Permanent Court of International Justice.[26]

Weeks passed before Dewey, as Levinson's intellectual spokesman, responded to Lippmann's charges. Two articles, published in the *New Republic* in October, comprised Dewey's rejoinder. "What Outlawry of War Is Not" and "War and a Code of Law" were ringing defenses of the outlawry position. "It does not say that law and war are the only methods of settling disputes," he pointed out in his first article, "but the only way of *compelling* their settlement–quite a different proposition, and one that I shall continue to believe until I am shown the contrary." Conference, conciliation, and mediation, according to Dewey, could be employed more effectively if recourse to war was recognized as a public crime. Here, in this particular article, it is readily apparent that Dewey was attempting to combine the traditional methods used in international diplomacy with the new instrument of outlawry. Moreover, a code of law, readers were informed in the second article, was indeed "manageable," necessary, and workable if war was to be declared illegal. Only when people realize the differences between "the present system of lawless and anarchic international political action and political action as it would become when associated with law," he vigorously maintained, could any measure of hope for lasting peace be counted on. Just as significant, this broadside did not propose to use the threat of force to produce peace. To Dewey, Lippmann's argument that outlawry could never be enforced was based on a false assumption about the concept of peace.

> When Mr. Lippmann says that diplomacy is required which works not only by conference and bargaining but "also in last analysis by the threat of force," he admits what he has previously denied: that law is in final analysis the only discovered alternative to force as a means of *compelling* settlement of disputes.

The urgent need is to substitute the method of judicial arbitration for the method of force. Such a proposition is not utopian, he noted, when one considers the number of past failures to prevent war. The time was ripe for a new idea and, "The friends of the outlawry of war hold that it is worth trying, and that unless it is capable of succeeding war will never be abolished." So effective was Dewey's rejoinder that the American Committee for the Outlawry of War considered the two articles an excellent exposition and defense of the outlawry plan and reprinted them in pamphlet form as *Outlawry of War: What It Is and Is Not*—distributing some twenty thousand copies.[27]

Dewey's defense of the outlawry of war position—which struck most realists as being completely nonpolitical in nature and too moralistic in sentiment—was nonetheless widely acclaimed by many advocates of peace. Justice Felix Frankfurter, later appointed to the Supreme Court, told Dewey that he had "rendered a service in exposing the false simplicity which his [Lippmann's] *Atlantic* article implied, to wit, that adjudication is co-extensive with 'law.' " James G. McDonald, chairman of the Foreign Policy Association, after having read an advance copy of Dewey's October 3 article, informed him "that many critics of the outlawry of war program do not understand it and . . . many others do not appreciate adequately its immediate possibilities in strengthening the peace movement everywhere or its potentialities as a factor in ultimately abolishing war altogether."

Levinson, above all, happily applauded Dewey's efforts, telling him that "your reply to Lippmann is masterly and withering. It serves to show how powerfully effective an analysis of an article can be." But Dewey's achievement was perhaps best summed up by a fellow outlawrist and Christian minister, Dr. John Haynes Holmes, who in a letter to Levinson, remarked: "The way Dewey's mind . . . has found weaknesses in Lippmann's armor is positively uncanny. All in all, Dewey's articles are the most brilliant pieces of controversial writing that I have ever seen. . . ." Having Dewey write for the movement, Holmes believed, was a tremendous asset for the outlawrists. "Think of what it means," he excitedly exclaimed to Levinson, "to have such an intellect on your side!"[28]

By the end of 1923 Dewey was extremely tired. Apart from his teaching duties, the numerous lectures, speeches, debates, and articles he had contributed to the outlawry crusade exacted a tremendous mental and physical toll—comparable to his activities during the war, only this time with an entirely different emphasis. By the middle of October he was cautiously parrying Levinson's constant overtures to undertake more speaking engagements. Remembering a letter he wrote to Scudder Klyce during World War I, in which he stated that "as a man I dislike taking responsibility," Dewey informed Levinson that his spare time could be more profitably employed in writing rather than lecturing. But weeks later Dewey retracted his earlier plea—as he would do during the Great Depression—and acceded to Levinson's wishes. "I am sure you can do an immense amount of good," Levinson encouraged Dewey, "by delivering blows in the strongholds of the East where there is so much pro-Leagueism. . . ." Assuming more responsibility, however, was a difficult task for the reticent and low-keyed Dewey. But in this particular case he had no choice. He was determined to atone for his past sins. Committed to the outlawry crusade and the overriding goal of achieving world peace, Dewey could only take satisfaction in knowing that in this case the end was clearly justified by the means.[29]

CHAPTER SEVEN

DIVERGENT PATHS TO PEACE

> The Outlawry of war movement is not a pacifist movement in the sense in which that term is currently used. It includes pacifists in its ranks, but it also includes those who are by no means convinced that a nation should not, so long as the war system is with us, be reasonably well prepared to defend itself in war. The whole controversy over pacifism is neither affected nor involved in the movement to outlaw war. Therefore, when the outlawrist says that the philosophy of peace by force is fallacious, and that a world organization for peace can rest only upon the plighted word of the nations, he speaks not as a pacifist but as a pragmatist, not as a perfectionist but as a practical realist.
>
> Charles Clayton Morrison, *The Outlawry of War*

Between the years 1923 and 1927 the outlawry of war crusade made tremendous gains. Receiving support from Protestant religious groups, various peace factions, and the Republican Party, the outlawrists began an all-out campaign to win the people over to their side. Like the Prohibitionists a few years earlier, the outlawrists appealed directly to the moral sentiments of mankind. In an era when social ideals took a back seat to economic prosperity and ultranationalism, the crusade to outlaw war represented the only reform movement that attempted to translate moral ideals into legal dictates. Their committed devotion to the crusade resembled that of a Prohibitionist who refused to compromise in any way his principles. Convinced of their destiny and determined to carry out Isaiah's proverb, the outlawrists sought to turn swords into plowshares on their own terms. Thus, with a combination of moral certitude and self-righteous indignation, the leaders of the outlawry crusade cautioned its followers not to become tainted by the corrupting influence of the League of Nations. They therefore encouraged their members to thwart any attempt League supporters might undertake to counter the movement's growing influence.

Nineteen twenty-three had been a rewarding year for Levinson and his followers. Initiated by the Borah resolution in the Senate and culminating in Dewey's reply to Walter Lippmann, the crusade to outlaw war quickly gained recognition among major peace groups and leading political figures throughout the country. Bolstered by their rapid successes, the outlawrists made it a point to demonstrate that their plan represented a constructive and viable path to international peace. Proud, combative, and perhaps even overaggressive, the outlawrists were determined more than ever to capture the hearts of all American lovers of peace.

With the outlawry crusade making tremendous inroads into the peace movement, Dewey quietly began slipping back into the academic world where he would remain for the next two years. Tired and worn by the past year's activities, he was now content to let Levinson and the rest of the outlawrists continue on their own for a while; he did not, however, refuse to speak on outlawing war whenever and wherever the opportunity presented itself. Satisfied with the progress they had made, he somehow felt reassured that the crusade could proceed without interruption while he devoted more time to his academic pursuits. He felt he had procrastinated long enough. He had already begun plans for a book when Levinson called upon him to lend his intellectual support to the cause. Having done just that, he now set himself to writing a book about the interrelationship between experience and nature, a book which many have labeled Dewey's greatest philosophical work.

In early January, 1924, while Dewey was writing *Experience and Nature* —a work that developed from the Paul Carus lectures which he delivered in December of 1922—a group of private American citizens met at the Columbia University Club. Called at the request of James T. Shotwell, professor of history at Columbia and general editor of the *Economic and Social History of the World War*, the meeting undertook to discuss various ways of strengthening great power cooperation at the League of Nations. Aware of the unsatisfactory state of the League's influence, Shotwell and the group focused their attention on the need for reconciling the difference between international disarmament and national security. Nineteenth-century power politics remained a basic part of their philosophy on international affairs. The main problem, according to Shotwell, was the fact that since 1920 the victorious European states had proved unable to settle their differences at Geneva. A deadlock had occurred, on the one hand, between France and the security-minded states, which sought guarantees of mutual aid, and on the other, Britain and the security-satisfied states, which demanded arms reduction. The object of the meeting, therefore, was to suggest ways of strengthening the League's power without damaging the nationalistic sentiments of the various European states involved in the dispute.

Shotwell, who was also director of research at the Carnegie Endowment for International Peace and a strong League advocate, introduced at the meeting a plan calling for three things: (1) outlawing of aggressive war; (2) use of "permissive sanctions" (according to Shotwell the League of Nations would automatically assume supervision over the colonial possessions of a belligerent nation); and finally (3) a definition of aggression which specifically stated that the failure of any aggressor nation to appear before the Permanent Court of International Justice within four days would immediately be charged with precipitating a war. The plan, largely the work of Shotwell, General Tasker H. Bliss, and David Hunter Miller—all three of whom served on Wilson's staff during the Treaty of Versailles—was unanimously agreed upon by the members at the meeting. The Draft Treaty of Disarmament and Security—as it was then called—proved to be an obvious attempt on the part of Shotwell and his committee to strenghthen the bargaining power of the League of Nations while at the same time heading off the gains the outlawry of war crusade had made.[1] Shotwell's plan—later adopted by the European nations as part of the Geneva Protocol—greatly upset Levinson and the Outlawrists. Fearful that Shotwell was attempting to sidetrack support for his plan, Levinson criticized Shotwell for his so-called blatant attempt to push the United States in the direction of involvement with the League of Nations.[2] What proved to be extremely disconcerting to Levinson, moreover, was Shotwell's obvious flirtation with the word "outlawry" within League circles. He was convinced that Shotwell was trying to use the word in order to manipulate public opinion to support his point of view. In addition, Shotwell's insistence on outlawing agressive war and defining acts of aggression was anathema to outlawrists. Attaching qualifications, Levinson argued, would only further detract from the legal concept of outlawry of *all* wars and would thus inevitably lead to more confusion. The basic point, he believed, was to keep things as simple as possible for the average layman to comprehend. Thus, Shotwell's support for collective security as embodied in the League of Nations and his incorporation of the word "outlawry" within League organizations was not favorably received by Levinson and the outlawrists. Somewhat selfishly, they saw it as a threat, rather than as a means of insuring peace.

Shotwell, however, was not to be deterred by Levinson and the American Committee for the Outlawry of War. In two articles, "The Problem of Security" and "What Is Meant by Security and Disarmament," he advocated armament reduction and support for the utilization of League sanctions as the most effective means for guaranteeing national security and international peace. The use of sanctions, Shotwell believed, would provide for national security by acting as a deterrent to future international conflicts. Equally important, he maintained that aggression and self-defense were terms which had to be defined and held firm in his position that collective security was the best means presently available for insuring national security and world peace. He was appalled, moreover, by what he considered to be the outlawrists' inability to grasp the political realities of the situation. Their unwillingness to support the use of sanctions while at the same time maintaining that their movement was not a pacifist one proved extremely perplexing to Shotwell. If they claimed not to be a pacifist organization, then why should they refuse to accept the use of sanctions as a means for maintaining peace? he asked. Outlawing war without any stipulations, Shotwell believed, was not only unrealistic but also very unpragmatic.[3] Yet Shotwell at the same time realized that a divided peace movement would minimize or lessen America's role in world affairs.

By 1925 Shotwell began making preparations for reconciling the differences between the two factions within the peace movement. A proposal which he called the Harmony Plan was introduced by him in mid-July. The plan established a Joint Committee composed of twenty-six prominent peace advocates throughout the country with Shotwell and Levinson as cochairmen. Other prominent members included Kirby Page, editor of *World Tomorrow*, Justice John H. Clark, Charles Clayton Morrison, Norman Thomas, Reinhold Niebuhr, and John Haynes Holmes. The purpose of the Harmony Plan was to initiate proceedings for the immediate entrance of the United States into the World Court on the basis of the Harding-Hughes-Coolidge reservations, with the added stipulation that if the nations of Europe, within a certain period of time, did not negotiate a general treaty outlawing war as a crime under the law of nations, the United States could withdraw its support from the Court. The plan, in effect, was simply a proposal to outlaw war by joining the World Court.

The Harmony Plan was viewed by some members within the outlawry camp, however, as another attempt on Shotwell's part to draw the United States into Europe's diplomatic sphere. Shotwell, who had always been sympathetic to the problems of European diplomacy, never quite recovered from the shock of America's refusal to join the League. He wanted desperately to make amends to Europe. The Harmony Plan, he believed, was one means of uniting opposing peace factions while at the same time demonstrating that the United States had not abandoned its responsibility as a leader in the movement for world peace. Even Shotwell's old adversary Salmon O. Levinson was anxious to cooperate with the plan. He too realized that it was essential for him to gain the cooperation of Shotwell's followers if his own plan was to have any chance of success. But the main objections to the plan came, as one might have expected, from Borah. The senator from Idaho had always been suspicious of any plan which tied the United States to what he regarded as the corrupt policies of the Old World. His isolationism as well as his opposition to the League of Nations was well known within Congressional circles. Shotwell, realizing this, was extremely anxious to gain Borah's compliance. He was well aware of the fact that without Borah's support very little would be accomplished in uniting the peace factions behind a single policy. Thus, in a letter to Borah, Shotwell cautiously pleaded with the senator to lend his support to the plan:

> I look forward to some difference of opinion with you with reference to the League of Nations. Yet it does not lessen in any degree my willingness to support heartily your present resolution in the Senate, so long as you are willing to give your support and encouragement to our Harmony Plan.

Borah, however, would not relax his opposition to the Harmony Plan despite the continuous pleas of both Levinson and Shotwell.[4]

Borah's refusal to go along with the plan placed Levinson in a tenuous position. Needing Shotwell's support to bolster his own movement in the eyes of peace advocates, he was also apprehensive about what might happen to outlawry if he lost the political backing of Borah. Thus, after serious consideration Levinson reached the conclusion that the purity of his program was more valuable to him than any virtues that might be derived from outlawing war by joining the World Court. He valued, moreover, the political support Borah gave to his movement and convinced himself that Shotwell's plan would eventually involve the danger of the United States joining the League of Nations through the back door. Consequently, by early February, 1926, Levinson turned sour on the Harmony Plan. In an article entitled "The World Court: A Polite Gesture," he argued against joining by pointing out that "if the United States goes into the Court it logically and inevitably follows that the United States will have a genuine relationship with the League." It was now obvious that Levinson had made up his mind to abandon Shotwell's plea for a unified peace movement. His suspicions about the League, coupled with Borah's objections to the Harmony Plan, thereby destroyed whatever chance the plan had of succeeding. Disappointment ran high within the Shotwell camp. Disagreement went deep. So deep in fact did it go that Shotwell later recounted in his *Autobiography*, "I finally came to the conclusion I could not work with them without compromising my own position."[5]

All during 1926 the tensions remained strong. The conflict between the two opposing peace groups over the idea of collective security and the degree of responsibility the United States should assume in world affairs appeared beyond resolve. So, having spent two relatively quiet and peaceful years in academic seclusion—writing *Experience and Nature* and making educational surveys for the governments of Turkey and Mexico—Dewey was once again summoned out of retirement by Levinson.[6]

Dewey, however, was not overenthusiastic about the new challenge; the major reason for his hesitation was that he admired and liked Shotwell. Although he may not have agreed with him on the use of sanctions and his support for the League, Dewey was extremely reluctant to destroy a friendship that had developed many years earlier when both he and Shotwell had marched down Fifth Avenue in New York City in a suffragette parade. But with Levinson's constant criticisms of Shotwell in his letters to Dewey and the apparent fact that Shotwell was attempting to undermine their cause, Dewey once again surrendered himself to Levinson's wishes. A friendship that extended over many years was gradually disintegrating. As Shotwell later reminisced: "Dewey and I had been close friends, but the friendship was strained by our disagreement."[7]

Two days before Christmas, 1926, Dewey issued his first warning to Shotwell and his followers. Recalling his own experience with the late war, Dewey pointed out that America's responsibility lay within the choice between two things and two things only—the outlawry of the war system, or its perpetuation. "The notion that we can really be of help to Europe by joining their affairs on terms that are set by their unhappy international and diplomatic heritage," he argued, "seems to me silly. We shall simply be drawn in, and our system assimilated to theirs." Furthermore, another warning appeared in the form of an introduction to Charles Clayton Morrison's book, *The Outlawry of War*, which was finally published in the summer of 1927; Dewey, however, had written the introduction in the early months of 1927. In the introduction Dewey pointed out that three things were necessary to guarantee world peace: "Emancipation of the International Spirit," "Liberation of Moral Force," and "Outlawry of War." Unlike Shotwell, who relied heavily on diplomatic bargaining and political statesmanship, Dewey argued that the people, not the politicians, would be responsible for creating an international spirit that would liberate the moral forces necessary to establish the outlawry of war system. In evangelical terms Dewey praised the virtues of the outlawry crusade yet cautioned against its quick application. "To regard the outlawry of war as mere prohibition of war akin to issuing edicts against earthquakes," Dewey reasoned, "is the most lazy and superficial kind of thinking." Institutions would have to be changed, ideals altered. In a most forthright fashion, moreover, Dewey now urged his readers to reorganize the present system of international diplomacy in order to implement the new diplomatic method of outlawry of war. "At present we are caught in the system, officials who make wars and peoples who suffer from them alike." Writing as if Randolph Bourne was his guiding spirit, Dewey criticized the state for its policy of making wars at the expense of the people and called upon all Americans "to cut the established alliance of law with war so as to put law decisively and irrevocably on the side of peace."[8]

Dewey's mounting offensive against the Shotwell faction during the spring and early summer of 1927 came to a sudden end with the death of his wife on July 14, 1927. The illness–a prolonged one–had been a constant problem for Dewey ever since their return from Mexico in the summer of 1926. Her condition became so bad that Dewey was forced to take a leave of absence from Columbia during the spring semester of 1927 in order to watch over her. The time he spent around the house–when not taking care of his wife–was devoted mainly to making new plans for countering Shotwell and his League supporters. But with her death Dewey's enthusiasm drained considerably. He no longer had the heart to continue the debate at this time.

Shotwell, however, angered by Levinson's attacks and Dewey's recent criticisms, was more than ever determined to outmaneuver the outlawrists. In a series of articles Shotwell introduced a new twist to the outlawry idea when he urged that a more practical proposal for achieving peace would be "to renounce war as an instrument of policy, not, as some pro-court proponents seemed to imply, 'to renounce war as an instrument of justice.' " The idea of renouncing war as an instrument of national policy struck a responsive chord. Many politicians and diplomatists were willing to admit that such a phrase contained political connotations which most statesmen could relate to. Somehow Shotwell's phrase was more appealing and exciting than "outlawry of war." The words "renounce," "instrument," and "national policy" were familiar terms commonly used within diplomatic circles–words which possessed realistic and practical application. Of greater consequence was the amount of publicity which Shotwell's phrase "renounce war as an instrument of national policy" received. It presented a serious threat to Levinson and his outlawry of war crusade. Thus, Shotwell, aware of the logical and political importance of such words, had scored–or so it seemed– a diplomatic triumph in his own right over his arch-rival Salmon O. Levinson.[9]

Shotwell's prestige, moreover, was greatly enhanced when during March

1927, while holding a professorship of international relations at the newly founded Hochschule für Politik at Berlin, he received an invitation to meet with the French foreign minister, Aristide Briand. Briand, who had been hoping to obtain a bilateral security pact with the United States, was intrigued with Shotwell's idea which called for the renunciation of war as an instrument of national policy. The meeting with Shotwell proved particularly satisfying to Briand. Thinking of a way to initiate a peace plan—as Shotwell hoped he would—that would not in any way jeopardize France's national security, Briand immediately decided upon making an appeal to American sentiments. Impressed, too, by Shotwell's overall sincerity in the matter, Briand thus sent a message to the American people asking for their support in the renunciation of war as an instrument of national policy (he used the words "outlaw war" but in reality accepted Shotwell's interpretation). The message was sent on April 6, 1927, ten years to the day after America first entered the Great War. Naturally, the message was worded and sent in such a manner as to arouse American peace sentiments. But what puzzled Briand and Shotwell for a brief period of time was the lack of popular interest in the proposal. Shotwell's suggestion that the appeal be made directly to the American people rather than through proper diplomatic channels—namely, the State Department—bore little fruit. Indeed, it was not until the appearance of Nicholas Murray Butler's April 25 letter to the *New York Times* that public appreciation for Briand's proposal first began to take effect.[10]

But if Butler's letter to the *Times* was the key that unlocked the door to renewed peace sentiment in America, it was Charles Lindbergh who turned the knob that opened the door all the way. Perhaps the greatest diplomatic achievement of the 1920s occurred on May 21, 1927, when Lucky Lindy landed his Spirit of St. Louis on an airfield just outside of Paris. The first solo transatlantic flight did more than anything else to strengthen Franco-American diplomatic ties. With renewed hope and greater appreciation between Frenchmen and Americans virtually assured, this feat of "airplane diplomacy," as one historian called it, provided the means for making the Briand proposal a reality.[11]

Yet Briand's proposal and Lindbergh's flight also gave renewed vitality to the outlawry crusade. In a letter to Dewey two days before his wife died, Levinson was ecstatic about the turn of events: "If a man had given me a million dollars four months ago to spend within that time for publicity relative to Outlawry I could not have gotten one-fifth the value out of it that has come from the Briand proposal." However, his enthusiasm was mixed with cautious skepticism. In another letter to Dewey early in September, he expressed concern over the recent efforts by Butler, Shotwell, and Joseph P. Chamberlain (professor of law at Columbia) to submit a new proposal to Undersecretary of State Robert E. Olds, calling for the renunciation of aggressive wars as an instrument of national policy. This they suggested should be part of Secretary of State Frank B. Kellogg's agenda in his upcoming discussions with Briand. Dewey, pleased by the recent turn of events, also shared with Levinson an annoyance at the activities of the League of Nations supporters. Dewey was particularly piqued by Butler's role in the matter, remarking to Levinson that Butler "was born with a reserved seat on the Band Wagon." Butler's recent actions, therefore, like those of Shotwell, became of growing concern to the outlawrists. In another *New York Times* letter, for example, Butler referred to the Briand proposal as a great diplomatic weapon by which to renounce war as an instrument of national policy. To the dismay of both Levinson and Dewey, Butler did not once use the word "outlawry."[12]

Levinson's fears about the recent tactics of his opponents increased when word got out that Senator Arthur Capper, a Republican from Kansas, had announced that he would introduce his own outlawry proposal in the Senate. The reason for Levinson's apprehension was the fact that Capper's proposed resolution was more favorable to the Shotwell point of view than it was to the outlawrists' way of thinking. In an appeal to Senator Borah, Levinson once again asked him to reintroduce his Senate resolution on the outlawry of war. Borah, needing very little persuasion at this point, readily consented to Levinson's demand. Realizing that the ground was being cut out from under his feet politically, Borah began making preparations to head off the Capper resolution. On November 10, 1927, Borah made public his plans for a multipower outlawry pact. The pact would not be bilateral, as the French had expected, Borah pointed out, but a multilaterial pact in which all nations would pledge their solemn word to declare war a crime. He followed that proposal with the reintroduction of Senate Resolution 441 on December 12, 1927. Having thus apparently offset Capper's drive for political immortality while at the same time regaining his own political prestige in the process, Borah began taking the lead in calling for the delegalization of war.

Borah scored a diplomatic triumph over the Shotwell faction even though it may have been for political purposes. By demanding a multipower outlawry pact, Borah was, in effect, discrediting Shotwell's position in the eyes of the French minister, who had hoped to achieve a diplomatic coup. Being forced into a position in which many nations would sign a pact outlawing war was not what Briand had in mind. He was upset with himself for having taken Shotwell's advice. But he also realized that it would be extremely embarrassing for the French government to back out of the negotiations at this crucial juncture. Moreover, Briand fully realized that Borah's move played directly into the hands of Secretary of State Frank B. Kellogg, who earlier had been looking for a way to avoid his proposal. He was extremely disturbed, therefore, by the new course the negotiations were taking.

Kellogg, who had been visibly upset at those "—— ——pacifists" for their relentless campaign supporting the Briand offer, breathed a bit easier now that Borah had made his proposal public. Borah's demand for a multi-power outlawry pact, Kellogg thought, was just the perfect move that was needed to offset Briand's real intentions while at the same time giving lip-service to the peace groups. Having been faced with the possibility that France would be the sole beneficiary from such an agreement, Kellogg purposely outwitted Briand's overture by demanding that the proposed treaty "include all peace-loving nations." All of Briand's suspicions about Kellogg's role in the negotiations were now confirmed. The bilateral security pact he had hoped for was now out of the question. Thus Kellogg, by deliberately utilizing Borah's proposal to his own advantage, not only diplomatically outmaneuvered Briand, but also paved the way for American acceptance of the Pact of Paris.[13]

Borah's role in the outlawry crusade meanwhile assumed increasing importance during the winter months of 1928. In early February, for example, his article "One Great Treaty to Outlaw All Wars," which appeared in the *New York Times*, considerably strengthened the outlawrists' position in their struggle with Shotwell and the League supporters. By skillfully managing to neutralize and in effect completely silence the Shotwell faction's criticisms of the State Department's refusal to define aggression in the pact then under discussion, Borah's article provided the outlawrists with more favorable publicity. Besides casting Shotwell and his pro-League supporters in the role of obstructionists to peace, the article also dealt a serious blow to those who opposed the outlawry of war crusade. Thus, the amount of attention which the article received as well as the willingness of the State Department to reject pleas for a definition of aggressive war added to the prestige of Levinson's group. Equally significant, the amount of political clout which Borah gave to the outlawry crusade was of considerable importance in its campaign against the Shotwell faction. By early 1928, with Borah holding the reins of political power, the outlawrists had gained the upper hand in the movement for a peace treaty outlawing war.

Shotwell, by this time much angered at Borah's recent actions, lashed out against the outlawrists. He accused them of naiveté because of their unwillingness to consider the political problems inherent in international policymaking. Relying on the plighted word of nations without any guarantees for national security, Shotwell argued, is like asking a general to send his troops into battle without the use of weapons. The only way to achieve lasting peace, he maintained, was for each individual nation to feel secure within its own borders, thereby minimizing the fear and animosity it felt toward its neighbors. The means for accomplishing this goal was through the process of collective security. He viewed with scorn the outlawrists' argument that his approach to world peace was just another Wilsonian scheme to involve the United States in the corrupt practices of Old World politics. He believed that the establishment of procedural patterns and the initiation of scientific techniques into the outmoded system of international relations was the most effective means for creating a just world order, an order that would replace the inequality and destructiveness of the balance of power structure by a system of justice. Thus, his emphasis upon collective security as established in the League of Nations, quite naturally, earned him the wrath of the outlawrists. Furthermore, in spite of the State Department's reluctance to listen to his point of view and despite the headway then being made by Levinson and his group in their personal struggle with League supporters, Shotwell was able to retaliate by demanding that a definition of aggression in the pact would be necessary before he would give his consent to the Briand proposal.[14]

Upon hearing this, Levinson lost his temper. Already disturbed by Shotwell's pro-League attitude, he once again called upon Dewey to neutralize his Columbia colleague. Although Dewey was still recovering from his wife's death, he was now more than anxious to get back into the outlawry fight. Anything which diverted attention from his wife's death, he felt, would be a good thing. In a series of letters between Levinson and Dewey, one can readily see Dewey's eagerness to resume where he left off in mid-July of 1927. His aggressiveness became more noticeable as Levinson kept informing him about Shotwell's actions. It was no secret to Dewey that Levinson and Shotwell disliked each other intensely—each accused the other of deliberate attempts to destroy his program. Shotwell never forgave Levinson for walking out on his Harmony Plan. Levinson, on the other hand, was suspicious of Shotwell's obvious sympathies for the League of Nations. It is no wonder that Levinson's letters to Dewey regarding Shotwell were worded in such a manner as to convince Dewey that Shotwell was determined to destroy their cause. With this in mind, Dewey immediately rallied to Levinson's side.[15]

Tension between the opposing factions increased considerably during the months of February and March. During this period Dewey had been meeting regularly with Shotwell, Kirby Page, and Joseph P. Chamberlain.[16] At numerous luncheons they discussed the means to a compromise formula. Since the meetings were held in New York, Dewey was the sole representative of Levinson's views (John Haynes Holmes was not present at any of the meetings). Most of the time Dewey was the object of criticism. Not only was he outnumbered, but most of the peace advocates in the northeast were pro-League. Dewey, quite naturally, was placed in a tenuous position. Yet he managed to hold his own against the onslaughts of Shotwell and his adherents. Levinson, who was at the time keeping Senator Borah posted on Dewey's activities, informed him, "They have been bombarding Dewey, but to no effect."[17] The meetings, however, accomplished little. Dewey, acting as conciliator, realized that both sides were firmly committed to their own points of view. It was obvious to him that neither Shotwell nor Levinson was willing to compromise his principles. Recognizing the utter futility of the meetings, Dewey reluctantly abandoned any hope of uniting the peace forces behind a single policy.

In early March Dewey wrote an article firmly supporting the outlawrists' position. "As an Example to Other Nations" was not only a direct attack upon League supporters but also an appeal urging all American lovers of peace to back Kellogg's proposal for a "general treaty of renunciation of war, and thereby execute the spirit of Briand's original idea of setting an example to the nations of the world."[18] His article was not taken lightly by Shotwell. It was obvious to Shotwell that Dewey was not about to drop his support for Levinson's idea, despite his conciliatory attitude during their winter discussions. Then on March 28 Dewey and Shotwell finally came to sword's point in an editorial debate in the *New Republic* entitled "Divergent Paths to Peace."

Shotwell's major contention was that a definition of what constitutes self-defense and aggression did not imply an obligation to put down aggression. "The enforcement of peace," he argued, "is quite another problem from that of defense or aggression." Dewey, however, could not accept Shotwell's argument that there is a distinction between commitment to a definition and the question of what acceptance of the definition implies. Calling Shotwell's argument merely an "academic exercise," Dewey went on to conclude, "It is part of any realistic devotion to the cause of international peace to trust to future developments rather than to any magic inhering in antecedent definitions."

It seems that Dewey scored a major victory for the outlawrists in his debate with Shotwell. Dewey's appeal to the simpler approach to the problem of peace and his casting of Shotwell in an unfavorable light—one of an ivory tower academician solely concerned with precise definitions—added considerably to the prestige of the American Committee for the Outlawry of War. His argument that providing definitions for what constituted self-defense and aggression allowed just that excuse needed to justify starting a war, was in keeping with his pacifist approach to international politics. Antecedent definitions, he believed, were useless since each nation could shape a definition of aggression and self-defense to meet its own needs and desires. What was needed, Dewey felt, was for the people to trust their moral sentiments rather than their political inclinations for the means of bringing about a lasting peace. So effective was Dewey's rejoinder that Shotwell felt it was incumbent upon him to drop his earlier demand for a definition of aggression in the pact. The "divergent paths to peace" were now reunited by a road that was being paved by the outlawrists.[19]

But Dewey's debate with Shotwell terminated a long and close friendship. As Dewey commented to Levinson: "Shotwell was pretty resentful about my last article; that I was attributing to him personal motives of underhandedness, etc. . . . I am embarrassed by our personal relations because of long years of friendship of the families. . . ."[20] It was thus extremely difficult for Dewey to accept the loss of Shotwell's companionship. Yet he also realized that during the course of political and ideological battles, friendships are won and lost as rapidly as the seasons change. In the case of a lost friendship there is no compensation—only the fond memories of days gone by. For both men reconciliation was now out of the question.

As the Kellogg-Briand talks moved swiftly along, Dewey became somewhat more skeptical over the increasing diplomatic and political wrangling then going on among the statesmen participating in the peace talks. Already Sir Austen Chamberlain of Great Britain was calling for measures which would guarantee the right of self-defense for British colonial possessions. Even Secretary of State Kellogg readily consented to the views of Chamberlain and many other statesmen that measures of self-protection must be guaranteed in the treaty if it was to have any chance of success at all. No longer was Dewey worried about what Shotwell's next move might be. Rather, he was concerned about the political moves being made on the part of the diplomatists to safeguard their own national interests. It appeared to Dewey that all his efforts were now being wasted. Why all this talk about self-defense when the treaty was supposed to ban all wars forever, he asked? Once it was signed and became operative, there would be no need to protect territory, he added. But as it became increasingly apparent that diplomatic bargaining was supplanting moral sentiments, Dewey once again took his case directly to the people. In an article entitled "Outlawing Peace by Discussing War," which appeared in mid-May, Dewey gave his own reasons why the public must be well informed if the treaty was to have any impact on world peace. The public must be educated as to the possibilities of what outlawry involves, he told his *New Republic* readers. "The American public, and possibly some Senators," Dewey contended, "need to be prepared for subsequent efforts that will have to be made in order to provide the necessary pacific means of adjustment of disputes. Discussion in terms of what would happen in case of war distracts attention from the essential need." The public mind had to be educated, he believed, to offset the political rhetoric urging support for defensive wars. "If discussion does not prepare the public mind for the necessity and we are caught unawares, then when the treaty has been negotiated, we may well be in for another failure, a failure humiliating to our national self-respect and tragic in its consequences for the world."[21] Unfortunately, Dewey's plea went unheeded. The public, he felt, had not been and was not being properly informed.

During the early part of the summer, Dewey continued to test public opinion regarding knowledge of the text of the treaty. The results of his personal survey were disappointing. In a letter to Levinson he explained that he was very upset because "there had been little general education as to the idea of outlawry" and as a result "the public is not prepared." Little could have been done at this point, however, to halt the negotiations. On August 27, 1928, in Paris the Pact of Paris, or the Kellogg-Briand Pact, was signed. It was signed without Shotwell's reservations for definitions of self-defense and aggression–much to Levinson's satisfaction. Admitting the joys of Levinson and Borah–for victory had been theirs–on the day the pact was signed, Dewey sadly told a friend that "he was convinced the Pact would hinder not help the realization of the Outlawry objective." In Dewey's opinion the outlawrists had failed to stick to their guns. In their haste to sign a treaty, the outlawrists allowed the politicians to manipulate their idea, thus giving further proof that they did not really believe that the means they proposed to use–educating the moral sentiments of mankind–were integrated with the end they originally hoped to attain. The signing of the pact, he felt, which talked of outlawing war as an international crime while guaranteeing the right to wage defensive wars, was indeed paradoxical! Consequently, it would appear that both Shotwell and Dewey were the losers in this case–Shotwell because the diplomats at the peace talks chose to ignore his concern for definitions and Dewey because in his efforts to arouse the moral sentiments of mankind miscalculated the political wrangling involved in international policy-making. Perhaps if Dewey had been more willing to accept Shotwell's concern for a political definition of self-defense and aggressive war, he might have influenced the outlawrists to cast aside their personal differences with the pro-League faction and thus put pressure on the diplomats at Paris–backed by public support–to work for a lasting peace. Nevertheless, the die had been cast, much to Dewey's consternation, in favor of a security pact rather than a peace pact.[22]

The Pact of Paris offered very little in the way of securing world peace.

Once again it appeared to Dewey that the people had very little say in the game of international politics. Even more disconcerting was the fact that prior to the passage of the Pact of Paris in Congress, the Senate approved a bill authorizing the construction of fifteen naval vessels. As George W. Wickersham's article "Pact of Paris: A Gesture or a Pledge?" aptly pointed out eight months after the signing of the treaty:

> The consideration of a bill authorizing the building of fifteen cruisers merely accentuated the Senators' lack of conviction in the reality of the peace treaty, and moreover, demonstrated a willingness on the part of that august body to appear like the temple of Janus, with two heads—one contemplating peace and the other smiling at war![23]

Thus, it was readily apparent that the debate over Senate approval of the treaty paradoxically rested not upon moral sentiment, as Dewey had hoped, but upon the passage of a bill guaranteeing the construction of new ships.

Despite the overwhelming vote (85 to 1) in favor of the outlawry treaty, very few senators really had much faith in it. Only Senator John J. Blaine was honest enough publicly to express his outright disapproval. Others such as Senator George P. McLean of Connecticut voted for it while referring to the pact as "throwing peace paper wads at the dogs of war, expecting they will seriously injure the dogs of war or destroy their appetite for a more palatable diet." Moreover, as the "cynical, saw-voiced, silver thatched" Senator James A. Reed of Missouri satirically remarked, "What the proclamation of Sinai did not accomplish in four thousand years, what Christ's teachings have not achieved in twenty centuries of time, is to be produced by the magic stroke of Mr. Kellogg's pen."[24] Indeed, it would appear that political support for the pact was more of a gesture than a pledge.

But perhaps the major weakness of the pact and the reason for its lack of credibility among politicians was best noted by Yale Professor Edwin M. Borchard when he asked:

> In view of the fact that the treaty apparently leaves each country contemplating or exercising measures of force as well as the judge of what constitutes "self-defense," who could assert, therefore, that any signatory going to war under circumstances which it claims require "self-defense," is violating the Pact? Has any modern nation ever gone to war (and without any suggestion of bad faith) for any other motive? How then could this Pact ever be legally violated or for that matter diplomatically enforced?[25]

For politicians like Reed and McLean and academicians such as Borchard, the Pact of Paris represented some very unsophisticated popular enthusiasm for peace. In their haste to have a treaty outlawing war, peace advocates ignored educating the public as to the meaning of the pact and what it would involve. In fact, the failure to educate the public represented some unpractical and unrealistic thinking on the part of many over-zealous peace patriots.

Although Dewey was disillusioned with the results of the pact, he did not abandon his optimism—perhaps it would be preferable to say idealism—regarding the possibility of educating the public toward understanding the goals of the multilateral treaty against war. In a pamphlet he wrote on Salmon O. Levinson, in a revised edition of *Ethics*, and in an article entitled "Outlawry of War" which appeared in the *Encyclopedia of the Social Sciences,* Dewey maintained that "the campaign is only begun."[26] The preliminary step had been taken, Dewey pointed out, "with the ratification of the Pact." However, the task of discovering and instituting the means for making a working reality out of the idea, Dewey stressed, remained to be accomplished. "The codification of a new code of international law congruous with the fact of Outlawry and the institution of the Supreme Court of the nations of the World," he concluded, "are the great tasks of the future." Whether the pact would amount to a mere gesture or a serious pledge, Dewey reasoned, would depend primarily upon the weight of conviction behind it. Until the public is educated to a point where it comprehends that outlawry of war "provides an orderly channel through which moral conviction will express itself," the campaign for world peace, Dewey contended, would never be completed.[27]

But no sooner had Dewey expressed his opinions than, on the night of September 18, 1931, an explosion evidently staged by Japanese soldiers stationed in Manchuria, damaged the Japanese-controlled South Manchurian Railroad. The Japanese armed forces, in apparent retaliation against Chinese nationalists, quickly seized most of the strategic positions in southern Manchuria. The action was so decisive and executed with such precision that State Department officials quickly concluded that Japan had waged an elaborately preconceived plan of aggression.

Japan's action was an outright violation of the Kellogg-Briand Pact. The Mukden Incident proved extremely upsetting to Dewey. Japan's disregard for the pact, Dewey noted, indicated that world peace remained enslaved to the dictates of national sovereignty. Thus, by early 1932, after the Manchurian crisis threw the American peace movement into utter confusion, Dewey was more than ever convinced that the Kellogg-Briand Pact, in its present form, had been a tremendous educational failure. Yet his idealism prevented him from abandoning his postwar pacifist values. He still would not give up his hope for the efficacy of the Pact of Paris. In a speech before the League for Industrial Democracy, Dewey told his listeners that

> the issue is whether the measures which the world has taken since the end of the great war to develop means for settling international disputes without resort to war have any force [force in terms of moral conviction, not armaments], or whether they can be blown aside like feathers when the air of animosity and national ambition is fanned into a breeze.

His reluctance to advocate military force was praised by the League for Industrial Democracy. And even though he signed the Princeton Pledge promising not to "purchase . . . Japanese silk or other products until peace has been secured in China on a basis in accord with existing international obligations," Dewey refused to support any measure which called for military action.[28]

The Japanese invasion of Manchuria did, however, prompt Dewey to undertake once more a campaign to educate the people concerning the virtues of the Pact of Paris. Shaken by the recent turn of events but nonetheless ready and willing to try again, Dewey informed his old colleague Salmon O. Levinson that "I always felt there was some danger that the Paris Pact was premature, being too much of an official diplomatic act without enough previous popular education, but now is the time probably to start something that will give a popular education and take the Pact out of the category of paper official documents." He was anxious to renew the campaign. Aware that the time had arrived for him to resume the responsibility of educating the public, Dewey set about writing a piece for the *New Republic*. Three weeks after his letter to Levinson, Dewey's article appeared in the March 23 issue. The article, "Peace by Pact or Covenant," was a public plea for all Americans to pledge their moral support for the Pact of Paris. Pointing out that the pact had been prematurely adopted and that it represented the "termination of the maneuvers of diplomats" instead of the conclusion of "an irresistible public demand," Dewey cautiously warned that "there has . . . always been the danger that official adoption of the outlawry idea would turn out to be an embalming of the idea rather than an embodiment of it." The recent action in Manchuria, he maintained, demonstrated that "the public's grasp of and belief in the Kellogg-Briand Pact is still lamentably superficial." Yet he would not concede that the pact had lost its appeal. In an impassioned way, Dewey pleaded for lovers of peace to concentrate their attention upon the peace pact. "They should deny themselves," Dewey reasoned, "the use of all methods of agitation and appeal which are contrary to its letter and spirit." If this were done, he believed, the work of public education "which was interrupted by the more or less premature official adoption of the Pact" could be resumed and undertaken more vigorously than before.[29]

While calling for the renewal of the public's awareness of the Pact of Paris, Dewey also maintained his pacifist stance against those calling for the use of military sanctions against Japan. In June, 1932, Dewey debated Raymond Leslie Buell, research director of the Foreign Policy Association, on the question of whether or not sanctions were necessary to international organization. Objecting to Buell's contention that sanctions were a concrete means for stopping war, Dewey countered by arguing that sanctions were impractical and precipitated wars rather than preventing them—a far cry from his World War I days. "Enforcement of Peace," Dewey pointed out, was a phrase combining two contradictory ideas. To rely upon sanctions, Dewey told Buell, would only increase conflicts, not lessen them. "I can think of no one thing more hostile to the development of this needed harmony and community than the overhanging menace of coercive force." Blockades and other war measures, Dewey believed, ran counter to the spirit of the Paris pact. The Manchurian crisis could be resolved, he contended, not through the use of sanctions as embodied in the League of Nations but by appealing to the liberal peace sympathizers in Japan and China. The task of educating the public as to the peaceful merits of the Paris pact, according to Dewey, remained unfinished.[30]

Dewey was pleased when, in August, Secretary of State Henry L. Stimson issued his doctrine of nonrecognition with respect to Japan's military aggression in Manchuria. In a letter to Levinson explaining the article he was about to write for the *Encyclopedia of the Social Sciences*, Dewey called attention to the fact that "the Stimson doctrine is a logical development of the outlawry of war crusade."[31] He had been delighted by Stimson's efforts to link nonrecognition to the outlawry idea and believed that the pact was far from dead. But he also realized that a tremendous educational campaign had to be waged in order to unite moral sentiment behind the pact. Unfortunately, by the fall of 1932, the severity of the depression at home and the rise of totalitarianism abroad destroyed whatever chance outlawry of war had for capturing the hearts of American lovers of peace.

CHAPTER EIGHT

SOCIAL JUSTICE AND THE EMPTY POCKET

> Every thinker puts some portion of an apparently stable world in peril, and no one can wholly predict what will emerge in its place.
>
> Dewey, *Characters and Events*

> There is the Dewey who revolted against formalism and who feared the consequences of setting up inalienable rights and self-evident principles for political and moral action. Then there is the Dewey who wanted to be a social engineer but did not succeed. One might have hoped that the second Dewey would stimulate students and disciples to build this technology, but where are they?
>
> Morton White, *Social Thought in America*

In 1949 a young socialist writer for the *New Leader* and former New York City high school teacher by the name of Jim Cork wrote a letter to John Dewey. Cork, who had been an admirer of Dewey, was puzzled by what he thought was an apparent inconsistency in the former Columbia University professor's philosophy. In the letter he asked Dewey if he would be kind enough to explain how it was possible for him to argue in *Liberalism and Social Action* that "liberalism must now become radical" and then only four years later condemn radicalism (the kind espoused in Marxian tenets) in *Freedom and Culture.* The uncertainty and confusion in Dewey's social analysis annoyed Cork. Why wasn't Dewey sympathetic to Marx's philosophy? Did not Dewey's philosophy reflect many of the things Marx advocated? These questions and many more rushed through the mind of Jim Cork as he wrote the letter.

Dewey's response came a few days later. It was less than satisfying to Cork. Dewey informed him: "I think that on the basis of *Liberalism and Social Action*, and to some extent *Individualism Old and New*, I can be classed as a democratic socialist. If I were permitted to define 'socialism' and 'socialist' I would classify myself today a supporter of that principle. . . ." But then he went on to say something imprecise: "I think that the issue is not as yet sufficiently definite to permit of any answer save that it has to be worked out experimentally. Probably my experimentation goes deeper than any other ism!" Cork was disappointed with Dewey's response. As a young socialist he had hoped that Dewey would provide some clue as to what his democratic socialism implied. If only Dewey would recognize the values of Marxism and employ his own philosophy along these lines, Cork thought, then perhaps society could be improved. It was Dewey's unwillingness—despite his liberal beliefs—to commit himself that bothered Cork. To point out existing ills and yet offer no solutions was most disheartening. For a young idealist like Jim Cork it was a tragedy.[1]

Yet Dewey's letter to Cork does provide a clue to the nature of Dewey's radicalism. If anything, Dewey was a liberal who looked for solutions without resorting to inflexible dogma or violence. His philosophy called for the reconstruction of society on a continuous and peaceful basis. There were no "absolutes" in his philosophy. All aspects of life, he maintained, had to be continually redefined and improved. It was "open-ended"; it had no specific ends in mind. His liberalism—which was more optimistic than that of his old colleague at the University of Chicago, Thorstein Veblen—was a natural outgrowth of his lingering sympathies for nineteenth-century liberalism. Somewhat ironically, however, he called for more governmental action in society without allowing his philosophy to assume the role of arbiter in the reconstruction he called for. Since his pragmatism was based on the assumption that goals were shaped by means, Dewey therefore opposed all "isms" (Marxism, fascism, totalitarianism, etc.) because he felt that they were illiberal. More important, his refusal to allow his philosophy to be entrapped by *a priori* tenets or fixed ends was a basic part of his liberal sympathy for the democratic way of life. For Dewey, there were no predetermined ends; there were merely parts of a continuous process in the reconstruction of society. However, his unwillingness to utilize his philosophy to give his complete support either to the socialists or to the experimentalism of the New Deal, despite his own involvement in the crusade for social justice, clearly demonstrated Dewey's own confusion as to which path to follow. At a time when Dewey's philosophy could have been most effective it was not. Why not?

By 1929 the golden days of normalcy were at an end. Prosperity suddenly gave way to depression. Only darkness now appeared at the other end of the tunnel. Public pessimism increased as rapidly as the stock market precipitously declined. Between 1929 and 1933 the annual national income fell from $81 billion to $49 billion while per capita income, which was constantly being adjusted to the cost of living, declined dramatically from $681 to $495. Gross farm income decreased during the same period from nearly $12 billion annually to $5.3 billion. At the same time the value of stocks on the New York exchange shrank from an estimated $87 billion in 1929 to $19 billion in 1933. All over, deflation ran rampant and business activity continually diminished. Unemployment, a key factor in determining an economic recession, totaled almost 3 million persons by the spring of 1930; nearly 4 million by the fall of that same year; 6.8 million a year later; and close to 11 million in 1932. By the time 1933 rolled around, therefore, nearly one out of every four members in the labor force was unemployed, and the gross national product was practically a third less than it had been four years earlier.

The financial crisis and ensuing economic depression, the worst in the nation's history, helped to bolster the views of those who had been critical of the reigning business and political philosophy of the twenties. The plaudits supporting technological innovation for its vaunted efficiency and unlimited productive capacities were no longer voiced. Instead, enthusiasm for social justice and governmental action became the battle cry of the reformer. Uncertain of the fate of both democracy and capitalism, prominent American thinkers led by John Dewey turned hopefully to some form of economic collectivism and scientific planning.

Dewey's concern for social justice was a natural outgrowth of his philosophical interests. As early as the 1880s Dewey had expressed a certain amount of interest in social problems. While teaching at the University of Michigan, he came in contact with a former Wall Street analyst by the name of Franklin Ford, who was something of an eccentric journalist seeking notoriety. Soured by his firsthand experiences of greed and corruption, Ford became a severe critic of the practices of Wall Street. The activities of Rockefeller, Morgan, and Vanderbilt intensified Ford's disdain for the predatory instincts of the American economic system. His criticisms of Wall Street, moreover, expanded outward until they included the whole capitalistic system.

Dewey, who had been attempting to apply his philosophy to social problems, was impressed by what Ford had to say about the need for the socialization of intelligence. The economic expansion of America was creating problems in the form of overcrowded cities, poor health conditions, and unsafe factory conditions. Even social democracy was suffering as a result of the inequality of wealth. Only intelligent social action, Dewey believed, could effectively counter the rapid increase in social and economic problems. Keeping Ford's criticisms in mind, Dewey began his own campaign against the existing ills of America's so-called democratic society. In a paper delivered at the University of Michigan in 1888, Dewey had criticized the existing form of economic aristocracy (the Vanderbilts, Rockefellers, and the like), claiming that civil and political democracy were meaningless without economic and industrial democracy. Industrial relations should serve the interests of all society's members. "All industrial relations," he told his listeners, "are to be regarded as subordinate to human relations, to the law of personality." The "Ethics of Democracy," he pointed out, depended on the ability of society to share its wealth equally. Political democracy rested upon economic democracy. Without social and economic equality, Dewey maintained, democracy does not exist at all.[2]

His interest in social problems continued throughout the Populist and Progressive periods. At a time when social and political ferment was reaching tremendous proportions in both city and countryside, Dewey quickly adjusted his philosophical and educational principles to meet the existing crisis. While at the University of Chicago he started the first experimental school in progressive education. The purpose of Dewey's experimental school was to enable young students to learn more about their environment while at the same time applying the skills which they learned in the classroom to social and economic problems. According to Dewey, the school was not only an extension of democracy but also an integral part of the social fabric. Thus, for example, in *Schools of Tomorrow* Dewey informed his new converts to progressive education that "the statement that the schools exist for a democratic purpose, for the good of citizenship, becomes an obvious formula. A community which perceives what a strong factor its school is in civic activities, is quick to give support and assistance in return. . . ."[3] Consequently, the school and the community were interactive and mutually interdependent. Both, therefore, needed each other's support.

In addition to his interest in education as an answer to the progressive call for social readjustment, Dewey was also very active in the affairs of Hull House. His interest in Hull House, not unexpectedly, was a natural outgrowth of his views on the school as part of the social settlement. Furthermore, his firsthand experience and awareness of industrial ills grew considerably from his association with Hull House. His many debates and lectures with socialists, anarchists, and single taxers emphasized the need for social cooperation and social change. His experience at Hull House was a rich and rewarding one. Dewey's fondness and admiration for Jane Addams, moreover, led him to name one of his daughters after the founder of Hull House.

Dewey's continuing interest in social justice played an important role during his early years at Columbia. Upon moving to New York in 1904, Dewey became active in Lillian Wald's Henry Street Settlement and served as chairman of the educational committee at Mary Simkhovitch's Greenwich House. New York's rich cultural heritage was also influential in shaping Dewey's philosophical approach to social problems. His books, especially *Ethics* (with James H. Tufts), *Schools of Tomorrow,* and *Democracy and Education*, point out the marked development of Dewey's attitude toward social reconstruction. The continuous renovation of society through experimentation and socialized intelligence was, for Dewey, the key for making democracy a living reality. Unfortunately, the war diverted Dewey's attention away from domestic progressivism at a time when he was establishing himself as the leading spokesman for the cause.

Dewey did not, however, like so many of the other spokesmen for social reconstruction, after the war abandon his progressive spirit. Still optimistic over the possibility that democracy could be made to work in America, Dewey divided much of his outside time between the issues of world peace and domestic social justice. In many respects, his views on social justice reflected his earnest desire to establish world peace. According to Dewey, economic inequality and social justice were major causes of domestic and international violence. Domestic tensions, he felt, encouraged governments to search for solutions outside the realm of social reconstruction. The conspiratorial view that governments embark upon aggressive foreign policies as a means of alleviating troubles at home was evident in his writings. Only by insuring social and economic equality on the home front, he believed, would the people feel secure enough to look upon one another as well as their international neighbors in a more favorable light. Years later, in an interview with the historian Merle Curti in 1932, Dewey expressed this feeling when he explained to him that the failure of the World War to achieve an extension of democracy, together with the Russian Revolution, convinced him that economic democracy was an "indispensable basis for political and cultural democracy." Without social and economic justice at home, world peace was an impossibility.[4] Consequently, during the 1920s Dewey became increasingly active in attempting to utilize his philosophy to promote social betterment.

In late 1921, after returning from China, Dewey was directly responsible for helping to organize and establish the Brookwood Labor College at Katonah, New York. Located in the scenic upper part of Westchester County, the college was financed by leading social progressives and various labor unions. The director of the school was a young socialist and Christian minister named A. J. Muste. The purpose of the school was to educate laborers to a better understanding of social problems and a greater appreciation of their jobs. Much of the school's program was simply an extension of Dewey's educational philosophy applied to the field of industrial relations. Having participated in the "X" Club, organized in 1903 by W. J. Ghent and including such people as Lincoln Steffens, Norman Hapgood, Hamilton Holt, Charles Beard, Owen R. Lovejoy, Walter Weyl, Morris Hillquit, Algernon Lee, and William English Walling, Dewey had gained a greater understanding and sympathy for the socialist point of view. Brookwood Labor College was Dewey's attempt not only to educate workers in gaining a better understanding of existing industrial and social problems but also to enable them to gain the respect of the community—a kind of "social scientific means applied to uplift." It appealed directly to socialists and labor groups seeking a change in the existing social structure in America. By the early thirties, however, the college came under increasing attack from the right for being a haven for communists and socialists. Losing financial and public support, it was forced to close its doors.

Dewey's activities in the field of domestic reconstruction blossomed by the mid-twenties. In 1925 he joined the League for Industrial Democracy and along with John Haynes Holmes and Harry Emerson Fosdick backed Norman Thomas, the Socialist candidate for New York City mayor. Two years later his radicalism became more noticeable in a speech to the National Consumers' League at the Hotel Astor in New York City. Upset at the proposal of leading manufacturers to take the unfit from the schools and employ them in factories, Dewey's humanitarian instincts caused him to lash out at what he considered to be an unethical and barbarian idea. "Many of these manufacturers," he told his audience, "are on the governing boards of universities. I have not heard them as such urging the families whose children by social custom go to college that their children should be enjoying the superior values of the factories."[5] It was imperative if democracy were to function properly that social equality be made a reality. The newly acquired prosperity, Dewey argued, had made people insensitive to the social ills around them. The lack of concern for fellow Americans and the predatory instincts of a greedy class of manufacturers, bent upon acquiring a leisurely way of life, did not set well with Dewey's progressive spirit. Like Thorstein Veblen, Dewey could only look with disdain on the waste of "conspicuous consumption."

Although Dewey was extremely disturbed by the economic exploitation in a rising industrial society, he was more concerned about the psychological problem resulting from changing life styles. The twisting and warping of human experience was, according to Dewey, the primary evil of capitalism. The monotony, drudgery, ugliness, and emptiness of most industrial jobs he saw as a serious threat to American civilization. Even industrial leaders lacked the spiritual and social involvements necessary for democratic cooperation. A feeling of uncertainty and bewilderment pervaded the American scene. The new technology and science, he urged, must be converted to social gains; he realized that the submarine and airplane were examples of the detrimental side of technology, and he urged that scientific investigation be directed away from military purposes. Technology placed man in a position where he was caught in the sweep of forces too vast to understand. "Our concern at this time," he told students in a series of lectures delivered at Kenyon College in June, 1926, and published the next year as *The Public and Its Problems,* "is to state how it is that the machine age in developing the Great Society had invaded and partially disintegrated the small communities of former times without generating a Great Community."[6] The contradictions and paradoxes of community disintegration caused by technological innovation had divided American civilization within and against itself. The nineteenth-century tradition of rural agrarianism, a tradition Dewey was accustomed to as a youth growing up in the small town of Burlington, Vermont, was being rapidly supplanted by the twentieth-century pattern of industrial technology. For democracy to survive and meet the changing conditions, a readjustment of preexisting notions was needed. Dewey knew this and encouraged it.

In two articles written during the late twenties, "A Critique of American Civilization" and "Philosophy," Dewey encouraged a change in American mentality. He realized that the twentieth-century realities of industrial technology were here to stay. Progress could not be stopped without serious damage to the economic structure of American capitalism. The old individualistic, laissez faire mentality had to adjust itself to the new problems and uncertain situations of twentieth-century America. A serious threat was now confronting our democratic traditions. "This intimate union of science and technology, realized in mechanical civilization," Dewey skeptically pointed out, "is a challenge to our most cherished philosophic tradition." The problem therefore was somehow to preserve the Jeffersonian notion of individualist values that characterized the older community and to transmit them into a new form of social or collective democracy compatible with the realities of present-day America. What was needed was a new philosophic tradition—one which called for a new form of integrated individuality. Thus, in a series of articles in the *New Republic*, later reprinted in book form as *Individualism Old and New*, Dewey advocated a new type of individualism which he preferred to call "corporateness." The collective age which America had entered was, Dewey accurately noted, no longer suited to the nineteenth-century rhetoric of "rugged individualism." Insecurity and uncertainty had to be replaced by a certain "quest for certainty"—namely, by a new corporate individualism. "By accepting the corporate and industrial world in which we live," Dewey perceptively pointed out, "and by thus fulfilling the preconditions for interaction with it, we, who are also parts of the moving present, create ourselves as we create an unknown future." The solution for the crisis in American society, Dewey sincerely believed, was the "creation of a new individualism as significant for modern conditions as the old individualism at its best was for its day and place," or an integrated individuality through democratic socialism. Such was Dewey's response to a most serious challenge.[7]

Dewey's dedicated concern for a social reconstruction extended into the political arena as well. In the 1928 presidential election he voted for Al Smith, much to the consternation of socialists and progressives, partly because he felt sympathetic to Smith's genuine concern for the urban poor and underprivileged, and partly because he disapproved of the way in which previous Republican administrations handled existing social and economic problems. His support for Smith was not taken lightly by his old outlawry companion Salmon O. Levinson, who let it be known to Dewey that "you and I are lined up on opposite political sides." Nonetheless, Dewey was convinced that Smith's approach to social problems was "humane and sympathetic" unlike Hoover's hard "efficiency," an efficiency that "works out to strengthen the position of just those economic interests that most need weakening instead of strengthening."[8]

His actions, however, were not limited to the editorial field. In late 1929 Norman Thomas and Paul Blanshard, looking for ways to reform New York City's political system as a result of the flamboyant and corrupt practices of the Jimmie Walker administration, organized the League for Independent Political Action. LIPA, as it was referred to, was a progressive-pacifist organization set up to serve as a liberal pressure group upon which to build a new political party. Its appeal was directed to the left of the political spectrum, and it recruited many socialists and Farmer-Labor progressives. Its platform was a curious combination of socialist tenets and pacifist appeals, ranging from demands for the public ownership of utilities and a high progressive income tax, an inheritance tax and increases in land values, to the independence of the Philippines and a determined effort to eliminate the economic, psychological, and political causes of war. Thus, in response to the League's call for a leader who would be willing to speak out on the issues of world peace and social and economic justice, Dewey readily accepted the prestigious position of chairman of LIPA. Incidentally, other leaders included James Maurer, president of the Pennsylvania Federation of Labor, Paul Douglas, professor of Industrial Relations at the University of Chicago, W. E. B. Du Bois, leading black educator, Oswald Garrison Villard, editor of the *Nation*, Devere Allen, editor of the *World Tomorrow*, and Howard Yolm Williams, a Minnesota clergyman.

Dewey's association with LIPA came by way of his criticisms of the unequal distribution of the national income. An admirer of both Edward Bellamy, whom he called "a great American prophet," and Henry George, who "understood the basic relationship betwen control of property and control of the community, and understood that an economy of abundance, allowing for democratic cooperation on every level, could follow rational management of resources by the general community," Dewey in his own fashion set out to emulate the spirit of these two social critics.[9] Backed by liberal intellectuals, plus some labor and socialist support, Dewey and the League proposed to establish a new political alignment based on the principle of social planning and control in an effort to counteract the two established political parties already deeply entrenched in conservatism. Operating under the same principles set forth by Bellamy and George, Dewey looked forward to the day when progressivism would replace conservatism within the American political process.

The stock market crash in October, 1929, and the realization that there would be no chicken in every pot nor a car in every garage, gave added incentive to the drive for a new political party. Meeting regularly at the Advertising Club of New York with Charney Vladeck as host, LIPA pushed forward with its plan for a new party. Recommending a planned economy with the possible socialization of public utilities, banks, and other enterprises, Dewey urged Hoover to move in the direction of further governmental action. Hoover, however, had decided to rely on his policy of "voluntary cooperatism" and was therefore unwilling to push the government toward the goal of a socialized economy. Dewey, dismayed by Hoover's obvious reluctance to experiment, criticized the president for his failure to act and demanded the creation of a new party "which will bring that sense of reality in present politics which is now absent."[10]

With the depression worsening, Dewey, as the leading spokesman for LIPA, wrote a letter to Senator George W. Norris of Nebraska asking him to assume the leadership of a new third party.

> The terrible suffering in this unemployment crisis, the increasing fear of insecurity, the exploitation by public utility companies and other monopolies resulting in our unjust distribution of wealth, and the nationalism and militarism which brought on the World War [Dewey pointed out to Norris], will be repeated under the present political leadership. A new party with your philosophy of life could stop these evils.

Norris, though, refused to sacrifice his position of security within the Republican Party, claiming that he could serve the cause of social justice more effectively within the established party system of which he was an elected representative. Although sympathetic to liberal sentiments and progressive appeals, Norris could not help remarking that the invitation lacked political realism. "Isn't that funny?" he commented to one of his aides when referring to Dewey's invitation. Perhaps even more discomfiting than Norris's declination, however, was the resignation of A. J. Muste from his position of leadership within the organization because of his disapproval of Dewey's appeal to Norris.[11]

Dewey's political radicalism increased after his retirement from Columbia in June, 1930. In addition to his affiliation with LIPA, he assumed the presidency of the People's Lobby, an organization opposed principally to monopolistic practices. As leader of both, Dewey continued to push for the formation of a new political party. At one point his enthusiasm went so far that at a speech before two thousand people at a meeting of the New Historical Society at the Community Church on Park Avenue and Thirty-fourth Street (John Haynes Holmes's congregation) he publicly called Senators Norris and Borah "snipers" for their reluctance to push Congress in the direction of solving the depression. Throughout 1930 and 1931 Dewey constantly criticized the Hoover administration and Congress for their foot-dragging and inability to move quickly and decisively. For *Common Sense*, the official voice of the League for Independent Political Action, the *People's Lobby Bulletin*, the organ of the People's Lobby, and the *New Republic*, Dewey wrote articles condemning not only both major parties but the whole political process.[12]

With an election year approaching Dewey and LIPA made public their "Four-Year Presidential Plan." The plan itself represented most of the progressive policies which LIPA had advocated two years earlier. It recommended three to five million dollars for public works, higher taxes for corporations and higher-bracket incomes, child labor legislation, worker's insurance, public ownership of the power utilities and, in the area of foreign policy, diplomatic recognition of Russia. The plan was indeed a bold one. Yet, as a biologist from Los Angeles County remarked in responding to the proposals: "None offers a realistic or convincing plan of *how* such reforms could be initiated or what specific assistance the plain citizen might give. *They are aids to talk rather than to action.*"[13]

With the plan unveiled, Dewey began pushing for a new party. In a series of articles in the *New Republic* during March and April, 1932, he argued that the two old parties were politically inept. "The reason," Dewey contended, "lies . . . deeper than the self-interest which binds leaders and office holders so closely to business that they can be freed only by acts of treachery. Conservatism tends to come with age, and the two parties are old." In late June he addressed the nation over the National Broadcasting Corporation radio network, arguing that "we cannot continue to do political business in the age of the radio, airplane, and electric motor with the political methods which have come down to us from the era of the stagecoach and tallow dip." His radio speech, however, appeared too radical to some Americans and prompted one person from Texas to write to NBC complaining that Dewey was one of the most dangerous men in America. One can only guess what this person thought of such demagogic leaders as Huey Long and Father Charles Coughlin! Despite some adverse criticism, Dewey continued to advocate more governmental participation in the regulation of the economy, along with the socialization of basic industries, while at the same time urging a new political party to come and replace the old and worn out Democratic and Republican parties.[14]

Yet, by mid-July at the Progressive Convention in Cleveland little had been accomplished in the way of forming a new political party. LIPA had no success whatsoever in the area of political organization. After nearly three years of calling for a rectification of "the incredible inequality in distribution of the national income," all the League could do was to educate and criticize. It proved to be a failure in the political game of survival of the fittest. As a *New York Times* editorial stated: "Professor Dewey feels that the constituency is waiting; the response is waiting. Most of us—and the majorities are said by some advanced thinkers to be always wrong—will surmise that the League is waiting and may have a long wait."[15]

In the 1932 presidential election Dewey voted for the Socialist candidate, Norman Thomas. Why, after three years of proposing nonpartisan or new party radical measures, did Dewey finally endorse the Socialist candidate? What is more interesting, however, is why Dewey did not unite his LIPA with the Socialist Party. It seems strange that with all of Dewey's outspokenness on the issue of strengthening democratic capitalism through social experimentation he would then decide to vote for the only political party that was perhaps most militant in its demands for class warfare. One possible explanation would seem to be that Dewey voted for the Socialists simply out of disdain for the two other major parties. Another explanation might be that he felt certain that by supporting Thomas, who was himself a devout pacifist, he would not in any way be compromising his own pacifist values. But perhaps the most important explanation for Dewey's electoral support for the Socialist Party in 1932 was the fact that the plans he proposed were almost identical to those sponsored by the Socialists. Only the Socialists' dogmatic insistence on the inevitability of class warfare prevented Dewey from assuming a more active role in the Socialist cause. Dewey's political activities mark a definite progression from the shy, almost introverted, and reluctant professor of philosophy in the early twenties to the outspoken, almost militant—indeed militant in nonviolent terms—activist of the thirties. Abandoning his earlier role of nonresponsibility, Dewey became increasingly radical with regard to his views on the economic and political problems of society. No longer willing to sit back and let others do the job, as he once proudly admitted to Scudder Klyce, Dewey was more than ready to enter the political fray by the time Franklin D. Roosevelt assumed office.

Dewey's initial reaction to Franklin Roosevelt was largely one of skepticism and uncertainty. Because Roosevelt represented one of the old, conservative political parties in America, Dewey did not believe that he could do much to combat the depression. Yet Roosevelt's political instincts and administrative resourcefulness enabled him to cast aside the stigma of conformity and legislative "do-nothingness." The New Deal was President Roosevelt's answer to skeptics like Dewey. Calling for more government regulation of the economy through plans like the National Recovery Administration, created to help stabilize the economy by fixing prices and fair labor standards, the Agricultural Adjustment Administration, which sought to raise farm prices through limits on production, the Public Works Administration, a program designed to employ workers for public service projects, the Civilian Conservation Corps, a semimilitary reforestation organization, and others, it appeared that Roosevelt was determined to buttress the capitalistic system by bold new plans of experimentation. His willingness to combat the depression through governmental action was a welcomed change from Hoover's program of "corporate voluntarism." Unfortunately, despite its legislative innovativeness, the New Deal did little to alter Dewey's previous assumptions about the American political process. In his opinion, Roosevelt's plan was not radical enough.

As early as the fall of 1933, Dewey expressed his disappointment over the New Deal's form of experimentalism. His skepticism of Roosevelt's program increased as the economy continued to suffer more serious setbacks. The planning and experimentalism of the National Recovery Act, the legislative backbone of the New Deal, Dewey felt, was a program filled with political paralysis and "unreflective realism."[16] In addition, the inability or unwillingness on the part of President Roosevelt to push the government in a more radical direction, Dewey argued, offered little in the way of concrete relief for the poorer classes. Voicing the same sentiments as Senator Huey Long of Louisiana and Francis Townsend, Dewey called for a "sharing of the wealth." According to Dewey, the most effective way of countering the depression as well as minimizing the burdens of the poorer classes was for the government to assume complete control over all industries, banks, and public utilites. Such a position smacked of socialism. Interestingly enough, though, Dewey did not advocate the destruction of the capitalistic system but merely its restructuring along more equal economic lines. The New Deal, he loudly proclaimed, was merely shuffling the same old cards. Thus, in a series of presidential statements in the *People's Lobby Bulletin* from October, 1933 to March, 1935, Dewey continued to make known his disappointment with a "new deal" stacked with improvisation rather than innovation.[17] He renewed his earlier campaign for the creation of a new political party with full restoration of power to the people.

> The one great question before the American people [Dewey pointed out], is whether it is going to trust to various measures of hocus-pocus to ensure against an even more tragic return of our abominable and unnecessary calamities, or whether it has the intelligence and courage to take over the basic agencies of public welfare and manage them for the welfare of all the people.

Unfortunately, in arguing that the "New Deal permitted power and rule to remain essentially in the same hands as those that had brought the country to its present state," Dewey offered little more than a plea for intelligence.[18]

But, if Dewey felt that the New Deal was not the answer to his hopes for democratic socialism, why did he not join the Marxist left? Perhaps the simplest answer would be his liberal opposition to all forms of "isms" which he believed were dogmatic. The real answer may be somewhat more complicated. Given the change in Dewey's pragmatic idealism after the war, it is possible to argue that he opposed Marxist philosophy primarily because of its belief in class warfare. Even though he was sympathetic to socialist goals—a fact which made it even more distressing to his long-time friend and cophilosopher Sidney Hook, who was himself a socialist and admirer of Marx—he became disillusioned with the militant tactics of the Communist Party under Stalin. The Russian Revolution convinced Dewey that the doctrine of violent class struggle held sway within all centers of Marxist activism. Their obsession with violence and class struggle as a fixed end unnerved Dewey. The socialist doctrine of class warfare based on *a priori* principles was incompatible with Dewey's philosophy of experimentalism and his belief that socialized intelligence afforded a better means for promoting social justice. Ironically, however, when Dewey's pragmatic justification for the use of violent force could have nicely served the socialist goal of working class equality, it did not. His refusal to support class warfare or violence was indicative of the change in attitude Dewey's pragmatism assumed after the war. In the midst of the worst depression this nation has encountered, Dewey still steadfastly refused to sacrifice his philosophy to the socialist cause. Committed to the democratic way of life—even though one would be correct in classifying him a peaceful socialist—he remained opposed to all philosophies which advocated the destruction of the capitalistic system. And although sympathetic to the goals of Norman Thomas's party, he shared with Thomas a pacific intolerance for all forms of organized violence. Thus, as a peaceful socialist, Dewey remained trapped between his desire for economic equality and social justice, which could only have been gained by the use of armed force, and his unyielding support for nonviolent measures, which proved thoroughly unsatisfying to the Socialist Party. His middle ground position pleased no one, including himself!

By 1935 Dewey had become increasingly cynical about the American political process. Disillusioned because the New Deal did not go far enough in the direction of creating his ideal of democratic socialism, Dewey called for a new type of "radicalized liberalism." In his book *Liberalism and Social Action,* which he dedicated to Jane Addams, Dewey argued that liberalism must be linked with radicalism if it was to have any chance of surviving the rigors of twentieth-century change as well as serving as a guide for the solution of social and economic problems.

Organized social planning, put into effect for the creation of an order in which industry and finance are socially directed in behalf of institutions that provide the material basis for the cultural liberation and growth of individuals is now the sole method of social action by which liberalism can realize its professed aims.[19]

Organized, cooperative, socialized intelligence—as opposed to the use of violence (force)—was the key, Dewey felt, for getting America back on her feet. The appeal to intelligence, however, failed to win the day. War, not intelligence, nor even the New Deal, lifted America from the trough of depression.

Dewey's failure to support either the New Deal or the Socialist Party represented, as one historian put it, a "dissociation from the centers of power and high drama."[20] It also demonstrated just how far Dewey had traveled away from his earlier belief in the pragmatic justification of the use of armed force to achieve new ends. And although Dewey may have recognized the fruitful service of socialism to America, he did little more than to suggest that one major step to economic recovery would be to read the works of Henry George; obviously he felt that reading would be more beneficial than fighting for economic justice. The sad reality of the entire situation was that with the exception of the H. G. Wells Society which printed a few cheap editions, very few of the unemployed had enough money even to purchase a copy of George's works.

Although, after 1935, Dewey directed his attention away from the depression to the threat of war in Europe, he nonetheless remained dissatisfied with the New Deal's program of scientific experimentation and governmental interventionism in the economy. Despite the major transition in a more radical direction which the New Deal underwent midway through Roosevelt's first term in office, Dewey still refused to change his mind. Granted that Roosevelt's major objective had been to preserve the capitalistic system at all costs, Dewey could no longer relate to what he considered to be a conservative political process which continually replastered the cracking walls without building new ones. Yet what alternatives did he offer? If it was not socialism, then what was it? To Dewey the solution was a liberalized, radicalized, and socialized intelligence. But intelligence alone was not enough to restore economic vitality and strength to a society wracked by the severest depression in its history. It may have been an essential prerequisite, as Dewey conscientiously pointed out, but it was by no means enough. Only by demonstrating the desirability of "free intelligence" to social and economic interrelationships rather than self-interest would Dewey's solution have proved successful. Unfortunately, the economic calamity of the 1930s proved too great an obstacle for Dewey's suggestions to make any lasting or enduring impression. As Reinhold Niebuhr so perceptively pointed out when writing about the pathos of Dewey's passive radicalism:

> Every argument used in developing his theme of the function of "free intelligence" in social change betrays a constitutional weakness in the liberal approach to politics. It does not recognize the relation of social and economic interest to the play of intelligence upon social problems. It does not perceive the perennial and inevitable character of the subordination of reason to interest in the social struggle.[21]

Unwilling and uncertain as to which road to choose, Dewey sat at the crossroads pondering America's fate.

CHAPTER NINE

A SHATTERED HOPE

> Our international system (since, with all its disorder, it *is* a system) presents another example, writ large, of the restriction of experience created by exclusiveness and isolation. . . . Peoples and nations exist in a state of latent antagonism when not engaged in overt conflict. This state of affairs narrows and impoverishes the experience of every individual in countless ways. An outward symbol of this restriction is found in the oft-cited fact that 80% of our national expenditure goes to pay for the results of past wars and preparing for future wars.
>
> Dewey, "What I Believe"

> Dewey's softening on the war issue did not extend to advocacy of intervention. Rather, he joined with Oswald Garrison Villard, John Haynes Holmes, and others of like mind to attack the idea of American involvement. Willful risking of American lives through concerted aid to the Allies seemed immoral; and the notion that America's involvement in war, which would surely weaken her materially and spiritually, would increase her ability to help reconstruct the postwar world on a just basis seemed to Dewey mistaken.
>
> Alan Lawson, *The Failure of Independent Liberalism*

The pragmatic faith in the idea of social progress proved a failure. The inability of socialized intelligence to bind the nation's wounds wracked by depression and political divisiveness proved particularly distressing to Dewey. But with the rise of military dictatorships in Europe during the thirties, Dewey began devoting more of his time to the pressing problems plaguing world peace. Although he was displeased by the lack of progress on the domestic front, Dewey had not abandoned his hope that the application of intelligence to international politics could prove helpful in bringing about permanent peace. Thus, with the rise to political power of Hitler and Mussolini, Dewey decided to work even harder for the creation of a world order in which peace rather than conflict would be the normal way of life.

Even though Dewey vigorously opposed all forms of totalitarianism as being illiberal and undemocratic, he would not—as he had during the last war—actively support the call for American military action. The war to end war quite clearly had not been properly understood nor adequately defined. Dewey now reached the conclusion that, since the war had not been fought for a liberal peace as originally hoped, it would be a terrible mistake to consider involvement in another one. It does appear somewhat paradoxical, though, that Dewey would abandon his pragmatic justification of militant force in the face of such a serious threat as totalitarianism. It is especially significant since such political ideology relied on armed force to achieve its ends. Yet, his experience with the World War proved to be enough for him. His thinking on the matter now paralleled that of the radical peace groups. Instead of trying to counter the forces of Hitler and Mussolini in the embryonic stage, Dewey supported those who strongly backed a nonmilitary, neutralist position.

Although dismayed by the failure of socialized intelligence and scientific technology to create a more just and equitable society, Dewey nevertheless continued to press for intelligent solutions with which to meet the increasing challenge of war. Dewey's energies in the area of world peace, therefore, did not end with the Pact of Paris. When he assumed the positions of leadership in the League for Independent Political Action and the People's Lobby, Dewey urged the creation of a new political party which would support measures such as international peace, debt revision, recognition of Soviet Russia, and friendlier relations with Latin America. Peace was a goal that was uppermost in his mind. He cherished it; he wanted it. Largely through Dewey's efforts, both LIPA and the People's Lobby pushed for world peace and cooperated with pacifist groups. In a letter to the pacifist editor Oswald Garrison Villard, for example, Dewey informed him that "the People's Lobby cooperates with all other peace organizations and is more than anxious to initiate new proposals for establishing a lasting peace throughout the world." Thus, by 1932 when a new third party platform was introduced at a convention of leading social progressives, it was not surprising to see proposals calling for the reduction of American military and naval expenditures by 50 percent, a national referendum to declare war, a readjustment of reparations and war debts, recognition of Soviet Russia, freedom for the Philippines, and abandonment of imperialistic policies toward Latin America. Dewey, as the acknowledged spokesman of the third party movement, heartily endorsed these proposals as a realistic step towards world peace.[1]

There was one issue, however, which bothered Dewey during the early thirties. That was the issue of war debts and reparations. Both the Dawes and Young plans of the twenties proved to be only stopgaps in solving the problem of international debts and reparations. The so-called Dawes plan of 1924 had originated in the mind of a well-known Chicago banker, General Charles G. Dawes, whose habitual profanity and picturesque brashness brought him untold headlines. In an effort to get Germany back on her financial feet after the unfair reparations settlement imposed upon her at Versailles as well as after the seizure of the Ruhr Valley in 1923 by the French and Belgian armies, the Dawes plan recommended a loan of $200 million, half of which was to come from American private bankers. Reparations payments were to begin with about $250 million a year and in five years reach up to $600 million a year. The total sum was left undecided. But the Dawes plan proved incapable of lifting Germany out of her economic woes. Consequently, in 1929 it was replaced by the Young plan. This new scheme bore the name of an unofficial American expert, Owen D. Young, chairman of the board of General Electric Company. The plan required that Germany make annual reparations payments for fifty-nine years, by which time she should have paid close to $9 billion in principal and $17 billion in interest. The $9 billion represented a drastic reduction from the $32 billion originally called for. Unfortunately, the Young plan also lacked the necessary economic firepower that was needed to settle the debt and reparations controversy.

Although both plans represented some form of economic restriction or compassion toward Germany, they did not go far enough in terms of alleviating the tension and distrust which the German people felt towards the victorious Allies. The feeling that Germany had to pay for her mistakes was bitterly resented by a majority of Germans. Economic aid for the sole purpose of paying off debts and reparations was not compensation for an economy already wracked by recession and unemployment. Consequently, Dewey sympathized with the German people in their suspicions of the "noble intentions" behind the Dawes and Young plans. He was particularly disturbed by what he thought was an "intolerable selfish attitude" on the part of the United States and the Allies. Moreover, the unwillingness of the United States to give up its war debt claims and the Allies' reluctance to forgo German reparations Dewey viewed as a serious international problem that could bear unforeseen consequences. He was extremely upset, therefore, upon reading Senator Borah's article in *Collier's* magazine.

Borah, a former outlawry associate, opposed any reconsideration of interallied debt revision because he believed that the money the Europeans would save would merely be plowed back into the manufacture of armaments. As spokesman for the People's Lobby, Dewey challenged Borah's argument. In a separate section of the *People's Lobby Bulletin* reserved for presidential addresses, Dewey lashed out at Borah by asking him:

> In view of the fact that we are separated by oceans from any nation strong enough to fight us and are spending several hundred million dollars a year more for war purposes than before the World War, do you not think we should pluck the beam of military aggression out of our own eye before we use the mote of military protection or even aggression of our neighbors as an excuse for refusing to consider the readjustment of the financial hang-over of four years of international stupidity?

Borah's argument he found ludicrous. It represented just that kind of philistine, nationalistic self-interest, Dewey believed, which led to international animosity. How could Borah point the finger at our allies without examining our own military expenditures? Superficial treatment of the debt question would fail, Dewey maintained, because each nation would continue to pursue its own economic ambitions. What was needed to quell Borah and those holding like-minded sentiments, Dewey felt, was a practical policy of international cooperation on all levels of economic exchange. In order to accomplish this goal, he called for a thorough reexamination and reorganization of the entire economic structure of the world market. "This means," Dewey stated, "adjustment of international debts, of loans from capital export to capital import countries, of titles to natural resources, and of concessions held by foreigners as well as adjustment of tariffs and other barriers to freedom of exchange." The means for implementing such a bold program, he pointed out, would be a new and popular political party which supported the policy of peace, not chauvinism.[2]

Apart from the problem of debts and reparations, Dewey was also concerned about the problem of military expenditures. He was still recoiling from the support he gave to scientific technology in the search for new weapons during the last war. In 1931 Congress approved the creation of a Joint Cabinet-Congressional Commission on War Policies, commonly referred to as the War Policies Commission. The establishment of this commision represented a serious threat to the efforts then being undertaken on the part of major peace groups to win the support of politicians, for it gave the military a strong lobbying position in Congress. Dewey, as leader of the People's Lobby, was particularly exasperated. In May, 1931, he pointed out that the United States held the largest military air maneuvers ever staged anywhere, in conjunction with mock naval and army battles. Equally appalling was the plan Major General Douglas MacArthur presented to the War Policies Commission requesting the conscription of four million men, with seven million more in reserve. Where would the money come from for such a force, Dewey asked in the *People's Lobby Bulletin?* The total strength of the army and National Guard at the time the armistice was signed, he declared, was only 3,757,000 men. Now, less than fourteen years later, Dewey noted, "our military, naval and other future war expenditures are several hundred million dollars a year larger than before the 'War to End War.'"[3] To him it appeared as though military preparedness was more important in the minds of most Congressmen than social justice and world peace.

By 1933 it became increasingly apparent that war clouds were on the horizon. Where only a year ago he had looked with scorn on the militant arguments of Adm. Bradley A. Fiske and Gen. Amos A. Fries, while chairing a debate on the preparedness issue at Carnegie Hall in New York City, now he read with displeasure the words of his friend Salmon O. Levinson: "If Japan and Germany are going to continue on the war path, I will have to shade my pacifism considerably." Dewey was upset also by the rise to power of Hitler in Germany. The threat to peace now seemed much more imminent. In a speech at the World's Fair held in Chicago, Dewey reflected the pessimism of many of his fellow Americans regarding the future when he stated that "the international situation is in the mind of every thoughtful person today. Fifteen years ago we closed the war that was to end war. Yet everywhere to-day there are prophecies of a *new* and more *deadly* war. . . ." He was disconsolate that after so many years of earnest effort in attempting to achieve lasting peace nothing had been gained. He was angry and embittered at what was taking place in Germany. Thus, by March, 1934, at a luncheon at the Empire State Club in New York, Dewey warned his listeners that Hitler and Hitlerism were "by all odds the greatest threat to world peace today."[4]

Nineteen thirty-four offered little hope to those anxious to preserve and protect world peace. The Italian invasion of Ethiopia, the impending revolution in Spain, and Hitler's increasing militancy weighed heavily on Dewey's mind. The situation was even more complicated for Dewey by the revelations then being made public in the Senate caucus room. Gerald P. Nye, a ranking Republican isolationist from North Dakota, had been conducting an investigation into the munitions industry. The results of the committee's findings, though somewhat ambivalent because of political ties and nationwide publicity, tended to be highly critical of the munitions manufacturers. In addition, with the publication of H.C. Engelbrecht's and F.C. Hanighen's *Merchants of Death* in the same year, Dewey became even more pessimistic about the prospects of a lasting peace. Torn between his hatred for Hitler and the predatory instincts of munitions makers,

Dewey was faced with a serious dilemma. Convinced that peace was in the balance, he chose to avoid the issue rather than meet it head on.

During 1935, however, Dewey made up his mind. He would not allow his philosophy to be used for any militaristic purposes. In early February in an article "International Cooperation or International Chaos," he pointed out that "these merchants of death are but symptoms of the present disorder and anarchy in international relations." Better trade conditions, he mused, would be the only cure for such a disease.

> We have heard much of late of the international munitions trade, and of the fact that international organizations in the armament and munition industries supply, for a profit, even their potential enemies in war. While we blame the munition-makers let us recall that these "merchants of death" are symptoms of the present disorder and anarchy in international relations. If we really want to put an end to this one flourishing form of international trade we must establish that cooperation among nations that will cut the ground out from under their feet. As long as nations fear each other, and every nation sees in other nations, and with good reason, danger of lowered standards of living in their home population, governments will have no difficulty in persuading even an impoverished nation to buy the arms and munitions by which the merchants of death wax fat and bloated.

He was convinced that the current economic disorder would inevitably pave the way for a growing martial spirit which would, in a matter of time, gradually take hold of the American mind. What was needed, and needed immediately, was the establishment of an international conference to work on the problems of free trade and world cooperation.

> It is for us, the people, first to develop a genuine co-operative spirit and sense of the mutual interests that bind the nations of the world together for weal or woe—and at the present time so largely for woe. The principle of good neighborliness is as fundamental in international matters as in the village and city. The principle has now ceased by force of events to be simply an ethical ideal. It has become an economic necessity. We shall refuse to live up to it at our peril, the peril of depression, unemployment, degraded standard of living, and of war that will kill millions more and destroy billions more of property.

Two month later, moreover, he was thanking his old outlawry companion and leader Salmon O. Levinson for sending him a copy of Louis Ludlow's (representative from Indiana) proposed amendment for a national referendum on the war issue. And by late June, in answer to a questionnaire sponsored by the periodical *Modern Monthly* entitled "When American Goes to War," in which Van Wyck Brooks, Charles Beard, Archibald MacLeish, and Reinhold Niebuhr participated, Dewey categorically stated that he was not in favor of American military participation in any war.[5]

What a striking turn of events took place in the peace psychology of John Dewey! Just twenty years earlier he was attempting to find ways to put his pragmatism to work in support of the war effort. Now at this crucial juncture—1935—the greater the threat of war, the quicker Dewey retreated to a pacifist position. He revolted at the suggestion that military force was the only answer to halt the spread of totalitarianism as found in Germany and Italy. His book *Liberalism and Social Action* was dedicated to a pacifist, Jane Addams, giving further evidence of his own pacifist sympathies. Its pages are filled with ringing condemnations of violence, class struggles, and wars. In words Jane Addams herself would have appreciated, he let his position be known:

> Modern warfare is destructive beyond anything known in older times. This increased destructiveness is due primarily, of course, to the fact that science has raised to a new pitch of destructive power all the agencies of armed hostility. But it is also due to the much greater interdependence of all the elements of society. The bonds that hold modern communities and states together are as delicate as they are numerous. The self-sufficiency and independence of a local community, characteristic of more primitive societies, have disappeared in every highly industrialized country. The gulf that once separated the civilian population from the military has virtually gone. War involves paralysis of all normal social activities, and not merely the meeting of armed forces in the field.

No longer would he sacrifice his pragmatic idealism to the technique of armed force. The key to peace, he warned, was through cooperative social action, both on a national and international scale.

> Organized social planning, put into effect for the creation of an order in which industry and finance are socially directed in behalf of institutions that provide the material basis for the cultural liberation and growth of individuals, is now the sole method of social action by which liberalism can realize its professed aims.

Ironically, his pragmatism now had more in common with the ideals of Randolph Bourne than he would have cared to admit. Having been burned once, he felt, was enough.

> It has long been part of the technique of politicians who wish to maintain themselves in power to foster the idea that the alternative is the danger of being conquered by an enemy. Nor does what has been suggested slur over in any way the effect of powerful and unremitting propaganda.

Therefore, by the end of the year, he happily related to his colleagues at the annual meeting of the American Association of University Professors in Washington, D.C., that "there are plenty of persons and groups, who will present and will urge with vigor nationalistic, political, economic, and ideological interests of different kinds. It is our business to stand up with at least equal vigor and aggressiveness for the cause of freedom and objectivity of mind [to] which our profession commits us." Teachers and scholars are soldiers also, he concluded, fighting in behalf of peace and international understanding.[6]

Although, militarily speaking, nationalist socialism and fascism presented the greatest threat to world peace, Dewey was not overenthusiastic about the system of government under Stalin in Soviet Russia. In 1937 he traveled to Mexico as chairman of an inquiry into the political activities of Leon Trotsky. Trotsky, who was then living in exile, had been banned from the Soviet Union by Stalin. Embittered by his inability to get a fair hearing in his mother country, Trotsky pled his case to the outside world of Western democracy. He claimed that the charges against him—secretly plotting with the fascists to overthrow Stalin was the main charge—in the Moscow Treason Trials of 1936 were false. He argued that his exile was chiefly motivated by his political differences with Stalin rather than by any treasonous acts. Putting aside writing his new philosophical work, *Logic: The Theory of Inquiry,* Dewey, now nearly eighty years old, accepted the onerous task of seeking justice.

It was a difficult mission for Dewey. He admired the "will power" of the Soviet people, and his work *Impressions of Soviet Russia,* which was serialized in the *New Republic* during 1929, had won him the admiration of many liberals in the United States. His vivid accounts of Soviet life and his high praise for the efficiency of their educational system endeared Dewey to the hearts of many political leftists. But he had been and still was extremely critical of the authoritarian practices of the Soviet government as well as of its philosophical justification of class warfare. He was repulsed by the tactics of the Stalinists when it came to suppression of civil liberties. Despite his own pragmatic bias towards efficiency and methodology, he was not overpleased by the way the Russian government had managed to carry out its Five-Year Plans. As the leading spokesman for democratic liberalism in the West, Dewey saw marked similarities between communism and fascism. "How Communism can continue to advocate the kind of economic change it desires by means of civil war, armed insurrection, and iron dictatorship in the face of what has happened in Italy and Germany," he wrote, "I cannot at all understand." The vicious element in their systems he emphasized, is that the end is so important that it justifies the use of any means. "Doctrines, whether proceeding from Mussolini or from Marx, which assume that because certain ends are desirable therefore those ends and nothing else will result from the use of force to attain them," Dewey sadly contended, "is but another example of the limitations put upon intelligence by any absolute theory." What had to be done, according to Dewey, was the application of democratic methods to social progress:

> For democracy means not only the ends which even dictatorships now assert are their ends, [that is] security for individuals and opportunity for their development as personalities. It signifies also primary emphasis upon the means to which it is devoted become the voluntary activities of individuals in opposition to coercion; they are [namely] the force of intelligent organization versus that of organization imposed from outside and above. The fundamental principle of democracy is that the ends of freedom and individuality for all can be attained only by means that accord with those ends.

Specifically, nonviolent means were what Dewey had in mind.[7]

Communist sympathizers in America, especially, were angry at Dewey, claiming that his commission was nothing more than a capitalist showcase designed to vindicate Trotsky. Dewey's dogmatic allegiance to democracy, they pointed out, would prevent him from siding with the verdict handed down at the Moscow trials. Both the *Nation* and the *New Republic* were extremely critical of Dewey's actions, and Dewey in time became so angry at the *New Republic* that he resigned from its editorial staff. It was even more difficult for Dewey to accept such criticism in view of the fact that his philosophical principles were unalterably opposed to those of Leon Trotsky's. Yet it was not unusual for Dewey to defend someone he ideologically opposed. Three years later he would defend the principle of acadmic freedom, as he had done during World War I, in the case of Bertrand Russell, a man he considered his worst intellectual enemy. The issue of freedom and justice, therefore, was his major concern and nothing more. In a letter to another former outlawry associate, Raymond Robins, Dewey stated his reasons for taking the case. "It is not pleasant," he told Robins, "to have to make a choice between the ideas that practically every early revolutionary became a traitor to the cause for which he fought and that those in power are deliberately employing cruel frame-ups to get rid of criticism and opposition." The complete suppression of dissent, Dewey told Robins, should not be tolerated. It ran contrary to everything he believed in. Thus, the commission, after some internal squabbling (Carleton Beals resigned, claiming that the committee was a setup in support of Trotsky) and thirteen sessions of testimony from the defense, reached the verdict that Trotsky was the scapegoat of Stalin's oppressive terrors and that therefore he was innocent. Nevertheless, it was the Soviet system and not Trotsky's guilt or innocence in the long run that most concerned Dewey. "If war is delayed for a few years," he told *Washington Post* correspondent Agnes E. Meyer, "it is not inconceivable that Russia and Germany will again be allies. We have to face this possibility." Ironically, the fulfillment of his prediction was only a year off.[8]

As the thirties came to an end, Dewey himself became increasingly pessimistic about the growing forces of intolerance and unreason that he observed around him. More and more he sympathized with his old Columbia colleague Charles Austin Beard, whose *Devil Theory of War* embodied the confession of one who had serious misgivings about his earlier support for war. Indeed, Dewey was equally sympathetic to Carl Becker's plea that "in the end, all depends upon the people, the interests they cherish, the opinions they hold, the instinctive emotional responses that give them satisfaction. The enlightenment of the people is the main thing; admittedly a slow business, but not to be advanced by beating their brains out." Over and over again he kept asking himself the very same question Becker raised: Since we all love peace, why do we wage war? He could no longer side with his friend and outlawry leader Sol Levinson, who was now chiding him for his reluctance to assume a more militant stance against fascism. He found it difficult, psychologically speaking, to rationalize his pragmatic justification of military force in the face of an impending crisis. Rather than take the chance again, he willingly accepted the role of an "irresponsible" who "leaves the present and returns across the past, where all the men are marble." One mistake, he believed was enough![9]

By early 1938 Dewey was seeking his own answers as to why men wage war. In an article entitled "Does Human Nature Change?" Dewey argued that it was indeed changeable. Unlike William James, however, who pursued a psychological approach to human nature, Dewey's approach was strictly environmental. Wars do not exist, he believed, because man possesses combative instincts but rather because of social conditions.

> Take the institution of war, one of the oldest, most socially reputable of all human institutions. Efforts for stable peace are often opposed on the ground that man is by nature a fighting animal and that this phase of his nature is unalterable. The failure of peace movements in the past can be cited in support of this view. In fact, however, war is as much a social pattern as is the domestic slavery which the ancients thought to be an immutable fact.

It was the environmental factors, camouflaged by past experience and social practice, which generated and sustained man's inclination to fight.

> The time may be far off [Dewey warned] when men will cease to fulfill their need for combat by destroying each other and when they will manifest it in common and combined efforts against the forces that are enemies of all men equally. But the difficulties in the way are found in the persistence of certain acquired social customs and not in the unchangeability of the demand for combat.

His inclination for social reconstruction was in keeping with his pragmatic philosophical position. The inability of the pacifists to win the day was due largely to inherited social customs rather than to any doctrine of unattainable ends.

> The point is that the obstacles in the way are put there by social forces which do change from time to time, not by fixed elements of human nature. This fact is also illustrated in the failures of pacifists to achieve their ends by appeal simply to sympathy and pity. For while, as I have said, the kindly emotions are also fixed constituents of human nature, the channel they take is dependent upon social conditions.

Like Becker, James, and H. G. Wells, who said that "human history becomes more and more a race between education and catastrophe," he did not believe that to acquire harmony men would have to beat one another's brains out. Enlightenment was the key. Though it might take some time, Dewey was confident it could be achieved.[10]

Dewey's isolationism and pacifism came to the fore during the latter stages of 1938. The Sudetenland crisis, in which Hitler demanded that Czechoslovakia surrender to him all of the German-populated Sudetenland area, caused Dewey considerable consternation. His professed sympathy for the Czechs, however, was balanced by his greater concern for world peace. He believed that the conflict could be contained within the perimeters of the European continent, and that the United States could best serve its own interests as well as the rest of the world by refusing to become a partner to this growing catastrophe. He strongly supported the pacifist Keep America Out of War Congress (KAOW) which had been organized earlier in the year by Socialist Party leader Norman Thomas. The KAOW Congress, whose slogan called for "the maximum American cooperation for peace; the maximum isolation from war," was the only national organization formed specifically to advocate American nonintervention in the European war. Dewey anxiously looked upon the KAOW Congress as an effective sounding board for organizing public opinion against the possibility of American intervention across the Atlantic. He was now obsessed with keeping America out of war and viewed the KAOW Congress as the instrument by which to achieve that end. His association with the KAOW, moreover, was spurred on by his fear that if the United States once again became involved in another World War it would almost certainly guarantee the triumph of patriotic emotionalism over democratic reason.

As a social critic, Dewey's effectiveness was by no means diminished by this latest threat. In fact, his influence increased because of this new challenge. Seeing no compensatory gain for the world by encouraging American military participation, Dewey maintained that the most effective way to keep America out of war and thereby insure some form of world peace was to establish public control over governmental institutions. War, he pointed out, is a destroyer, not a builder. He therefore urged the people to encourage Congress to enact more stringent neutrality laws in order to outlaw even minimal trade with the warring powers. The people had to put pressure on the Congress. He argued that war trade with any of the combatants would result in direct American involvement. He wanted America to work instead for a negotiated peace in order to prevent a recurrence of what had taken place some twenty years earlier.

The following year Dewey presented a stronger defense for his conviction against American involvement in another war. Reversing the position he had taken during the Great Crusade, he declared that the serious threat to democracy was not the existence of foreign totalitarian states but the "existence [of fascist instincts] within our own personal attitudes and within our own institutions. . . . The battlefield is also accordingly here—within ourselves and our institutions." In the spirit of Bourne, who once argued that "war is the health of the state," Dewey was now saying, "war under existing conditions compels nations, even those professedly the most democratic, to turn authoritarian and totalitarian as the World War of 1914-1918 resulted in fascist totalitarianism in nondemocratic Russia, and promoted political, economic, and intellectual reaction in this country." He believed that mobilizing the nation's social and economic resources for war would postpone indefinitely the social advances America was attempting to make. He argued that the last war had all but destroyed the Progressive movement underway just prior to World War I and that in all probability it would also happen to the liberal movement then taking place. "We are forgetting that the years before the last war were a time of growth for a strong and genuine progressivism in this country, and that if its career had not been interrupted we should have made whatever gains have been accomplished by the New Deal much earlier and in a much less costly way."[11] He feared that the political, economic, and military organizations that would be created to prosecute a war successfully would remain in existence following the war, much to the impairment of democratic liberties. The fear of a reactionary government assuming political power in America if war became a reality was a major theme in his book *Freedom and Culture.* "Resort to military force," he warned, "is the first sure sign that we are giving up the struggle for the democratic way of life. . . ."[12]

As the war clouds darkened, Dewey continued to press for a neutralist position. "It is not a question for us of isolationism," he maintained, "although the physical factors which make possible physical isolation from the warring ambitions of Europe are a factor to be cherished in an emergency." President Roosevelt's gradual, then increasing, efforts to get the United States to assume a more positive role in the conflict were not taken lightly by Dewey. Aware of the political machinations involved in decision making, Dewey looked with suspicion on Roosevelt's neutrality acts. To Dewey they represented more a back door to war than a genuine effort to work for a negotiated peace in Europe. Afraid, therefore, that Roosevelt was determined to take the United States out of the throes of its depression by becoming militarily involved in the conflagration in Europe, Dewey became more and more apprehensive about what might happen to the social fabric of American society. His significance as a social critic in the late thirties stemmed from his warning that American participation in another World War would virtually spell the end of all hopes for a progressive regeneration of individual liberties free from the restraining hand of governmental control. Fearful that a dictatorship could happen here in America, he told his fellow American citizens:

> It is quite conceivable that after the next war we should have in this country a semi-military, semi-financial autocracy, which would fasten class divisions on this country for untold years. In any case we should have the suppression of all the democratic values for the sake of which we professedly went to war.

By the end of the year, after the announcement in August that the Nazis had signed a nonaggression pact with Soviet Russia, thereby allowing Hitler to invade Poland a month later and igniting the flames of total war in Europe, Dewey's convictions were further strengthened when he remarked sadly: "I cannot rid myself of the belief that the existing war situation strengthens a nationalistic spirit, which is already too strong." Yet the answer for Dewey, in the face of another World War, was simple: "No Matter What Happens–Stay Out!"[13]

By early 1940 Dewey despaired of keeping the United States out of the war.

> Talking and writing seem a little futile just now, [he wrote to a pacifist friend], but not only are they better than guns but they may be a kind of needed important work under present conditions. . . .As far as the Congressional debates are concerned I would wish there was less talk to the general effect that this or that Congressional act was the way to keep out of war, and more realization that action one way or the other was of less importance than the resolve of the people at large that no matter what we won't go in. . . .I'm afraid, however, that little can be done at this point to change people's minds. The appeal to national honor seems to outweigh that of international understanding and goodwill.[14]

A "holy war" of democracy against totalitarianism was uppermost in the minds of a majority of Americans. The crusade in defense of America's democratic traditions became more and more a badge of patriotic loyalty that demanded action for war rather than the resolve to keep the peace.

Beginning in March, Hitler's military forces conquered Denmark and Norway, the Low Countries, and France in precision fashion. The French army was decimated by the superior mechanized and well-trained forces of the Nazi army. The British barely escaped annihilation by a miraculous evacuation at Dunkirk. By late June it appeared as though Hitler had all but wrapped up his military objectives. Even this threat of Nazi world domination did not change Dewey's mind, however. He was still vehemently opposed to the war, which he felt was in large part due to the Versailles tragedy. The Allied misfortunes, and there were many, only led Dewey to fight harder against the hysteria which he feared might lead the United States once again into war. Thus, in the fall presidential election race, Dewey clearly and openly demonstrated his pacifist inclinations by organizing a committee of liberal intellectuals which included such important personages as Van Wyck Brooks, V. F. Calverton, Henry Pratt Fairchild, Benjamin Huebsch, John Haynes Holmes, Sidney Hook, A. J. Muste, and John Sloan. Dewey's purpose for organizing the committee was to gather support for the Socialist candidate, Norman Thomas, who urged that the United States stay out of the war. The committee's own plank was in line with the Socialist candidate's views by calling for American isolation from the war in Europe. Since Roosevelt seemed more and more likely to embark upon another overseas adventure, Dewey urged that the American people cast their precious ballots for Thomas as an expression of American solidarity for noninvolvement and peace. Despite the awesome power displayed by the German army and the threat it posed to the preservation of democracy, Dewey was by no means convinced that a farewell to peace was now in order.

The last two years before American involvement, however, proved to be years of despair for Dewey. Already eighty years old, he could now do very little but sit back and wait for the inevitable surge of patriotic fervor to sweep over the land like an onrushing hurricane. In a number of letters to his close friend Max Otto, professor of philosophy at the University of Wisconsin, Dewey continued to voice his hope that, against great odds, America could stay out. In one particular missive to Otto, Dewey noted: "I think—as far as I can make out—the feeling against our getting into war is deeper because [it is] much better informed than twenty years ago, but the work has to be kept up. . . ." But his enthusiasm and optimism gradually waned as America began gearing up its war machinery. Despite his own hopes and desires he was well aware as a practicing pragmatist that in the final analysis realities take precedence over idealistic wishes. His hopes shattered, therefore, Dewey indicated that the present struggle for world peace would have to be carried on by those younger and more physically fit crusaders who are desirous of achieving a lasting peace. As he wrote to his Wisconsin correspondent: "Well Otto, it's up to you and others–and the still younger–generation to do the job that has to be done about the conditions for the interactions needed to produce democratic human beings. After all I am 80–this isn't an apology but just a statement of fact." After Pearl Harbor, Dewey had very little to look forward to. The future state of civilization remained, for him, a pressing problem.

> The course of the age [Dewey told Otto] will decide whether it will take five hundred years to work out of the present situation or whether the skies . . . will clear fairly rapidly, [perhaps in] a generation or two. It's impossible for me to imagine it remaining anything like the same, an epoch has come to an end, I think, but what is beginning is too much for me.

It was now possible for Dewey to understand what Matthew Arnold meant in writing "Wandering between two worlds, one dead, The other powerless to be born." Indeed, limbo was not a very pleasant place for a man like Dewey.[15]

CHAPTER TEN

TROUBLED PHILOSOPHER

> Let us perfect ourselves within, and in due season changes in society will come of themselves, is the teaching. And while saints are engaged in introspection, burly sinners run the world.
>
> While some thirty years ago the idea of a war to end war should have been taken seriously we now indulge only in the modest hope of being able to establish a peace that will last a generation or two.
>
> Dewey, *Reconstruction in Philosophy;*
> "Democratic versus Coercive International Organization"

The war years were trying times for John Dewey. Unhappiness and uncertainty characterized his mood. "Thanks as always," he told Max Otto in 1942, "for your words of cheer. They help make life more bearable in a distracted world." But the distracted world proved harder to bear for Dewey than most people realized. "I fear," he wrote the former Amherst president Alexander Meiklejohn in the fall of 1942, "there is already under way a prospect for political-social reaction after the war." And by the end of the year his pessimism grew to such a degree that he warned Max Otto that "the immediate future after the war, international and domestic, doesn't look rosy."[1]

Neither did the present appear any better. By the close of 1942 the war was at a standstill, and 1943 brought no change. But in the following year the Axis powers began to show signs of weakness.

In the Pacific, under the leadership of General Douglas MacArthur, the Allied forces had already begun their campaign of island hopping. The marines, sustaining heavy casualties, managed to catch the Japanese troops off guard at Guadalcanal. It was a costly but important victory. Next came Tarawa. This was the battle America almost lost. During the course of a day's battle three thousand marines were killed. From Tarawa MacArthur's forces moved on to Saipan, which proved to be the costliest battle in the entire campaign. Over fifteen thousand Americans sacrificed their lives for this strategic island, while the Japanese lost some twenty-five thousand troops. After Saipan came Tinian and then finally Guam. By the summer of 1944 the Allies were on the threshold of victory in the Pacific. The Tojo cabinet knew this and subsequently fell from power.

At the same time that MacArthur's forces in the Pacific were advancing, General Dwight D. Eisenhower was preparing to storm the impregnable German defenses at Normandy. On June 6, 1944, thousands of Allied troops moved across the sandy beaches of Normandy, and D-Day had begun. The fighting was intense, with both sides suffering heavy losses. But after three days the Nazis were forced to give up their first line of coastal defenses, and for the first time Americans saw a way to victory in Europe, and were heartened. For the first time they also saw a way to peace.

On the domestic front, however, news of Allied victories in no way bolstered Dewey's spirits. He was bothered not only by the weakened prospects for world peace, but also by the quality of freedom and liberty that would exist in America after the war ended. The evacuation of over 100,000 Japanese-Americans on the west coast to relocation centers, and the passage of the Smith Act in 1940, were glaring examples, Dewey thought, of the government's attempt to suspend civil liberties and check dissent. In no way was Dewey happy with the government's conduct during the war.

Prior to American military involvement, Dewey already had an inkling of what was in store for Americans when, in 1940, the board of trustees at the City University (CCNY) yielded to conservative pressures, led by the Right Reverend William T. Manning, Episcopal bishop of New York, and New York Supreme Court Judge John E. McGeehan, a Tammany appointee, and refused to allow Bertrand Russell to assume the chairmanship of the philosophy department. Dewey, who personally disliked Russell, nevertheless felt it was incumbent upon him to argue the case of academic freedom. As the leading spokesman of the Committee for Cultural Freedom, Dewey argued that the court case against Russell was perpetrated by philistine moralists who were more interested in preserving their own virginity and nationalistic prejudices than they were in guaranteeing some form of academic enlightenment. Because Russell was a pacifist and atheist, many Americans resented his presence and feared he would corrupt the minds of young college students. To Dewey such an argument was sheer nonsense.

The action of the justice, who stood steadily in the way of permitting an appeal to a higher court and in the way of allowing Mr. Russell to exercise the supposedly elementary right of self defense, [Dewey fumed] is but the technical manifestation of an underlying attempt to apply the lynch law of popular outcry to settle an issue. . . .

The decision against allowing Russell to teach only led Dewey to conclude that "it would be a bitter irony if protest against totalitarianism abroad should be a factor in fostering recourse to totalitarian methods in this country."[2]

More and more, it seems, therefore, that the spirit of Randolph Bourne manifested itself in Dewey's letters and writings. Like Bourne, he had a basic distrust in the suppression of dissent and the suspension of civil liberties that accompany a war.

To take as far as possible every conflict which arises—and they are bound to arise—out of the atmosphere and medium of force, of violence as a means of settlement, into that of discussion and of intelligence, is to treat those who disagree—even profoundly—with us as those from whom we may learn, and in so far, as friends. A genuinely democratic faith in peace is faith in the possibility of conducting disputes, controversies, and conflicts as cooperative undertakings in which both parties learn by giving the other a chance to express itself, instead of having one party conquer by forceful suppression of the other—a suppression which is nonetheless one of violence when it takes place by psychological means of ridicule, abuse, intimidation, instead of by overt imprisonment or in concentration camps.[3]

Mindful of what had taken place in America during and after World War I, he began worrying about the possibility of another domestic "witch hunt" comparable to the Palmer raids of 1919. The rise of a totalitarian or garrison state in America deeply troubled him. Throughout the course of the war, Dewey concentrated his efforts on bringing Americans to accept a more tolerant attitude toward those who opposed the consensual mode of thought. His writings—he made very few speeches during the war because of his age and physical health—reflect his growing concern for domestic tolerance. For as the war progressed on the battlefields, it was a different story at home. He saw for himself that civil liberties were being readily sacrificed on the altar of Mars. The displacement experience of the Japanese-Americans, the herding of hundreds of conscientious objectors into public service camps, and the increased and constant surveillance of civilians by the Federal Bureau of Investigation convinced Dewey that a period of reactionary conservatism and ultranationalism, far more dangerous than that of the 1920's, was beginning to take shape. Like Bourne also, he now accepted the dictum that "war is the health of the State," and freedom of conscience a forgotten right.

Dewey, like most intellectuals, however, looked forward to an Allied victory in spite of the increase in patriotic intolerance. Like his associates on Sidney Hook's Committee for Cultural Freedom, he hoped inwardly for the defeat of the Axis powers. His opposition to antidemocratic forces was the main reason why he joined the committee, which was organized in the spring of 1939 as a bastion against fascism and totalitarianism. Moreover, his willingness to join the Committee for Cultural Freedom was spurred on by his distrust for organizations like America First, which he felt represented a threat to the basic values and loyalties of democracy: "Nationalism, expressed in our country in such phrases as 'America First,' is one of the strongest factors in producing existing totalitarianism, just as a promise of doing away with it has caused some misguided persons to be sympathetic with Nazism." Along with Hook, Dewey and other members of the committee drew up a manifesto that was published in the *Nation.* This was a ringing defense of the principles of democratic liberalism and called attention to the suppression of freedom and culture in Germany, Italy, Russia, Japan, and Spain. It is also warned that similar curtailments of civil liberties were beginning to take shape in the United States. In response to the growing threat to individual freedoms and democratic rights in the "land of the free," the manifesto proposed "to expose repression of intellectual freedom under whatever pretext, to defend individuals and groups victimized by totalitarian practices anywhere, and to propagate courageously the ideal of untrammeled intellectual activity."[4] The establishment of democratic freedom was Dewey's main goal. He abhorred the Nazi mentality and wished to see it crushed.

Yet, in spite of his chairmanship of the Committee for Cultural Freedom and his intense dislike for totalitarianism and fascism, Dewey's support of the war was half-hearted. Age and disillusionment now tempered his enthusiasms. Aside from a propaganda leaflet to the Chinese people which he wrote for the Army Air Force in 1942 and a new introduction that same year to *German Philosophy and Politics,* entitled "The One-World of Hitler's National Socialism," one can find little evidence–in contrast to what his official biographer asserts–of Dewey's energies being devoted vigorously to support of the war.[5] In fact, the theme of world peace dominated his writings. "Our common struggle and sacrifice," he told the Chinese people, "have united our two great nations in their determination to bring into being a new world–a world in which there will be no ruthless coercion, but an embracing society characterized by love and friendship and sympathy."[6] One will not find a pragmatic justification for the use of military force even though–as a result of Pearl Harbor and the Nazi atrocities–most Americans would have been willing to accept it. One will not find a criticism of conscientious objectors for their refusal to fight. Nor will one find any articles filled with the optimistic rhetoric that once called upon all Americans to participate in a glorious campaign for peace and democracy. A quarter century earlier that would have been the case. But not in 1941 and the years following.

Although Dewey's pragmatic idealism would have been more suited to the realities of the second World War than it was in 1917-18, there is a noticeable consistency in Dewey's peace psychology between the wars. Logically, his philosophy could easily have been adapted to meet the realities of 1941-45 without much criticism. Yet, ideologically speaking, his sympathies were with the pacifists. It would seem, therefore, that Dewey now believed pacifism to be a useful and vital ideological tool by which to sustain humanitarian values.[7] The role of intelligence, he contended, was more compatible with the method of nonviolence than it was with the technique of force. In a letter to Miss Emily Balch regarding the introduction he was writing for Jane Addams's 1922 work *Peace and Bread in Time of War,* he defended the usefulness of Jane Addams's pacifism and the "wisdom of her analyses of war-situations. . .with their extraordinary applicability to the dangers. . .of the present war, and of the peace we hope may follow."[8] The hope—a modest hope at that—of establishing a peace that would last a generation or two was all Dewey would look forward to. But for him even that was enough!

Toward the end of the war Dewey pressed for some kind of democratic international organization. In the introduction to *Peace and Bread in Time of War,* appropriately entitled "Democratic Versus Coercive International Organization: The Realism of Jane Addams," Dewey called for a type of organization that would meet human needs. "The instruction concerns the need for adoption of methods which break with political tradition and which courageously adventure in lines that are new in diplomacy and in the political relations of governments and which are consonant with the vast social changes going on everywhere else." The method for achieving such a goal, he asserted, was the utilization of intelligence as a means for informing the public as to the need for an organization that would guarantee lasting peace. His mood, however, was one of disillusionment and clearly implied that the world had lost ground in its effort to secure international peace. The reality of the present situation, he pointed out, was largely a choice between establishing an international organization based on coercion which would be "sure to collapse when old stresses and strains recur in new shapes" and a democratic organization that was "vital and dynamic" in responding to the needs of human beings. Although the hope for peace was not very encouraging, Dewey did not give up. The task was not an easy one, he maintained, but it had to be faced. It was imperative, now more than ever, to go ahead with the challenge and build a new democratic organization in which human beings, not citizens of different nations, would have a say in the execution of world peace. To Dewey that was the ultimate task of mankind.[9]

On May 8, 1945, Harry Truman's sixty-first birthday, the German government officially surrendered. Suddenly it was V-E Day. Everywhere people were in the streets, in Times Square, hurling tons of ticker tape out of Wall Street windows, dancing in the Chicago loop, Boston Common, on Pennsylvania Avenue in the Nation's capital, on campuses, and wherever there was room to dance and celebrate. Joyous celebration was proclaimed the order of the day. The war in Europe was finally at an end. But the World War was not.

Throughout the spring and early summer the Allied forces were gradually making their way toward the Japanese mainland. The question which entered the minds of most military strategists, however, was how many more lives would have to be sacrificed before Japan would finally be forced to give up the fight. After much conscious decision making and many sleepless nights, it was finally decided that the project then under way at Los Alamos, New Mexico, be given the green light. It was then only a matter of time. Having surrendered to expediency, President Truman gathered up all his moral and physical strength for the dark days ahead. Then it happened. At 9:14 on the morning of August 6, the populous and thriving city of Hiroshima was pulverized by an atomic bomb. The secret was now out—unleashed in a most terrifying manner. Three days later a second nuclear device exploded over Nagasaki. On August 14 Emperor Hirohito announced to his loyal subjects that Japan had quit.

As the U. S. S. *Missouri* sailed into Tokyo Bay, much like Admiral Perry's ship less than a hundred years earlier, to accept the Japanese surrender, Americans began worrying about their future role as the arsenal of democracy. Although the surrender ceremonies aboard the *Missouri* on September 2 marked the official end of World War II, no one seemed enthusiastic on such a momentous occasion. V-J Day was not the same as V-E Day. The atomic bomb saw to that. Happiness and joy gave way to uncertainty and pessimism. Unfortunately, the immediate joy of victory had become permanently clouded by the present realities of nuclear warfare.

After the war Dewey remained pessimistic about the prospects of a lasting peace. The hopeful, if fleeting, wartime view that United States foreign policy might become more democratic and more in accord with an informed public opinion, ran counter to the bitter realities of the Cold War. Congressional reaction to and press criticism of communism and Russia's supposed expansionist tendencies precluded the use of liberal democracy as a viable adjunct of American diplomatic policymaking. The American people, reflecting nostalgically once again on the peace and security they had enjoyed in the past, were moved to support an aggressive United States foreign policy only in the negative sense of resisting the spread of communism. The fear, animosity, and patriotic fervor generated by the ideology of the Cold War, Dewey sadly pointed out, turned what was an essentially pragmatic policy into a moralistic crusade in defense of democracy right or wrong.

The atomic bomb, he also pointed out, didn't brighten the situation. In 1948 when writing a new introduction to *Reconstruction in Philosophy* he offered very little hope to his readers.

> The First World War was a decided shock to the earlier period of optimism, in which there prevailed widespread belief in continued progress toward mutual understanding among peoples and classes, and hence a sure movement to harmony and peace. Today the shock is incredibly greater. Insecurity and strife are so general that the prevailing attitude as to what the future has in store casts its heavy black shadow over all aspects of the present.[10]

The past thirty years, he lamented, had proved unsuccessful in the movement for world peace. It seemed incredible to him that the progression from the construction of tanks and submarines of the first World War to the invention of the atomic bomb in World War II was regarded by many as a major scientific advance. Was this progress, he asked? Why would anyone even want to consider the atomic bomb a scientific advance, Dewey sadly asked, with the threat of the world's destruction hanging over our heads? Yet, the same technological success and scientific expansionism of Western society that Dewey once endorsed had now encouraged the increasing economic and political conflict of nations. Quite clearly, Dewey saw this as a step backward rather than a genuine leap forward in the improvement of the human race. Mankind as a whole, and not the scientists alone, had to make what would be not technical but major political and social decisions. Intelligence, according to Dewey, would thus have to play its part in countering the evil effects of nuclear weapons.

> The lesson to be learned is that human attitudes and efforts are the strategic center for promotion of the generous aims of peace among nations; promotion of economic security; the use of political means in order to advance freedom and equality; and the world wide cause of democratic institutions. Anyone who starts from this premise is bound to see that it carries with it the basic importance of education in creating the habits and the outlook that are able and eager to secure the ends of peace, democracy, and economic stability.

An informed public opinion, Dewey concluded, was the most effective means for achieving the goal of world peace. But, with nuclear annihilation a real possibility, peace remained at best an uncertainty.[11]

Dewey's role during World War II, both before and after Pearl Harbor, was as consistent as it was dogmatic. His politics from 1939 to 1945 were directed toward waging battles in behalf of civil liberties and civil rights as well as toward a program to avert future war. Before American involvement Dewey believed that the United States could best serve the purposes of freedom by remaining aloof from the European crisis. This was an assumption that merely emphasized his pacifist leanings which he had inherited from his unhappy World War I experience. Given this premise, plus his belief that American military participation would spell the doom of democratic liberties, there does not appear to have been any alternative open to Dewey but isolationism. His assumptions, however, were lacking in any realistic assessment of the war situation. True, American involvement would mean the suspension and perhaps the total extinction of many civil liberties, but the alternative was total enslavement under Hitler and his fascist allies. Perhaps the United States could have done more to revive Europe, as Dewey believed, if it had not become directly involved in the fighting; yet it is probable, indeed likely, that the Europe left to be rejuvenated would have been little more than a decimated concentration camp filled with starved, psychologically distraught slaves lacking the willpower to revitalize their homelands. Dewey's unfortunate predicament was that his former pragmatic argument for coercive force would now have been greeted with almost universal acceptance, in contrast to the days of the first World War; his reasoning certainly could have been employed more effectively and with greater assurance had he publicly chosen to support the principle of military intervention. Yet his conscience would not allow him to support the dual doctrines of expediency and armed force.

Yet if Dewey's weakness was his refusal to invoke his pragmatism to counter the evil effects of Nazism it also, though somewhat ironically, represented his greatest strength. The argument for realism is in fact a double-edged sword. On the one hand, one can argue logically that Dewey's failure to back vigorously the war effort represented the complete breakdown of his pragmatism in light of the ongoing events in Europe. No doubt, as many have argued, Hitler had to be stopped at all costs, regardless of the sacrifices involved. On the other hand, it is possible to defend Dewey's position from the standpoint of long-term effects. According to Dewey, the defeat of Hitler and his allies represented only a temporary cure. The real goal, a lasting peace, he accurately pointed out, would not be attained with the defeat of the Axis powers. In a much more realistic —in fact one could say pragmatic—way, Dewey was correct when he argued that a war to end present and future wars has never worked. What was needed, he believed, was the development of pacifist sympathies as the only real hope of escape from mankind's perennial dilemma. Given the present threat of nuclear annihilation, Dewey's position appears all the more realistic. In many ways, the pacifist opponents of war have proved themselves to be the ultimate realists of the twentieth century. Perhaps the only hope of escape from complete destruction, as Dewey foresaw, was that, if the awful prospect of nuclear annihilation could not make men saints, as he had hoped, it might at least save the world by making them cowards. But even faced with this gloomy predicament, Dewey was still uncertain as to what lay in store for future generations. To guess would have been too painful.

EPILOGUE

The post-World War II years offered no lasting hope to an aging philosopher that peoples throughout the world would finally join hands and engage in a process of peaceful cooperation. Not only had the recent war demoralized the will power of many an ardent peace advocate, but it had also brought forth new uncertainties with the advent of atomic weapons. The possibility, indeed the imminent threat, that millions of people would be destroyed by the push of a button aroused the fears of even the most warlike person. Fear more than hope characterized the American scene after 1945.

Though the prospects looked dim, Dewey continued to believe that pacifism could serve as a significant social force. Sharing the values and ideals which motivated the liberal pacifist A. J. Muste, Dewey looked upon pacifism as a method which would challenge the convictions and assumptions as well as the power of the established order.[12] The past thirty years or so had taught him that violence not only invariably destroys the personal worth of human beings but also runs contrary to the democratic way of life. As a pragmatist-pacifist, Dewey argued that the relationship between ends and means, or peace and nonviolence, is appropriate to human nature not because men are naturally good, but rather because they are "potentially" good. It was this factor, and this factor alone, that enabled Dewey to carry on the struggle for peace and justice.

The fact that there existed a potential goodness in man was enough of an incentive for Dewey to search for new ways in which education could be made to explore and redefine in specific situations the method of nonviolence. Unlike many, if not most, of his contemporary liberal pacifists who lacked any specific program or tactic as to how to approach the problem of war and peace, Dewey recognized the potentiality of educational peace research.[13] The need for peace studies, Dewey believed, was greater now than ever before. The threat of another war, one even more destructive than the previous two, led Dewey to call for greater interest in this field. The world leaders, he still felt, were more attuned to their own political ambitions than they were to the needs and feelings of the people. The time was ripe, he urged, to educate the mind against thinking in terms of militant force and violence. Moreover, as a practicing pragmatist, Dewey realized the essential relationship between the establishment of a democratic society based on peace and understanding as the end and nonviolence as the means. Education, as a process which functions to broaden the mind, Dewey hoped, would serve as the vehicle for bringing about an enlightened public opinion that would work for the creation of a peaceful world order.

John Dewey died on June 1, 1952, not quite forty years after the war that made him a pacifist. His passing was widely mourned, as leading newspapers throughout the world carried notices and tributes. Everyone who recorded his influence recalled the many contributions he had made in the field of education. But, noticeable as these tributes were, there was little mention of his association with the peace movement. In large measure this was due to his outspokenness in support of American war aims during World War I. Yet the conversion of John Dewey to pacifist values presents an interesting sidelight on the man who, for nearly three-quarters of a century, searched for the best means by which to improve the quality of life. Happily, he had found it in the method of nonviolence. For Dewey there was no other way.

NOTES

INTRODUCTION

1. Personal letter from Mrs. Roberta Dewey (Dewey's long-time secretary and second wife) to author, May 8, 1969.
2. John Dewey, "Lessons from the War: In Philosophy." Typed transcript of speech delivered at Cooper Union in New York City on December 7, 1941. The transcript is located in the Dewey Collection, Morris Library, Southern Illinois University.
3. Dewey's mood and disposition on the night of December 7, 1941, were conveyed to the author in a letter written by Mrs. Roberta Dewey on May 8, 1969.
4. John Dewey, "The Need for a Recovery of Philosophy," in John Dewey et al., *Creative Intelligence: Essays in the Pragmatic Attitude* (New York: Henry Holt & Co., 1917), p. 63.
5. John Dewey, *Characters and Events* (New York: Henry Holt & Co., 1929), vol. 2, pp. 636-41, 782-89.
6. Alan Cywar, "John Dewey in World War I: Patriotism and International Progressivism," *American Quarterly* 21 (June, 1969): 579-80.
7. Randolph Bourne, "Twilight of Idols," in Carl Resek, ed., *War and the Intellectuals* (New York: Harper & Row, 1964), pp. 60-61.
8. John Dewey. *The Problems of Men* (New York: Philosophical Library, 1946), p. 44.
9. John Dewey, "Democracy Is Radical. . .As an End, and the Means Cannot Be Divorced from the End," *Common Sense* 6 (January, 1937).
10. Oral history project, Butler Library, Columbia University.
11. John Dewey, *Democracy and Education* (New York: Macmillan & Co., 1916), p. 359.
12. George Dykhuizen. *The Life and Mind of John Dewey* (Carbondale: Southern Illinois University Press, 1973), p. xiv. This particular quotation is from Harold Taylor, a philosopher and friend of Dewey's.

1. THE MAKING OF A SOCIAL CRITIC

1. George Dykhuizen, *The Life and Mind of John Dewey* (Carbondale: Southern Illinois University Press, 1973), pp. 1-2.

2. In the past there has been some confusion with regard to Dewey's social origins. Many people have been under the impression that he came from a humble farm family (Irwin Edman, "Our Foremost Philosopher at Seventy," *New York Times Magazine,* October 13, 1929). Such is not the case however. In fact, Dewey was born into a relatively prosperous, upper middle class family.
3. *The Life and Mind of John Dewey,* p. 11
4. Ibid., p. 42
5. Richard Bernstein, *John Dewey* (New York: Washington Square Press, 1967), pp. 183-84.
6. Jo Ann Boydston et al., *The Early Works of John Dewey,* (Carbondale: Southern Illinois University Press, 1969), vol. 1, p. 246
7. *Ethics of Democracy* was originally published in 1888 by Andrews and Company of Ann Arbor, Michigan. It was delivered as part of the University of Michigan Philosophical Papers.
8. John Dewey, *Outlines of a Critical Theory of Ethics* (New York: Greenwood Press, 1969), pp. 127, 129-30.
9. Syllabus for philosophy of a social and political theory. Dewey notes, Butler Library, Columbia University.
10. John Dewey, *The School and Society* (Chicago: University of Chicago Press, 1899), p. 75.
11. Ibid., p. 99.
12. Ibid., p. 12.

2. DISAPPOINTMENT

1. John Dewey, *Pscyhology* (New York: Harper & Bros., 1886), p. 336; *Outlines of a Critical Theory of Ethics* (New York: Greenwood Press, 1969), p. 32; Dewey and James Hayden Tufts, *Ethics* (New York: Henry Holt & Co., 1908), p. 410.
2. Joseph Ratner, ed., *Intelligence in the Modern World* (New York: Modern Library, 1939), p. 40.
3. John Dewey, *My Pedagogic Creed* (Washington: Progressive Education Association, 1897, 1927), p. 8; *The School and Society* (Chicago: University of Chicago Press, 1899), p. 12; *Moral Principles in Education* (Boston: Houghton Mifflin Co., 1909) p. 8.
4. Jane Dewey, "John Dewey: A Biography," in Paul A. Schilip, ed., *The Philosophy of John Dewey* (Evanston: Northwestern University Press, 1939), pp. 29-30. See also Wayne R. Leys, "Dewey's Social, Political, and Legal Philosophy," in Jo Ann Boydston, ed., *Guide to the Works of John Dewey* (Carbondale: Southern Illinois University Press, 1970), pp. 145-46; Dewey and Tufts, *Ethics,* p. 482.
5. John Dewey, *German Philosophy and Politics* (New York: G. P. Putnam's Sons, 1915, 1942), p. 108; Max Lerner, ed., *Veblen* (New York: Viking Press, 1958), p. 548; John Dewey to Scudder Klyce, June 19, 1915, Scudder Klyce papers, Library of Congress; John Dewey, "On Understanding the Mind of Germany," *Atlantic Monthy* 117 (February, 1916): 262.
6. *Characters and Events* (New York: Henry Holt & Co., 1929), vol 2, p. 637; vol. 1, p. 577.
7. *Characters and Events,* vol. 2, p. 637, 581; Alan Cywar, "John Dewey in World War I: Patriotism and International Progressivism," *American Quarterly* 21 (June 1969): 579-89. Dewey's reference to his son's rank in the U. S. Army can be found in a letter to Edwin H. Wilson, dated April 6, 1938. The letter is among the Dewey papers, Morris Library, Southern Illinois University.
8. Sidney Kaplan, "Social Engineers as Saviors: Effects of World War I on Some American Liberals," *Journal of the History of Ideas* 17 (June, 1956): 360.
9. *Characters and Events,* vol. 1 p. 477; Christopher Lasch, *The New Radicalism in America,* 1889-1963 (New York: Alfred A. Knopf, 1965), pp. 203-12; Morton White, *Social Thought in America; The Revolt against Formalism* (Boston: Beacon

Press, 1947), ch. 11, pp. 161-79. White uses the term "destructive intelligence" as distinguished from "creative intelligence." His purpose is to point out Dewey's ambivalent stand regarding his philosophical support for war. White's basic argument is that Dewey attempted to link his pragmatism with support of war by arguing that armed force was a realistic and useful means for establishing world peace. The fallacy in Dewey's argument, White notes, is that armed force itself tends to breed more armed force rather than lasting peaceful settlements. For further analysis consult pages 160-64.

10. *Characters and Events,* vol. 2, pp. 579, 564, 569; *Social Thought in America,* pp. 168-69.

11. *Characters and Events,* vol. 2, p. 565.

12. Joseph Ratner, ed., *Education Today* (New York: G. P. Putnam's Sons, 1940) p. 116

13. *Characters and Events,* vol. 2, pp. 537-39.

14. Ibid., pp. 745-59.

15. Ibid., pp. 554, 560.

16. John Dewey, "A League of Nations and the New Diplomacy," *Dial* 65 (November 30, 1918): 608-09.

17. John Dewey, "A League of Nations and Economic Freedom," *Dial* 65 (December 14, 1918): 613-14.

18. Arthur A. Ekirch, Jr., *The Challenge of American Democracy* (Belmont, Calif.: Wadsworth Publishing Co., 1974) p. 197

19. *New York Times,* February 14, 1917, p. 5.

20. Dewey to A. A. Young, October, 1917 (exact date undetermined), Dewey papers, Butler Library, Columbia University. There exist some of Dewey's papers at Columbia. They deal primarily with correspondence to fellow faculty members. Most of the Dewey correspondence, however, can be located at the Morris Library, Southern Illinois University.

21. *New York Times,* October 9, 1917, p. 1; Dewey wrote a personal letter to Beard at the time of the resignation. He was extermely upset with Beard's decision to leave Columbia, yet respected him for the stand he took. Dewey to Beard, October 9, 1917, Dewey papers, Morris Library, Southern Illinois University.

22. *New York Times,* December 16, 1917, section 2, p. 5.

23. John Dewey, "Public Education on Trial," *New Republic* 12 (December 29, 1917); 245.

24. *Characters and Events,* vol. 2, pp. 577-78, 571.

25. Staughton Lynd, ed., *Nonviolence in America* (Indianapolis: Bobbs-Merril Co., 1966), p. 185.

26. Norman Thomas, *War's Heretics: A Plea for the Conscientious Objector* (New York: American Union against Militarism, 1917), p. 3.

27. Randolph Bourne, "Conscience and Intelligence in War," *Dial* 63 (September 13, 1917): 193-95; Cywar, "John Dewey in World War I: Patriotism and International Progressivism," p. 579; Jane Addams to Randolph Bourne, June 30, 1917, Bourne Papers, Butler Library, Columbia University.

28. Cywar, "John Dewey in World War I, p. 579; White, *Social Thought in America,* p.170; Randolph Bourne to Van Wyck Brooks, March 27, 1918, Bourne papers, Butler Library, Columbia University.

29. Corliss Lamont, ed., *Dialogue on John Dewey* (New York: Horizon Press, 1959), pp. 25,30,

30. John Dewey, *Human Nature and Conduct* (New York: Henry Holt & Co., 1922), p. 101.

31. John Dewey, *Experience and Nature* (New York: Dover Publications, 1958), p. 296.

32. Dewey and Tufts, *Ethics,* pp. 9, 229, 252.

33. Max Eastman, "John Dewey," *Atlantic Monthly* 168 (December, 1941): 682-88.

34. *Characters and Events,* vol. 2, pp. 630-31.

35. Ibid., p. 634
36. Ibid., pp. 634-35.
37. Walter Lippmann, *Early Writings* (New York: Liveright, 1970), p. 89.
38. John Dewey, *Reconstruction in Philosophy* (Boston: Beacon Press, 1948), p. 128.
39. *Characters and Events,* vol. 2, p. 619.

3. DEMOCRACY'S AMBASSADOR TO THE FAR EAST

1. Dewey to Salmon O. Levinson, December 9, 1918, Salmon O. Levinson papers, Joseph R. Regenstein Library, University of Chicago. See also Evelyn Dewey, ed., *Letters from China and Japan* (New York: E. P. Dutton & Co., 1920).
2. Hu Shih received his Ph. D. degree in philosophy at Columbia University. He became a leading Chinese educator as well as a strong advocate of the pragmatic method and remained a close friend to Dewey.
3. Dewey to John Jacob Coss, January 13, 1920, Dewey papers, Butler Library, Columbia University.
4. Robert W. Clopton and Tsuin-Chen Ou, eds., *John Dewey: Lectures in China, 1919-1920* (Honolulu: University of Hawaii Press, 1973), p. 98. See also John Blewett, ed., *John Dewey: His Thought and Influence* (New York: Fordham University Press, 1960), p. 207.
5. Dewey to Coss, January 13, 1920.
6. *John Dewey: Lectures in China,* pp. 93-94.
7. Ibid., p. 93.
8. John Dewey, *Conditions among the Poles in the United States* (Washington: Government Printing Office, 1918)
9. Dewey to Colonel Drysdale, December 1, 1920, service report on Bolshevism in China, National Archives, State Department.
10. *Letters from China and Japan,* p. 168.
11. Ibid., pp. 180-81.
12. John Dewey, "The Far Eastern Deadlock," *New Republic* 26 (March 16, 1921): 71; see also the following articles by Dewey: "The International Duel in China," *New Republic* 20 (August 27, 1919); "The American Opportunity in China," *New Republic* 21 (December 3, 1919); "China's Nightmare," *New Republic* 23 (June 30, 1920); and "Japan and America," *Dial* 66 (May 17, 1919).
13. John Dewey, "The Far Eastern Deadlock, " *New Republic* 26 (March 16, 1921): 71.
14. John Dewey, *China, Japan and the U. S. A.: Present-day Conditions in the Far East and Their Bearing on The Washington Conference* (New York: Republic Publishing Co., 1921).
15. Arthur S. Link and William B. Catton, *American Epoch* (New York: Alfred A. Knopf, Inc., 1967), vol. 2, p. 339.
16. Frederick L. Paxson, *American Democracy and the World War* (New York: Cooper Square, Inc., 1966), p. 235.
17. Ibid., pp. 235-36.
18. Oswald Garrison Villard, "The Conference: The Second Phase," *Nation* 113 (November 30, 1921): 619.
19. Nathaniel Peffer, "Versailles, 1919-Washington, 1921," *Nation* 113 (December 14, 1921): 697.
20. *New York Times,* October 11, 1921, p. 21.
21. John Dewey, "China and Disarmament," *Chinese Students' Monthly* 17 (November 1921): 16.
22. John Dewey, "The Pacific Conference," *Kaizo* 3 (September, 1921) : 235-40.
23. *China, Japan and the U. S. A.,* p. 64.
24. *Baltimore Sun,* November 17, 1921, p. 7.
25. Ibid., p. 7.

26. The following articles appeared in the *Baltimore Sun:* "Shrewd Tactics are Shown in Chinese Plea" (November 18, 1921); "Underground Burrows Must Be Dug Open" (November 29, 1921); "Four Principles for China Regarded as But Framework" (November 23, 1921); "Chinese Resignations" (December 9, 1921); "Three Results of the Treaty" (December 10, 1921); "A Few Second Thoughts on the Four-Power Pact" (December 16, 1921).
27. *Baltimore Sun,* November 29, 1921, p. 6.
28. Sado Asada, "Japan's 'Special Interests' and the Washington Conference, 1921-1922," *American Historical Review* 67 (October, 1961): 62.
29. John Dewey, *Characters and Events* (New York: Henry Holt & Co., 1929), vol. 2, pp. 200-201.
30. John Dewey, "America and the Far East," *Survey* 56 (May 1, 1926): 188.
31. John Dewey, "Is China a Nation or a Market?" *New Republic* vol. 44 (November 11, 1925), p. 321.
32. John Dewey, "Intervention: A Challenge to Nationalism," *Current History* 28 (May 1928): 323.

4. EDUCATION FOR PEACE AND DEMOCRACY

1. John Dewey, *The School and Society* (Chicago: University of Chicago Press, 1899), p. 28.
2. For an excellent account of the history of the philosophy department and description of the courses Dewey taught, consult the following work by John H. Randall, Jr., and Jacques Barzun, eds., *A History of the Faculty of Philosophy–Columbia University* (New York: Columbia University Press, 1957). See also syllabi of Dewey's courses with complete descriptions located at Seth Low Library, Columbia University.
3. Irwin Edman, *Philosopher's Holiday* (New York: Viking Press, 1939), pp. 138-39.
4. Oral history project, Butler Library, Columbia University.
5. Syllabus for Philosophy 131-132 (Social and Political Philosophy), Seth Low Library, Columbia University.
6. Ibid.
7. John Dewey, *Reconstruction in Philosophy* (New York: Henry Holt & Co., 1921), pp. 125-26.
8. John Dewey, *My Pedagogic Creed* (Washington, D. C.: The Progressive Education Association, 1897, 1929), p. 3. *The School and Society,* p. 48; *Moral Principles in Education* (Boston: Houghton & Mifflin Co., 1909), p. 65; *Democracy and Education* (New York: Macmillan Co., 1916), p. 20.
9. Robert W. Clopton and Tsuin-Chen Ou, eds., *John Dewey: Lectures in China, 1919-1920* (Honolulu: University of Hawaii Press, 1973), pp. 210-13.
10. *The School and Society* p. 151; *Democracy and Education,* pp. 213-14, 217. Dewey was also following the advice of David Starr Jordan, president of Stanford University, who wrote:

> To teach history is a part of our business. Only by knowing the past can we create the future. But to know the past we must attach ourselves to realities. The reality in life is growth and achievement, not destruction. War is always the destroyer. It is comparable to a great lava flow laying desolate the fertile fields, branching in every direction, scorching all vegetation, weeds with the flowers, thistles with the fruits, and leaving a trail of evil not removed for years or centuries.

("The Teacher and War," *School and Society* 2, [August 28, 1915], 289).
11. *John Dewey: Lectures in China, 1919-1920,* p. 277.
12. Syllabus of Philosophy 131 for the academic year 1923, Seth Low Library. See also John Dewey, "Ethics and Internation Relations," *Foreign Affairs* 1 (March 15, 1923): 85-95.

13. Joseph Ratner, ed., *Education Today* (New York: G. P. Putnam's Sons, 1940), pp. 112-20.
14. John Dewey, "The Schools as a Means of Developing a Social Consciousness and Social Ideals in Children," *Journal of Social Forces* 1 (September 1923): 516.
15. Merle Curti, "John Dewey and Nationalism," *Orbis* 10 (Winter, 1967): 1109. Curti's article is an excellent description of Dewey's understanding and definition of the term "nationalism."
16. Ibid.
17. Merle Curti, *The Social Ideas of American Educators* (Totowa, N.J.: Littlefield, Adams & Co., 1959), p. 500.
18. Syllabus for Philosophy 131-132.
19. John Dewey, "Education as Politics," *New Republic* 32 (October 4, 1922): 776-81.
20. John Dewey, "A Sick World," *New Republic* 33 (January 24, 1923): 217.
21. *New York Times,* April 25, 1927, p. 14.
22. John Dewey, *Characters and Events* (New York: Henry Holt & Co., 1929) vol. 2, 526-36.
23. Ibid., p. 803.
24. *The Social Ideas of American Educators,* p. 500.

5. EDUCATION FOR UNDERSTANDING, NOT FOR WAR

1. John Dewey, *How We Think* (Chicago: Henry Regnery & Co., 1971), p. 53; *The School and Society* (Chicago: University of Chicago Press, 1971), p. 34.
2. Minutes of the faculty, November 21, 1877, Guy W. Bailey Library, University of Vermont. See also George Dykhuizen, *The Life and Mind of John Dewey* (Carbondale: Southern Illinois University Press, 1973), p. 11.
3. Merle Curti, *Peace or War: The American Struggle,* 1636–1936 (New York: W. W. Norton & Co., 1936), p. 235; John Dewey, *Characters and Events,* (New York: Henry Holt & Co., 1929), vol. 1, pp. 494-95.
4. *Characters and Events,* vol. 1, pp. 467-77.
5. John Dewey, *Enlistment for the Farm,* Columbia war papers, series 1, no. 1, (Division of Intelligence and Publicity of Columbia University Press, 1917), pp. 1-10.
6. William Heard Kilpatrick, oral history project, Butler Library, Columbia University.
7. John Dewey, "Vocational Education in the Light of the World War," *Vocational Education of the Middle West Bulletin,* no. 4 (January 1918), pp. 4-7; see also William James, "Moral Equivalent of War," in Ralph B. Perry, ed., *Essays on Faith and Morals* (New York: World Publishing Co., 1962), p. 325; Randolph Bourne, "A Moral Equivalent for Universal Military Service," in Carl Resek, ed., *War and the Intellectuals* (New York: Harper & Row, 1964), p. 145.
8. Winthrop D. Lane, *Military Training in Schools and Colleges in the United States* (Washington, D. C.: Committee on Militarism in Education, 1926); John Dewey, introduction to Charles Clayton Morrison's *The Outlawry of War* (Chicago: Willett, Clark & Colby Inc., 1927), p. xiv; *New York Times,* December 7, 1925, p. 29.
9. John Dewey, introduction to Barnes's *Militarizing Our Youth,* pp. 1-4.
10. Otto Nathan and Heinz Norden, eds., *Einstein on Peace* (New York: Simon & Schuster Inc., 1960), pp. 113-14; Joseph Ratner, ed., *Education Today* (New York: G. P. Putnam's Sons, 1940), pp. 245 & 262.
11. See the following articles by Dewey in *Social Frontier:* "Youth in a Confused World" (May, 1935); "Toward a National System of Education" (June, 1935); "The Social Significance of Academic Freedom" (March, 1936); "Education and Social Change" (May, 1937). Most of these are reprinted in *Education Today.*
12. John Dewey, "The Crucial Role of Intelligence," *Social Frontier* 1 (February, 1935): 9-10.
13. *New York Times,* July 9, 1940, p. 4.

6. OUTLAWRY OF WAR: A NEW APPROACH TO WORLD PEACE

1. See the following works: Robert E. Ferrell, *Peace in Their Time: The Origins of the Kellogg-Briand Pact* (New Haven: Yale University Press, 1953); Robert E. Osgood, *Ideas and Self-Interest in American Foreign Policy* (Chicago: University of Chicago Press, 1953); and Arthur A. Ekirch, *Ideas and Ideals in American Diplomacy* (New York: Appleton-Century-Crofts, 1966).
2. John E. Stoner, *S. O. Levinson and the Pact of Paris* (Chicago: University of Chicago Press, 1943), pp. 184, 195; see also Alexander De Conde, ed., *Isolation and Security* (Durham: Duke University Press, 1959).
3. Walter Lippmann, *Men of Destiny* (New York: Macmillan Co., 1928), pp. 160-61.
4. William Hard, "Raymond Robins," *New Republic* 16 (August, 10, 1918): 39.
5. Levinson to Dewey, April 27, 1923, S. O. Levinson papers, Joseph Regenstein Library, University of Chicago.
6. Charles De Benedetti, "American Internationalism in the 1920's: Shotwell and the Outlawrists," (unpublished Ph. D. thesis, University of Illinois, 1968), p. 41.
7. John Dewey, *Outlawry of War: What It Is and Is Not* (Chicago: American Committee for the Outlawry of War, 1923), pp. 9 & 16.
8. George Herbert Mead argued that "outlawry" was idealistic since it went only half-way toward its great goal. As long, he noted, as there are provisos or stipulations about self-defense and readiness to fight, "we have the proud sense of being willing to stake everything on national self-hood." (*International Journal of Ethics,* July, 1929, pp. 406-7) ; Merle Curti, "John Dewey and Nationalism," *Orbis* 10 (Winter, 1967), 1117.
9. Levinson to Dewey, February 8, 1918; Dewey to Levinson, February 14, 1918.
10. Salmon O. Levinson, "The Legal Status of War," *New Republic* 16 (March 9, 1918): 171-73.
11. John Dewey, *Characters and Events* (New York: Henry Holt & Co., 1929), vol 2, p. 649.
12. Levinson to Dewey, December 28, 1918.
13. Robert W. Clopton and Tsuin-Chen Ou, eds. *John Dewey: Lectures in China, 1919-1920* (Honolulu: University of Hawaii Press, 1973), pp. 159-63.
14. Levinson to Dewey, December 23, 1921; Dewey to Borah, March 6, 1922, Willaim E. Borah papers, Library of Congress; Borah to Dewey, March 15, 1922.
15. Congressional Record 64 (February 14, 1923): 3605-6; see also John C. Vinson, *William E. Borah and the Outlawry of War* (Athens: University of Georgia Press, 1957), pp. 74-75.
16. Levinson to Dewey, February 19, 1923; Levinson to Dewey, March 13, 1923.
17. Dunn to Dewey, February 8, 1923; Dewey to Dunn, February 12, 1923, Levinson papers; John Dewey, foreword in Salmon O. Levinson, *Outlawry of War* (Chicago: American Committee for the Outlawry of War, 1921), p. 7.
18. *Characters and Events,* vol. 2, pp. 139-40, 624; Levinson to Dewey, March 28, 1923.
19. *Characters and Events,* vol. 2, pp. 667-73.
20. Dewey to Levinson, March 30, 1923; Levinson to Dewey, April 2, 1923.
21. Dewey to Levinson, May 15, 1923.
22. *Intelligence in the Modern World,* p. 634.
23. John Dewey, "Shall the United States Join the World Court?" *Christian Century* 40 (October 25, 1923): 1369.
24. Levinson to Dewey, May 26, 1923.
25. Borchard to Dewey, May 22, 1923, Levinson papers; Albert B. Hart, "Amateur Diplomacy," *Current History* 26 (July, 1927) pp. 623-24; *Congressional Digest* 7 (March 1928) 87-89.
26. Walter Lippmann, "Outlawry of War," *Atlantic Monthly* 132 (August, 1923), pp. 245-53.

27. *Outlawry of War: What It Is and Is Not* (Chicago: American Committee for the Outlawry of War, 1923), 16 pp.
28. Frankfurter to Dewey, September 27, 1923, Levinson papers; McDonald to Dewey, October 1, 1923, Levinson papers; Levinson to Dewey, October 2,1923; Levinson to Dewey, October 4, 1923.
29. Dewey to Klyce, May 29, 1915, Scudder Klyce papers, Library of Congress; Dewey to Levinson, October 19, 1923; Levinson to Dewey, October 19 and November 3, 1923.

7. DIVERGENT PATHS TO PEACE

1. Charles De Benedetti, "The Origins of Neutrality Revision: The American Plan of 1924," *Historian* 25 (November, 1972): 75-89.
2. Salmon O. Levinson, "The Draft Treaty and the Outlawry of War," *New Republic* 39 (August 27, 1924): 383.
3. James T. Shotwell, "The Problem of Security," *Annals of the American Academy of Political Science* 120 (July, 1925), 159; "What Is Meant by Security and Disarmament," *Annals* 121 (July, 1926): 8.
4. Shotwell to Borah, November 26, 1924, Salmon O. Levinson papers, Joseph Regenstein Library, University of Chicago; Levinson to Borah, June 23,1925; Borah to Levinson, June 25, 1925; Shotwell to Borah, November 26, 1924 & November 30, 1924, Levinson papers.
5. Salmon O. Levinson, "The World Court: A Polite Gesture," *Nation* 122 (February 3, 1926): 113; James T. Shotwell, *The Autobiography of James T. Shotwell* (Indianapolis: Bobbs-Merrill Co., 1961), p. 196.
6. Levinson to Dewey, December 29, 1925.
7. *The Autobiography of James T. Shotwell,* pp. 71 & 196.
8. John Dewey, *Characters and Events* (New York: Henry Holt & Co., 1929), vol. 2, p. 693; introduction to Morrison's *The Outlawry of War,* pp. vii-xxv.
9. James T. Shotwell, "The Movement to Renounce War as a Diplomatic Weapon," *Current History* 27 (October, 1927); "Alternatives For War," *Foreign Affairs* 6 (April, 1928); "The Pact of Paris, with Historical Commentary," *International Conciliation* 243 (October, 1928).
10. *New York Times,* April 25, 1927, p. 2.
11. Robert Ferrell, *Peace in Their Time: The Origins of the Kellogg-Briand Pact* (New Haven: Yale University Press, 1953), pp. 90-93.
12. Levinson to Dewey, July 12, 1927; Dewey to Levinson, September 1, 1927; *New York Times,* September 30, 1927.
13. *Peace in Their Time,* p. 127; Foster Rhea Dulles, *America's Rise to World Power* (New York: Harper & Row, 1954), p. 159.
14. Charles De Benedetti, "American Internationalism in the 1920's: Shotwell and the Outlawrists," (unpublished Ph. D. thesis, University of Illinois, 1968), p. 341.
15. Levinson to Dewey, February 8, 1928; Dewey to Levinson, February 17, 1928; Levinson to Dewey, February 20, 1928; Dewey to Levinson, February 29, 1928; Levinson to Dewey, March 2, 1928.
16. Dewey to Levinson, February 29, 1928; Dewey to Levinson, March 5, 1928.
17. Levinson to Borah, March 2, 1928.
18. *Characters and Events,* vol 2, p. 702.
19. John Dewey and James T. Shotwell, "Divergent Paths to Peace," *New Republic* 54 (March 28, 1928): 194-96.
20. Dewey to Levinson, April 7, 1928.
21. *Characters and Events,* vol. 2, pp. 704-6.
22. Dewey to Levinson, June 8, 1928; *New York Times,* August 27, 1928, pp. 1ff; Joseph Ratner, ed., *Intelligence in the Modern World* (New York: Modern Library, 1939), p. 547.

23. George W. Wickersham, "Pact of Paris: A Gesture or a Pledge?" *Foreign Affairs* 7 (April, 1929): 355-56.
24. No author, "Strength and Weakness of the Kellogg Peace Pact," *Literary Digest* 100 (January 26, 1929), pp. 7-9.
25. Edwin M. Borchard, "The Multilateral Treaty for the Renunciation of War," *American Journal of International Law* 6 (January, 1929): 117.
26. John Dewey, *Apostles of War and Peace: Salmon O. Levinson* (New York: World Unity Publishing Co., 1929), 7 pp; *Ethics* (New York: Henry Holt & Co., rev. 1932); and "Outlawry of War," *Encyclopedia of the Social Sciences* (New York: Macmillan Co., 1933).
27. *Apostles of War and Peace,* p. 7; *Ethics,* p. 413.
28. *New York Times,* December 30, 1931, p. 30; March 3 & 4, 1932, p. 4.
29. Dewey to Levinson, March 1, 1932; Dewey, "Peace by Pact or Covenant?" *New Republic* 70 (March 23, 1932): 145-47.
30. John Dewey and Raymond L. Buell, *Are Sanctions Necessary to International Organization?* (New York: Foreign Policy Association, 1932), 36 pp.
31. Dewey to Levinson, November 1, 1932.

8. SOCIAL JUSTICE AND THE EMPTY POCKET

1. Jim Cork, "John Dewey, Karl Marx and Democratic Socialism," *Antioch Review* (December, 1949), pp. 435-52.
2. John Dewey, *The Ethics of Democracy* (Ann Arbor: University of Michigan Press, 1888), pp. 25-26.
3. John Dewey, *Schools of Tomorrow* (New York: E. P. Dutton & Co., 1915), p. 151.
4. Interview was held on December 21, 1932; see also Curti's *The Social Ideas of American Educators* (Totowa, N. J.: Littlefield, Adams & Co., 1959), p. 502.
5. *New York Times,* November 29, 1927, p. 26.
6. John Dewey, *The Public and Its Problems* (New York: Henry Holt & Co., 1927), pp. 126-27.
7. John Dewey, "Philosophy, " in Charles Beard, ed., *Whither Mankind* (New York: Longmans, Green & Co., 1928), p. 317; *Individualism Old and New* (New York: Capricorn Books, 1929), pp. 33-34, 171.
8. Levinson to Dewey, October 22, 1928, S. O. Levinson papers, Joseph Regenstein Library, University of Chicago; see also George Dykhuizen, *The Life and Mind of John Dewey* (Carbondale: Southern Illinois University Press, 1973), p. 228.
9. John Dewey, "A Great American Prophet," *Common Sense* 3 (April, 1934): 7; Introduction to Harry G. Brown, ed., *Significant Paragraphs from Henry George's Progress and Poverty* (New York: Macmillan Co., 1929); introduction to George R. Geiger, *The Philosophy of Henry George* (New York: Macmillan Co., 1933); *Steps to Economic Recovery* (New York: Robert Schalkenback Foundation, 1933); "Socialization of Ground Rent," *People's Lobby Bulletin* 4 (January, 1935), Dewey to James Truslow Adams, September 18, 1945, Dewey papers, Butler Library, Columbia University.
10. Corliss Lamont, ed., *Dialogue on John Dewey* (New York: Horizon Press, 1959), pp. 66-67; John Dewey, "What Do Liberals Want?" *Outlook* 153 (October 16, 1929): 261.
11. Dewey to Norris, December 23, 1930 (People's Lobby Bulletin contains a reprint of Dewey's letter to Norris; *New York Times,* December 27, 1930, p. 12 & December 30, 1930, p. 3.
12. *New York Times,* December 31, 1930, p. 3; John Dewey, "The Need for a New Third Party," *New Republic* 66 (March 18 & 25; April 1 & 8, 1931).
13. John Dewey, "A Third Party Platform," *New Republic* 69 (February 10, 1932): 335-56; no author, editorial in *Nation* 135 (March 16, 1932): 132.

14. "The Need for a New Third Party," p. 116; John Dewey, "The Place of Minor Parties in the American Scene," (Washington: Government Lecture Series, no. 13, 1932), p. 7; *Dialogue on John Dewey,* pp. 59-60.
15. *New York Times,* editorial, "A Philosopher in Politics," section 2 (July 24, 1932), p. 1.
16. Alan Lawson, "The Reform Psychology of John Dewey," unpublished paper delivered at the American Historial Association Convention, December 27, 1973.
17. Consult *People's Lobby Bulletin* for presidential statements by John Dewey.
18. John Dewey, "America's Public Ownership Program," *People's Lobby Bulletin* 3 (March, 1934): 1; see also "The Reform Psychology of John Dewey," p. 2, and Lawson's book, *The Failure of Independent Liberalism, 1930-1941* (New York: G. P. Putnam's Sons, 1971).
19. John Dewey, *Liberalism and Social Action* (New York: Capricorn Books, 1935), pp. 54-55; see also Dewey's article "Creative Democracy: The Task Before Us," in Sidney Ratner, ed., *The Philosopher of the Common Man: Essays in Honor of John Dewey to Celebrate His Eightieth Birthday* (New York: G. P. Putnam's Sons, 1940), p. 226; *Social Thought in America,* p. 165.
20. "The Reform Psychology of John Dewey," p. 1.
21. Reinhold Niebuhr, "The Pathos of Liberalism," *Nation* 144 (September 11, 1935): 303.

9. A SHATTERED HOPE

1. Dewey to Villard, January 16, 1929, Oswald Garrison Villard papers, Houghton Library, Harvard University; John Dewey, "A Third Party Platform," *New Republic* 63 (February 10, 1932): 336.
2. *People's Lobby Bulletin* 1 (July, 1931): 7-8; 3 (June 1933): 1.
3. *People's Lobby Bulletin* 1 (July, 1931): 6
4. Levinson to Dewey, May 6, 1933, Salmon O. Levinson papers, Joseph Regenstein Library, University of Chicago; Charles F. Weller, ed., *World Fellowship* (New York: Liveright, 1935) p. 121; *New York Times,* March 21, 1934, p. 10.
5. *People's Lobby Bulletin* 4 (February, 1935): 7; Dewey to Levinson, April 24, 1935; "When America Goes to War," statement by John Dewey in *Modern Monthly* 9 (June, 1935): 200.
6. John Dewey, *Liberalism and Social Action* (New York: Capricorn Books, 1935), pp. 54-55, 83-84; *Freedom and Culture* (New York: G. P. Putnam's Sons, 1939), p. 38; "Higher Learning and the War," *Bulletin of the American Association of University Professors* 25 (December, 1935): 614.
7. John Dewey, "Why I Am Not a Communist," *Modern Monthly* 7 (April, 1934): 136; "The Future of Liberalism," *Journal of Philosophy* 32 (April 25, 1935): 229; "Democracy Is Radical. . .As an End, and the Means Cannot Be Divorced from the End," *Common Sense* 6 (January, 1937): 11.
8. Dewey to Robins, June 3, 1937, Raymond Robins papers, Wisconsin State Historical Society, Madison, Wisconsin; "John Dewey, Great American Liberal, Denounces Russian Dictatorship," in the *Journal of International Conciliation* (February, 1938): 56; see also, *Washington Post,* December 17, 1937. [Interview with Agnes Ernst Meyer (Mrs. Eugene Meyer).]
9. Carl Becker, "Loving Peace and Waging War," *Yale Review* 26 (June, 1937): 668; Levinson to Dewey, April 25, 1938; Archibald MacLeish, "The Irresponsibles," *Nation* 150 (May 18, 1940): 622.
10. John Dewey, "Does Human Nature Change?" *Rotarian* 30 (February, 1938): 10.
11. John Dewey, "No Matter What Happens–Stay Out," *Common Sense* 8 (March, 1939): 11.
12. *Freedom and Culture,* p. 175.
13. *Freedom and Culture,* pp. 174-75; "No Matter What Happens–Stay Out," p. 11; "The Basis For Hope," statement by John Dewey in *Common Sense* 8 (December, 1939): 9-10.

14. Dewey to Otto, October 23, 1939, Max Otto papers, Wisconsin State Historical Society, Madison, Wisconsin.
15. Dewey to Otto, October 23, 1939, November 28, 1939 and July 7, 1941; Matthew Arnold, "Stanzas From the Grand Chartreuse," as quoted in *Poetry and Criticism of Matthew Arnold* (Boston: Houghton Mifflin Co., 1961), A. Dwight Culler, editor, p. 187.

10. TROUBLED PHILOSOPHER

1. Dewey to Otto, November 8 & December 28, 1942, Max Otto papers, Wisconsin State Historical Society, Madison, Wisconsin; Dewey to Meiklejohn, September 25, 1942, Alexander Meiklejohn papers, Wisconsin State Historical Society, Madison, Wisconsin.
2. John Dewey and Horace M. Kallen, eds., *The Bertrand Russell Case* (New York: Viking Press, 1941), pp. 8-9.
3. John Dewey, "Creative Democracy: The Task Before Us," in Sidney Ratner, ed., *The Philosophy of the Common Man–Essays in Honor of John Dewey* (New York: Greenwood Press, 1968), p. 226.
4. John Dewey, "The Basic Values and Loyalties of Democracy," *American Teacher* 25 (May, 1941): 8-9; Corliss Lamont, ed., *Dialogue on John Dewey* (New York: Horizon Press, 1959), p. 84; George Dykhuizen, *The Life and Mind of John Dewey* (Carbondale: Southern Illinois University Press, 1973), pp. 294-95.
5. Robert W. Clopton and Tsuin-Chen Ou, eds., *John Dewey: Lectures in China, 1919-1920* (Honolulu: University of Hawaii Press, 1973), pp. 307-8; John Dewey, *German Philosophy and Politics* (New York: G. P. Putnam's Sons, rev. 1942); *The Life and Mind of John Dewey,* pp. 291-300.
6. *John Dewey: Lectures in China, 1919-1920,* p. 308.
7. In 1942 Dewey responded to a survey on the question of pacifism. The survey was drawn up by Professor George W. Hartmann of Teachers College, Columbia University. Dewey, along with seventy-four distinguished American philosophers, presented his views. His defense of pacifism is clearly demonstrated in the survey. See George W. Hartmann, "The Strength and Weakness of the Pacifist Position as Seen by American Philosophers," *Philosophical Review* 53 (March, 1944): 125-44.
8. Dewey to Balch, December 29, 1944, W. L. Werner Collection on World Peace, Pennsylvania State University Library, Pennsylvania State University.
9. John Dewey, "Democratic versus Coercive International Organization: The Realism of Jane Addams," in Jane Addams's *Peace and Bread in Time of War* (New York: King's Crown Press, 1945), pp. xvii-xviii. This is a worthwhile preface Dewey wrote for the Addams book.
10. John Dewey, "Reconstruction as Seen in Philosophy Twenty-five years Later" in *Reconstruction in Philosophy* (Boston: Beacon Press, rev. 1948), p. vi.
11. John Dewey, "Dualism and the Split Atom," *New Leader* 28 (November, 1945): 1, 4; *The Problems of Men* (New York: Philosophical Library, 1946), p. 30.
12. Charles Chatfield, *For Peace and Justice: Pacifism in America, 1914-1941* (Knoxville: University of Tennessee Press, 1971), 332-33.
13. Chatfield's last chapter in *For Peace and Justice* provides an interesting discussion of the liberal pacifists' failure to initiate any programs or proposals that might have been useful in bringing about their desired goals.

A NOTE ON SOURCES

These notes are confined to selected sources for the study of pacifism and John Dewey's role in the peace movement after World War I. Bibliographies helpful in broadening the area of research on John Dewey and world peace are Milton Halsey Thomas's *John Dewey: A Centennial Bibliography* (Chicago: University of Chicago Press, 1962), which is the most comprehensive and authoritative compilation on Dewey's writings and works about him; *A Guide to the Works of John Dewey,* edited by Jo An Boydston (Carbondale: Southern Illinois University Press, 1970), provides a useful checklist on Dewey's writings; and *The Early Works of John Dewey,* edited by Jo Ann Boydston and others (Carbondale: Southern Illinois University Press, 1969), represents the labors of many individuals at the Cooperative Research Center for Dewey Publications at Southern Illinois University. Useful works on the study of peace are *To End War,* edited by Robert Pickus and Robert Woito (San Francisco: World without War Council, 1970), and *Bibliography on Peace Research in History,* edited by Blanche W. Cook (Santa Barbara: ABC-Clio, 1969). Both works cover a broad range of topics and various disciplines.

MANUSCRIPT SOURCES

The richest repository of material on John Dewey is the Cooperative Research Center for Dewey Publications at Southern Illinois University. The project is under the direction of Dr. Jo Ann Boydston. Since Dewey wrote a great deal, there remains much material that has yet to be examined. Butler Library, Columbia University, also contains some Dewey correspondence. Most of it, however, is among fellow faculty members at Columbia. The Seth Low Library at Columbia contains most of Dewey's unpublished lecture notes as well as syllabi on the courses that he taught in the philosophy department and at Teachers College. The National Archives contains an important field report Dewey made during his journey to the Far East. The "Report on Bolshevism in China" was addressed to Colonel Drysdale, an intelligence officer in the State Department.

Other collections of importance are the Jane Addams papers at the Swarthmore College Peace Collection, Swarthmore College. There exists minor correspondence between Dewey and Addams dealing primarily with social issues around the turn of the century. The William E. Borah papers at the Manuscripts Division, Library of Congress, contain some correspondence dealing with the outlawry of war crusade. The Randolph Bourne papers, Butler Library, Columbia University, provide some information on Bourne's disillusionment with Dewey's support for World War I. The James McKeen Cattell papers and the Scudder Klyce papers are both in the Manuscripts Division, Library of Congress. They are helpful in pointing out some of Dewey's personality traits. They also touch upon philosophical and faculty questions. Perhaps the most important source of information contained in this book is the Salmon O. Levinson papers, located at the Joseph Regenstein Library, University of Chicago. They are invaluable in exploring Dewey's peace psychology as well as his activities in the outlawry of war crusade. Also important are the papers found at the Wisconsin State Historical Society, Madison, Wisconsin. The Merle Curti papers, the Alexander Meiklejohn papers, the Max Otto papers, and the Raymond Robins papers touch upon a wide area of topics from education to Russia and finally to world peace. There is a surprising amount of Dewey correspondence located at the Wisconsin State Historical Society. The James T. Shotwell papers at Butler Library, Columbia University, are useful in pointing out Shotwell's differences with Dewey on the outlawry issue. The Oswald Garrison Villard papers, Houghton Library, Harvard University, discuss the important social issues of the day. Dewey's contact with Villard is in relation to the League for Independent Political Action. The Howard Yolm Williams papers, Manuscripts Section, Minnesota Historical Society, offer some insight into Dewey's activities with third party movements in the twenties and thirties.

PERSONAL CORRESPONDENCE AND ORAL MEMOIRS

Dewey's long-time secretary and second wife, Roberta Dewey, was kind enough to present to me a vivid account of Dewey's speech at Cooper Union on the night of December 7, 1941. Howard Yolm Williams, executive secretary of the League for Independent Political Action, was generous in his recounting of Dewey's association with LIPA and other third party movements. Charles C. Griffin, professor emeritus at Vassar College, was also kind enough to relate to me his contact with John Dewey while studying for a graduate degree in history at Columbia University.

The oral history project in Butler Library, Columbia University, includes valuable reminiscences by Roger Baldwin, Harold F. Clark, William Heard Kilpatrick, and A. J. Muste. Most of these recollections discuss Dewey's role as a teacher and social critic. One of the tragedies is that Dewey died shortly before the initiation of the oral history project.

NEWSPAPERS AND PERIODICALS

Among the more useful newspapers are the *Baltimore Sun,* which carried feature articles by Dewey on the Washington Naval Conference and the Far East in 1921 and 1922; the *New York Evening Post,* which ran stories on Dewey's support for World War I; and the *New York Times,* which regularly presented articles and stories on Dewey during the interwar period.

Periodicals of interest include *Asia* (1919-28), which carried articles by Dewey on Far Eastern problems; *Atlantic Monthly* (1916-45), featuring the Dewey-Lippmann debate on outlawing war; *Christian Century* (1922-30), which under the direction of Charles C. Morrison was sympathetic to the outlawry crusade and pacifism in general; *Common Sense* (1932-39), a vehicle for Dewey's social ideas during the depression; *Dial* (1917-41), which regularly presented Dewey's writings on war, peace, and social injustice; *Nation* (1915-41), which under its pacifist editor, Oswald Garrison Villard called for social reform and the abolition of war; *New Republic* (1915-41), Dewey's primary organ of expression until a rift developed between him and the other members of the editorial staff during the Trotsky inquiry in Mexico in 1937; *People's Lobby Bulletin* (1931-36), Dewey's vehicle for criticizing the New Deal and calling for a new third party; *School and Society* (1915-40), an exceptional account of Dewey's views on education and social justice; and *Social Frontier* (1935-40), which ran a series of articles by Dewey opposing the rise of totalitarian states in Europe.

DEWEY'S WRITINGS

Dewey's philosophical writings are many. Those of a more technical nature are discussed here. *Psychology* (New York: Harper & Bros., 1886) is Dewey's first technical work on the discipline of philosophy. It does emphasize the importance of philosophy in its social context. *Outlines of a Critical Theory of Ethics* (New York: Greenwood Press, 1969), *The Study of Ethics: A Syllabus* (Ann Arbor: Register Publishing Co., 1894), and *Ethics* (New York: Henry Holt & Co., 1908) in collaboration with James Hayden Tufts, present a more detailed analysis of Dewey's social philosophy. The connection between experience and ideas is clearly demonstrated in these writings. They also point out the development of Dewey's pragmatism. Other works on the technical nature of his pragmatism include: *The Influence of Darwin on Philosophy* (New York: Henry Holt & Co., 1910); *How We Think* (Chicago: Henry Regnery Co., 1971); *Essays in Experimental Logic* (Chicago: University of Chicago Press, 1916); *Reconstruction in Philosophy* (New York: Henry Holt & Co., 1921, rev. 1946), which derived from his lectures at the Imperial University at Tokyo, Japan, and which is a clear presentation of his views on the function and importance of social philosophy; *Human Nature and Conduct* (New York: Henry Holt & Co., 1922), another important exposition of pragmatism in a social setting; *Experience and Nature* (New York: Dover Publications, 1958), which Oliver Wendell Holmes, Jr., proclaimed Dewey's greatest philosophical work despite the fact that he had to read the book three times before he finally understood it, because of its lack of clarity; *The Quest for Certainty* (New York: G. P. Putnam's Sons, 1929), a series of lectures delivered at the University of Edinburgh on philosophy and its present condition; *A Common Faith* (New Haven: Yale University Press, 1934), presented as the Terry Lectures at Yale University, explains Dewey's opposition to organized forms of Christianity; and *Logic: The Theory of Inquiry* (New York: Holt, Rinehart, & Winston, 1938), which is very technical and perhaps Dewey's most serious contribution to the study of philosophy.

Articles written by Dewey on his philosophy are "Moral Theory and Practice," *International Journal of Ethics* 2 (January, 1891), which presents a concise analysis of Dewey's theory of the interrelationship between morality and experience; "The Chaos in Moral Training," *Popular Science Monthly* 45 (August, 1894), which further elaborates this theme; and "The Reflex Arc Concept in Psychology," *Psychological Review* 3 (1896), which is the first clear indication of Dewey's outright espousal of the philosophy of pragmatism.

In the area of education Dewey has contributed a great deal. Some of his more important works are *My Pedagogic Creed* (Washington, D. C.: Progressive Education Association, 1897), which is an exposition of Dewey's educational theories; *The School and Society* (Chicago: University of Chicago Press, 1899), an explanation of Dewey's philosophy of progressive education which over the years has become distorted and bitterly attacked during the course of pedagogical disputes; *The Child and the Curriculum* (Chicago: University of Chicago Press, 1902), and *Moral Principles in Education* (Boston: Houghton Mifflin Co., 1909) are supplementary to *The School and Society; Schools of Tomorrow* (New York: E. P. Dutton & Co., 1915) was collaborated in by his daughter Evelyn Dewey and further elaborates Dewey's views on the child-centered school; and *Democracy and Education* (New York: Macmillan Co., 1916), which is Dewey's classic work on the subject and perhaps his most anthologized book. Of all Dewey's writing, this one is by far the most useful to those interested in exploring Dewey's social and educational ideas.

Edited works on Dewey's educational theories are found in Joseph Ratner's *The Philosophy of John Dewey* (New York: Henry Holt & Co., 1928), and *Education Today* (New York: G. P. Putnam's Sons, 1940). It would also be advisable to consult Robert W. Clopton and Tsuin-Chen Ou, eds., *John Dewey: Lectures in China, 1919-1920* (Honolulu: University of Hawaii Press, 1973).

Dewey's most important contribution was in the field of social affairs. It was there that he attempted to employ his pragmatic philosophy as a means for improving our democratic society. *Ethics of Democracy* (Ann Arbor: University of Michigan Press, 1888) is Dewey's earliest attack on social injustices in America and provides a clue to his definition of democracy; *The Public and Its Problems* (New York: Henry Holt & Co., 1927) derived from a series of lectures Dewey delivered at Kenyon College, Ohio, in the spring of 1926. The work is useful for pointing out the changes America was experiencing during the 1920's. The rise of technology and its impact on American traditions is the main theme. Both works are supplanted by *Individualism Old and New* (New York: Capricorn Books, 1929), a work of extreme importance, which attempts to encourage Americans to adapt to a more "collectivized" way of life. Also helpful are: *Education and the Social Order* (New York: League for Industrial Democracy, 1934), a pamphlet stressing the importance of education as a guide to social readjustment; *Liberalism and Social Action* (New York: Capricorn Books, 1935), a short propaganda piece which encourages a radicalized, nonviolent form of social action. It is a piece for its day and useful in explaining Dewey's increasing radicalism after 1930. *Freedom and Culture* (New York: G. P. Putnam's Sons, 1939), and *The Problems of Men* (New York: Philosophical Library, 1946) round out Dewey's views on the role of philosophy in society.

Dewey's more important articles in the area of social philosophy are the following: "Pragmatic America," *New Republic* 32 (April, 1922); "Education as Politics," *New Republic* 33 (October, 1922); "The Pragmatic Acquiesence," *New Republic* 49 (January, 1927); "A Critique of American Civilization," in *Recent Gains in American Civilization,* edited by Kirby Page (New York: Harcourt, Brace & Co., 1928); "Philosophy," in *Whither Mankind?* edited by Charles Beard (New York: Longmans, Green & Co., 1928); "Politics and Culture," *Modern Thinker* 2 (May, 1932); and "The Future of Liberalism," *Journal of Philosophy* 32 (April, 1935. One should also consult the *People's Lobby Bulletin* and *Common Sense,* since they contain numerous articles by Dewey on questions of social import. In addition, edited works of major importance include *The Early Works of John Dewey,* edited by Jo Ann Boydston et al., and Joseph Ratner's two important works, *Intelligence in the Modern World* (New York: Modern Library, 1939) and *Characters and Events,* 2 vols. (New York: Henry Holt & Co., 1929). They are invaluable for ascertaining information and ideas on Dewey the social critic.

Dewey's writings on peace and war encompass a wide range of topics. The more important writings on the subject have been neatly compiled in Joseph Ratner's two works, *Characters and Events* and *Intelligence in the Modern World.* Both works contain a great deal of information pertaining to Dewey's ideas on world peace. Aside from the edited writings, some of Dewey's major works on war and peace are *German Philosophy and Politics* (New York: G. P. Putnam's Sons, 1915, 1942), which provides a useful glimpse of Dewey's objections to German militarism and autocracy, and *China, Japan, and the U. S. A.: Present-day Conditions in the Far East and Their Bearing on the Washington Conference* (New York: Republic Publishing Co., 1921), which contains Dewey's views on the Far Eastern problem as well as his opposition to imperialism in China. Perhaps Dewey's major contribution to the peace movement, however, is contained in a pamphlet entitled *Outlawry of War: What It is and Is Not* (Chicago: American Committee for the Outlawry of War, 1923). This pamphlet proved to be a contributing factor to the success and popularity which the outlawry of war crusade enjoyed. It can be supplemented with *Apostles of War and Peace: Salmon O. Levinson* (New York: World Unity Publications, 1929), and *Are Sanctions Necessary to International Organization?* (New York: Foreign Policy Association, 1932), collaborator Raymond Leslie Buell, chairman of the Foreign Policy Association. Dewey and Buell presented opposing points of view on the question of sanctions.

Besides writing articles and pamphlets on world peace, Dewey wrote introductions to various peace works. They are the following: Salmon O.

Levinson, *Outlawry of War* (Chicago: American Committee for the Outlawry of War, 1921), Charles C. Morrison, *The Outlawry of War* (Chicago: Willett, Clark, & Colby, 1927); Roswell P. Barnes, *Militarizing Our Youth: The Significance of the Reserve Officers Training Corps in Our Schools and Colleges* (Washington, D. C.: Committee on Militarism in Education, 1927); and John E. Stoner, *S. O. Levinson and the Pact of Paris: A Study in the Technique of Influence* (Chicago: University of Chicago Press, 1943). The introductions are an important guide in determining the intensity Dewey expressed in the peace crusade.

Dewey's articles on peace are found primarily in the following periodicals and newspapers: *New Republic, Christian Century, Baltimore Sun, Survey, School and Society, People's Lobby Bulletin, New York Times, Journal of Philosophy, Common Sense,* and *Dial.* Other articles of special importance are: "Vocational Education in the Light of the World War," *Vocational Educational Association of the Middle West* 4 (January, 1918), which provides a Jamesian equivalent for war; "China and Disarmament," *Chinese Students' Monthly* 17 (November, 1921); "The Schools as a Means of Developing a Social Consciousness and Social Ideals in Children," *Journal of Social Forces* 1 (September, 1923), emphasizing the importance of educational peace research; "Outlawry of War," *Encyclopedia of the Social Sciences,* vol. 4 (New York: Macmillan & Co., 1933), substantiates in further detail his reasons for support of the movement; "When America Goes to War," *Modern Monthly* 9 (June, 1935); "Higher Learning and the War," *Bulletin of the American Association of University Professors* 25 (December, 1935); and "Democratic versus Coercive International Organization: The Realism of Jane Addams," an important preface to Jane Addams's *Peace and Bread in Time of War* (New York: King's Crown Press, rev. 1945). An unpublished transcript entitled "Lessons from the War: In Philosophy," which was a speech Dewey delivered at Cooper Union on December 7, 1941, is also a valuable reference source, particularly since it was given on the same day that U.S. ships were attacked by the Japanese at Pearl Harbor.

OTHER PRIMARY SOURCES

The World War I period and after brought about a flourishing of writings in opposition to war. The notion that war was immoral and destructive of human values was made public by Randolph Bourne in his scathing attacks on Dewey's pragmatic support for American military involvement during the first World War. His writings have been edited by Carl Resek, *War and the Intellectuals* (New York: Harper & Row, 1964), and Lillian Schlissel,

The World of Randolph Bourne (New York: E. P. Dutton & Co., 1965). Both are invaluable references. Norman Thomas's *War's Heretics: A Plea for the Conscientious Objector* (New York: American Union against Militarism, 1917), is primarily directed at Dewey's criticisms of conscientious objectors during World War I. Jane Addams's *Peace and Bread in Time of War* is especially significant for detailing the role of women's peace work.

Books dealing with the outlawry of war crusade and the Pact of Paris are plentiful. The more important ones have been written by peace advocates and legal experts. David Hunter Miller's *The Peace Pact of Paris* (New York: G. P. Putnam's Sons, 1928), is a legal analysis of the treaty and is nicely supplemented by James T. Shotwell's *War as an Instrument of National Policy: And Its Renunciation in the Pact of Paris* (New York: Harcourt, Brace & Co., 1929). Kirby Page's *An American Peace Policy* (New York: George H. Doran Co., 1925) and Charles Clayton Morrison's *The Outlawry of War: A Constructive Policy for World Peace* are particularly helpful in presenting alternative peace plans for the twenties. Both books were instrumental in paving the way for public acceptance of the Kellogg-Briand Pact, or the Pact of Paris.

Articles on the peace movement and, in particular, on the outlawry of war crusade are also numerous. Among the more significant are those written by Senator William E. Borah, Salmon O. Levinson, and James T. Shotwell. Borah's articles include "Toward the Outlawry of War," *New Republic* 39 (July, 1924); "Outlawry of War," *Historical Outlook* 16 (February, 1925); "One Great Treaty to Outlaw All Wars," *New York Times*, section 9 (February 5, 1928), and "Can War Be Outlawed?" *Congressional Digest* 7 (March, 1928). Levinson, the head of the outlawry crusade, wrote a considerable number of articles. Some are as follows: "The Legal Status of War," *New Republic* 14 (March, 1918); "Can Peace Be Enforced?" *Christian Century* 42 (January, 1925); "The World Court: A Polite Gesture," *Nation* 122 (February, 1926); "Can War Be Enforced?" *Congressional Digest* 7 (March, 1928); and "Sanctions of Peace," *Christian Century* 46 (December, 1929). Shotwell, Levinson's main adversary, responded in defense of the League of Nations with the following articles: "The Problem of Security," *Annals of the American Academy of Arts and Sciences* 120 (July, 1925); "What is Meant by Security and Disarmament?" *Academy of Political Science Proceedings* 12 (July, 1926); "The Problem of Disarmament," *Annals* 126 (July, 1926); and "The Movement to Renounce War as a Diplomatic Weapon," *Current History* 27 (October, 1927). The articles by Levinson and Shotwell are especially useful for demonstrating the incompatibility and ideological differences between the two peace prophets.

SECONDARY WORKS

It is impossible to list all the works on Dewey. Such a task would run into many pages. Yet there exist certain works that help to put Dewey in proper perspective. Richard Bernstein's *John Dewey* (New York: Washington Square Press, 1966) is part of the Great American Thinkers Series; it attempts to discuss Dewey's role as a social critic. Paul K. Conkin's *Puritans and Pragmatists: Eight Eminent American Thinkers* (New York: Dodd, Mead & Co., 1968), is an excellent intellectual and interpretive portrait of John Dewey's pragmatism, and fits in nicely with Merle Curti's *The Social Ideas of American Educators* (Totowa, N. J.: Littlefield, Adams & Co., 1959). The recently published *Life and Mind of John Dewey,* by George Dykhuizen (Carbondale: Southern Illinois University Press, 1973), is a factual account of Dewey's life. One would have hoped that Dykhuizen could be a bit more interpretive in his analysis of Dewey's long career. He is, nonetheless, helpful in ascertaining facts about Dewey. Sidney Hook's *John Dewey: An Intellectual Portrait* (New York: John Day Co., 1939) presents a sympathetic account of Dewey's philosophy of pragmatism up to the advent of World War II. It is rich in useful insights into the social aspects of Dewey's career and his philosophy. Richard Hofstadter's *Social Darwinism in American Thought* (Boston: Beacon Press, 1967) and *Anti-Intellectualism in American Life* (New York: Vintage Books, 1962) offer a more critical analysis of Dewey's pragmatic philosophy. Both works are complementary to Morton White's influential book, *Social Thought in America; The Revolt against Formalism* (Boston: Beacon Press, 1947). All three works are extremely discerning in their approach to a critical understanding of pragmatism.

Doctoral dissertations on Dewey are also numerous. Those of a more sophisticated and scholarly nature are the following: Charles S. Bednar, "John Dewey's Rationale for a Democratic Society" (Columbia University, 1960); Edward J. Bordeau, "The Practical Idealism of John Dewey's Political Philosophy" (Fordam University, 1969); Barry C. Keenan, "John Dewey in China: His Visit and the Reception of His Ideas, 1917-1927" (Claremont Graduate School, 1969); Harold McNitt, "John Dewey's Democratic Liberalism: Its Philosophical Foundations" (University of Michigan, 1956); and James Earl Weaver, "John Dewey: A Spokesman for Progressive Liberalism" (Brown University, 1963). These dissertations are particularly useful because of their historical orientation.

The history of pacifist organizations since World War I has been vividly recounted in Charles Chatfield's excellent work *For Peace and Justice:*

Pacifism in America, 1914-1941 (Knoxville: University of Tennessee Press, 1971). It should be read in conjunction with Merle Curti's classic *Peace or War: The American Struggle, 1636-1936* (New York: W. W. Norton & Co., 1936), which traces the entire history of the peace movement in America since its inception; Peter Brock's *Pacifism in the United States: From the Colonial Era to the First World War* (Princeton: Princeton University Press, 1968), a monumental study in its own right; C. Rolan Marchand's *The American Peace Movement and Social Reform, 1898-1918* (Princeton: Princeton University Press, 1972), an excellent analysis of peace organizations prior to the first World War; Alexander De Conde's edited work *Isolation and Security* (Durham: Duke University Press, 1957); and Sondra R. Herman's *Eleven against War: Studies in American Internationalist Thought, 1898-1921* (Stanford: Hoover Institute Press, 1969). All these works are influential in fostering interest in further peace research. In addition, Charles De Benedetti's "American Internationalism in the 1920's: Shotwell and Outlawrists" (Ph. D. thesis, University of Illinois, 1969) is also a valuable source of information on peace movements in the twenties.

Biographies and autobiographies of leading peace advocates are also available. Louis Filler's *Randolph Bourne* (Washington, D. C.: American Council on Public Affairs, 1943) remains the only scholarly biography of Bourne. Robert J. Maddox's *William E. Borah and American Foreign Policy* (Baton Rouge: LSU Press, 1969), Marian C. McKenna's *Borah* (Ann Arbor: University of Michigan Press, 1961), and John C. Vinson's *William E. Borah and the Outlawry of War* (Athens: University of Georgia Press 1957) are good accounts of the senator's views on foreign affairs. Of the three, Maddox's work is by far the most critical. John E. Stoner's *S. O. Levinson and the Pact of Paris: A Study in the Techniques of Influence* remains the only biography on the outlawry chief. Especially significant is Stoner's treatment of Levinson's utilization of the media as a means for bolstering his program. Two influential autobiographies that should be read in connection with the interwar peace movement are John Haynes Holmes's *I Speak for Myself: The Autobiography* (New York: Harper & Bros., 1959) and James T. Shotwell's *The Autobiography of James T. Shotwell* (Indianapolis: Bobbs-Merrill Co., 1961). Both are colorful presentations of dedicated and important figures in the peace movement after World War I.

Works of a general nature that deal with pacifism and world peace are Robert H. Ferrell's *Peace in Their Time: The Origins of the Kellogg-Briand Pact* (New Haven: Yale University Press, 1953), far and away the most authoritative study on the subject; Manfred Jonas, *Isolationism in America, 1935-1941* (Ithaca: Cornell University Press, 1966), a discussion of the neutrality controversy leading up to American involvement in World War II; and the two studies on antimilitarist thought, Arthur A. Ekirch's *The Civilian and the Military* (New York: Oxford University Press, 1956) and Samuel P. Huntington's *The Soldier and the State* (Cambridge: Belknap Press, 1964). Both are extremely informative accounts of military-civilian encounters.

There exist literally hundreds of articles on John Dewey. Those dealing with his peace activities have been narrowed down to a small number, among which are William Brickman's "Dewey's Social and Political Commentary" in *A Guide to the Works of John Dewey;* Merle Curti, "John Dewey and Nationalism," *Orbis* 10 (winter, 1967); Alan Cywar, "John Dewey in World War I: Patriotism and International Progressivism," *American Quarterly* 21 (June, 1969), and "John Dewey: Toward Democratic Reconstruction, 1915-1920," *Journal of the History of Ideas* 30 (December, 1969); Lewis Feuer, "John Dewey and the Back to the People Movement in American Thought," *Journal of the History of Ideas* 20 (October-December, 1959); Sidney Kaplan, "Social Engineers as Saviors: Effects of World War I on Some American Liberals," *Journal of the History of Ideas* 17 (June, 1956); and Wayne R. Lyes "Dewey's Social, Political, and Legal Philosophy" in *A Guide to the Works of John Dewey.* All these articles are useful in interpreting specific aspects of Dewey's thought with regard to the issue of war and peace.

In recent years writings on the peace movement in American history have emphasized what I would call an organizational approach. Various studies have been undertaken which attempt to point out the many and varied activities of different peace organizations. In-depth studies of how a peace organization came about, how it operated, where it received its funds, and what it accomplished have presently captured the interest of historians. Yet, little has been done in the way of studying the leaders of these organizations. Peace research in history should expand its focus by undertaking a more biographical approach. That is the purpose of this book. For no organization can move effectively without the leadership of its most important members.

INDEX

Addams, Jane, 11, 17, 35-36, 72-77, 117-18, 135
Adler, Felix, 6
Alexander, Matthias F., 37, 39
Allen, Devere, 122
American Committee for the Outlawry of War, 6, 67, 80-113; opposition to League, 80-81; New York Committee, 91-92
Angell, James B., 14
Angell, Norman, 30
Arnold, Matthew, 143

Balch, Emily, 148
Barnes, Roswell P., 76
Beale, Howard K., 78
Beals, Carleton, 137
Beard, Charles A., 34, 119, 134, 138, 156 n21
Becker, Carl, 138-39
Bellamy, Edward, 30, 122
Bemis, Edward W., 17
Blanshard, Paul, 121
Blaine, John J. (Sen.), 110
Bliss, Tasker H. (Gen.), 98
Borah, William E. (Sen.), 51, 76; outlawry, 82-88, 97-100, 104-05, 109; debts and reparations, 123, 131-32
Borchard, Edwin M., 93, 110
Bourne, Randolph, x, 4-5, 67, 74-75, 83, 89, 102, 135, 140, 146; opposes Dewey in WWI, 35-39, 44
Briand, Aristide, 102-112
Brooks, Van Wyck, 37, 134, 142
Brookwood Labor College, 118-19
Buckham, Matthew, 12
Buell, Raymond L., 112-13
Burke, Edward R. (Sen.), 78
Butler, Nicholas M., 33, 74, 103-04

Calverton, V. F., 142
Capper, Arthur (Sen.), 104
Carnegie Endowment for International Peace, 98
Carus, Paul, 97
Catt, Carrie, 76
Cattell, James McKeen, 33, 39, 74
Cecil, Robert (MP), 81
Chamberlain, Austen, 108
Chamberlain, Joseph P., 103-04, 106
Chatfield, E. Charles, x, 164 n13
Chen-Oui, Tsuin, 47
Chiang Kai-shek, 49
China, 43-57, 62-64, 86-87, 113, 118
Civil War, American, 11
Clark, Harold F., 60-61
Clark, John H. (Justice), 99
Clark, Reuben, 91
Clemenceau, Georges, 40
Clopton, Robert W., 47
Cold War (U. S. vs. U. S. S. R.), 149-50
Columbia University, 19-20, 51-59, 61-68, 71- 74, 87, 90, 97, 102, 118, 123, 156 n20, 158 n2; academic intolerance in WWI, 32-34
Committee for Cultural Freedom, 145-47

Committee on Militarism in Education (CME), 75-79
Connolly, Christopher P., 91
Coolidge, Calvin, 66, 91, 99
Cork, James, 114-15
Coss, John J., 47
Coughlin, Charles (Father), 124
Creel, George, 32; Committee on Public Information, 32, 67
Croly, Herbert, 33, 85
Crozier, William (Gen.), 57
Curti, Merle, ix, 78, 85, 118, 159 n15

Dana, Henry, 33, 39, 74
Darrow, Clarence, 27
Darwin, Charles, 12-13, 75
Dawes, Charles G. (Gen.), 131
Debs, Eugene V., 16
Declaration Against Conscription, 78-79
Dewey, Alice C., 15, 102
Dewey, Archibald, 9-11
Dewey, Frederick A., 27
Dewey, John: At Columbia University, 19-20, 50-71, 102, 118, 123; World War I, 20-42; Pragmatic Philosophy, 68-69, 126-27, 147-51 Early Life, 10-20; The Johns Hopkins University, 13-14, 25; At University of Michigan, 14-15, 116-17; At University of Chicago, 16-19, 72-73, 117-18; Social Philosophy, 12-19, 116-17; Educational Theories, 18-23, 58-73, 117, 152-53; Far East, 43-57; Outlawry of War, 80-113; Committee on Militarism in Education (CME), 75-79; On Sanctions, 48-49, 89, 101; League of Nations, 31-42, 89-90, 102; Kellogg-Briand Pact (Pact of Paris), 107-113; New Deal, 125-28, 140; Influence on Brookwood Labor College, 118-19; University of Vermont, 12-13, 72; Jane Addams and Hull House, 11, 17, 35, 72, 117-18, 135, 148; Democratic Beliefs, 5-6, 14-15, 18-19, 21-22, 45-47, 117-19, 140-41, 147-48, 152-53; High School Teacher in Oil City, Pennsylvania, 13; On Treaty of Versailles, 40-42; Trotsky Hearings, 37, 136-38; On Washington Naval Conference, 51-56; League for Independent Political Action (LIPA), 121-25; People's Lobby, 123-27, 130-32; World War II, 144-53; On Communism, 136-38, 145-50; On Atomic Bomb, 149-53; Death, 153
Dewey, Roberta, 154 n1, n3
Douglas, Paul, 122
Dreiser, Theodore Mrs., 91
Drysdale (Col.), 49
Du Bois, W. E. B., 122
Dunn, Arthur, 89

Eastman, Max, 39
Edman, Irwin, 60-61
Einstein, Albert, 77
Eisenhower, Dwight D. (Gen.), 145
Ekirch, Arthur A., Jr., x, xi
Engelbrecht, H. C., 133
Espionage Act (1917), 34

Fairchild, Henry Pratt, 142
Farrell, James T., 37
Fiske, Bradley A. (Adm.), 133
Ford, Franklin, 116-17
Foreign Policy Association, 91, 94, 112
Fosdick, Harry E., 119
Frankfurter, Felix, 94
Fraser, Leon, 33, 39, 74
Freud, Sigmund, 77
Fries, Amos A. (Gen.), 133

Geneva Protocol, 98
George, Henry, 16-17, 122, 127-28
George, Lloyd, 40
Germany, 20-42, 46, 65, 78, 131-37, 141-42, 147, 149
Ghent, W. J., 119
Gidding, Franklin, 26
Goodrich, Caspar F. (Adm.), 73
Great Depression (1930s), 95, 114-28
Greenwich House, 118
Grotius, Hugo, 85

Haire, Nellie B., 85
Hall, G. Stanley, 13
Hamilton, Alexander, 66
Hanighen, F. C., 133
Hapgood, Norman, 119
Hard, William, 82
Harding, Warren G., 51-52, 66, 91, 99
Harmony Plan (1925), 99-100, 106
Harper, William R., 16, 72
Hart, Albert B., 93
Hartmann, George W., 164 n7
Harvard University, 91, 93
Hay, John, 57
Haymarket Square, 14
Hayes, Carlton, 26
Hegel, G. W. F., 13
Henry Street Settlement, 118
Hillquit, Morris, 119

Hirohito, Emperor of Japan, 149
Hiroshima, 149
Hitler, Adolph, 78, 130, 133, 139-43, 146-48, 151
Holmes, John Haynes, 83, 95, 99, 106, 119, 123, 129, 142
Holmes, Oliver Wendell, Jr., 168
Holt, Hamilton, 119
Hook, Sidney, 126, 142; Committee for Cultural Freedom, 147
Hoover, Herbert, 66, 122-23, 125
Hudson, Manley O., 91-92
Huebsch, Benjamin, 142
Hughes, Charles Evans, 52, 55, 99
Hull House, 17, 35, 117-18
Hu Shih, 46, 157 n2
Huxley, Thomas H., 12

Imperial University (Japan), 45
Italy, 78, 133, 135-36, 147

Jackman, Wilbur S., 19
James, William, x, 7, 30, 74-75, 138-39
Japan, 43-57, 62-64, 86, 111-13, 133, 147, 149
Joint Peace Council, 77
Jordan, David Starr, 158 n10

Keep America Out of War Congress (KAOWC), 7, 139
Kellogg, Frank B., 104-12; Pact of Paris, 105-13
Kenyon College, 120
Kilpatrick, William Heard, 7, 74, 78
Klyce, Scudder, 25, 95, 125
Ku Klux Klan, 66

La Follette, Robert (Sen.), 76
Lane, Winthrop D., 76
Lansing, Robert, 93
Lasch, Christopher, x
League for Independent Political Action (LIPA), 121-25, 130
League of Nations, 6, 30-32, 40-42, 80-82, 86-87, 89, 93, 97-113
League for Industrial Democracy, 111
Lease, Mary, 16
Lee, Algernon, 119
Levinson, Salmon O., 81-82, 138; and Morrison, 83; and Dewey, 83-85, 87-89, 92, 95, 102-10, 112; and Shotwell, 98-102, 106-07; and outlawry, 81-113
Libby, Frederick, 76
Lincoln, Abraham, 11
Lindbergh, Charles, 103
Lippmann, Walter, 41, 82, 93-95, 97
Lloyd, Henry Demarest, 17
Long, Huey, 124-25
Lovejoy, Arthur O., 90
Lovejoy, Owen R., 119
Ludlow, Louis, 134

MacArthur, Douglas (Gen.), 132-33, 144-45
MacLeish, Archibald, 134
Manchu Dynasty, 47
Manchurian Crisis (Mukden Incident), 111-13
Mann, Horace, 66
Manning, William T., 145
Marx, Karl, 114-16, 126-28, 136
Maurer, James, 122
May Day Movement (China), 47
McDonald, James G., 82, 94
McGeehan, John E., 145
McLean, George P. (Sen.), 110
Mead, George H., 160 n8
Meiklejohn, Alexander, 73, 144
Mexico, 101-02, 136-37
Meyer, Agnes E., 137
Miller, David H., 98
More, Sir Thomas, 24
Morgan, John P., 116
Morris, George S., 13
Morrison, Charles C., 83; on outlawry, 83, 96, 99, 101
Moscow Treason Trials (1936), 136-37
Mufson, Thomas, 34
Munsey, Frank A., 91
Mussolini, Benito, 130, 136
Muste, Abraham J., xi, 78, 118, 123, 142, 152

Nagasaki, 149
National Defense Act (1920), 75-79
National Nanking Teachers College, 50
National Origins Act (1924), 56
National Peking Teachers College, 50
National Peking University, 46, 86
Nazi-Soviet Non-Aggression Pact (1939), 141
Newark Lawyers Club, 90
New Deal, 115, 125-30, 140
New Republic, 5, 27-28, 32-33, 35, 37 41, 50, 57-58, 68, 82-86, 90-91, 93, 107-08, 112, 120, 123, 136-37
Niebuhr, Reinhold, 99, 128, 134
Norris, George W., 122-23
Nye, Gerald P., 133-34

Olds, Robert E., 104
Open Door Policy, 51, 55, 57

Orlando, Vittorio, 40
Otto, Max, 142-44

Pacifism, 5-6, 80-113; Dewey's opposition, 26-29; Dewey's conversion, 37-38, 41-42, 111-13, 124-28, 135, 147-53; in schools (peace education), 57-79
Page, Kirby, 76, 81, 99, 106
Palmer, A. Mitchell, 68; raids (1919), 146
Parker, Theodore, 66
Pearl Harbor, 143, 147, 151
Peffer, Nathaniel, 52-53
People's Lobby, 123-27, 130-32
Perry, M. Thomas (Adm.), 149
Post, Adeline E., 91
Powell, John Reed, 33
Prince, John D., 33
Princeton Pledge, 111
Prohibition Movement, 66, 96

Reed, James A. (Sen.), 110
Reed, John, 26
Reserve Officers' Training Corps (R. O. T. C.), 75-79
Rich, Charles, 11
Rich, Davis, 11
Rich, Lucina Artemisia, 11
Riggs, Evalina, 15
Riggs, Frederick, 15
Robins, Raymond, 82, 88, 91, 137
Robinson, James Harvey, 33, 64
Rockefeller, John D., 116
Rodman, Henrietta, 26
Roosevelt, Franklin D., 78; on New Deal, 125-28; on World War II, 140-43
Roosevelt, Theodore, 24
Russell, Bertrand, 7, 77, 137; CCNY controversy, 145-46
Russia, 78, 82, 130, 137, 140, 147; Revolution of 1917, 118-26; Cold War, 149-50

Sacco, Nicola, 68
Saipan, 145
Santayana, George, 7
Sayre, John Nevin, 76
Schmalhausen, Samuel, 34
Schneer, A. Henry, 34
Schneider, Herbert W., 67
Senate Resolution 441, 88, 104
Shotwell, James T., 81; as Director of Carnegie Endowment for International Peace, 98; views on outlawry, 97-100, 104-05, 109; and Levinson, 98-102, 106-07; and Dewey, 101-02, 106-07, 109; and Briand, 102-08
Shunyu Maru, 45
Simkhovitch, Mary, 118
Sinclair, Upton, 77
Sloan, John, 142
Smith, Al, 121
Smith Act (1940), 145
Socialist Party, 124-28
Society for Ethical Culture, 6
Spain, 24, 147
Spanish-American War (1898), 24
Stalin, Josef, 126, 136-37
Starr, Frederick, 17
Stephen, Leslie, 12
Stimson, Henry L., 113
Straight, Willard Mrs., 91
Small, Albion, 17
Steffens, Lincoln, 119
Sudetenland, 139
Sumner, Charles, 83

Tarawa, 145
Thomas, Norman, 35, 73-74, 99, 119, 121, 124, 127, 139, 142
Thomas, W. I., 17
Tinian, 145
Tojo Cabinet (WWII), 145
Tolstoy, Leo, Count, 72
Tolstoy, Leo Jr., 33
Torrey, H. A. P., 12
Totalitarian Dictatorships, 129-43, 146-52
Townsend, Francis, 125
Treaty of Versailles, 40-41, 43, 47, 50, 55, 80-81, 86, 98, 131, 142
Trotsky, Leon, 37, 136-38
Truman, Harry, 149
Tufts, James H., 16-17, 118
Turkey, 101
Twenty-one Demands, 45, 50-51
Tyndall, George, 12

USS *Missouri,* 149
Universal Military Training, 75
University of California at Berkeley, 44-45
University of Chicago, 15-19, 25, 72, 81, 115-17
University of Michigan, 14-15, 45, 85, 116-17
University of Vermont, 12, 14, 72

V-E Day, 149
V-J Day, 149

Vanderbilt, Cornelius, 116
Vanzetti, Bartolomeo, 68
Veblen, Thorstein, 17, 25, 115, 119
Villard, Oswald G., 52-53, 73-74, 76, 78, 122, 129-30
Vladeck, Charney, 122

Wadsworth, James W., 78
Wald, Lillian, 73, 118
Walker, Jimmie, 121
Walling, William E., 119
War Policies Commission, 132-33
Washington Naval Conference (1921-2), 51-56; Four-Power Treaty, 54; Five-Power Treaty, 54-55; Nine-Power Treaty, 55
Wells, H. G. 77, 139; Society, 127
West Chester Normal School (Pa.), 68
Weyl, Walter, 119
White, Morton, x, 114, 155-56 n9
Wickersham, George W., 110
Williams, Howard Y., 122
Wilson, Woodrow, 26, 43, 51, 93; and WWI, 27-42; and Fourteen Points, 30; and League of Nations, 30-32, 82, 106; and Treaty of Versailles, 40-41, 98
Wood, Leonard (Gen.), 73, 75
World Court (Hague), 90-91, 99-100
World War I, 4-6, 67, 73, 78, 95, 103, 137, 146, 150; and Dewey, 20-42, 62, 78, 89, 112, 118, 130, 140, 151, 153; and Bourne, 35-39; and League, 30-32; and John H. Holmes, 83
World War II, 78, 141-53

"X" Club, 119

Yale University, 93
Young, A. A., 33
Young, Owen D., 131

Zimmermann, Alfred, 27